American Grand Strategy and East Asian Security in the Twenty-First Century

East Asia is richer, more integrated, and more stable than at any time in the past hundred years, while East Asian defense spending is now roughly half of what it was in 1990 and shows no sign of increasing. There is no evidence of any Asian arms race. All countries in the region are seeking diplomatic, not military, solutions with each other. Yet this East Asian reality still runs counter to a largely Western narrative that views China's rise as a threat and the region as increasingly unstable. In this important book, David C. Kang argues that American grand strategy should emphasize diplomatic and economic relations with the region, rather than military-first policies. Using longitudinal and comparative data, statistical analysis, and intensive research in selected East Asian countries, he suggests that East Asia is in sync with the American desire to share burdens and that the region may in fact be more stable than popularly believed.

DAVID C. KANG is Professor of International Relations, Business, and East Asian Languages and Cultures at the University of Southern California. He is author of numerous books, including *Crony Capitalism: Corruption and Development in South Korea and the Philippines* and *East Asia Before the West: Five Centuries of Trade and Tribute*. A regular consultant for U.S. government agencies and the military, he has written for the *New York Times*, the *Financial Times*, the *Washington Post*, and the *Los Angeles Times*, and appears regularly in broadcast media such as CNN, BBC, and NPR.

American Grand Strategy and East Asian Security in the Twenty-First Century

DAVID C. KANG

University of Southern California

CAMBRIDGE
UNIVERSITY PRESS

CAMBRIDGE
UNIVERSITY PRESS

University Printing House, Cambridge CB2 8BS, United Kingdom

One Liberty Plaza, 20th Floor, New York, NY 10006, USA

477 Williamstown Road, Port Melbourne, VIC 3207, Australia

314-321, 3rd Floor, Plot 3, Splendor Forum, Jasola District Centre, New Delhi - 110025, India

79 Anson Road, #06-04/06, Singapore 079906

Cambridge University Press is part of the University of Cambridge.

It furthers the University's mission by disseminating knowledge in the pursuit of education, learning and research at the highest international levels of excellence.

www.cambridge.org
Information on this title: www.cambridge.org/9781316616406
DOI: 10.1017/9781316711620

First published 2017

A catalogue record for this publication is available from the British Library

ISBN 978-1-107-16723-0 Hardback
ISBN 978-1-316-61640-6 Paperback

For William Hojin Kang

Contents

Figures

Tables

Acknowledgments

Many scholars read parts of this book, either in chapter form or as I was formulating the ideas through a various set of papers and presentations. I am grateful to all of them for their scholarly generosity and for taking the time and energy to help me improve and hone my thoughts. Thanks to Erin Baggot-Carter, Andrew Bertoli, Richard Bitzinger, Jae-ho Chung, Andrew Coe, Andrew Erickson, Erik Gartzke, Brad Glosserman, Evelyn Goh, Benjamin Graham, Steph Haggard, Chris Hanscom, Joey Huddleston, Pat James, Tom Jamieson, Hildi Kang (a.k.a. "Mom"), Saori Katada, Sean Kay, Scott Kennedy, Daisy Kim, Ellen Kim, Collin Koh Swee Lean, Alex Yu-ting Lin, Jon Lindsay, Dan Lynch, Jonathan Markowitz, Marco Milani, Inyoung Min, Brett Sheehan, Jihyun Shin, Allan Stam, and Andrew Yeo. Thanks also to Andrew Coe, Alexandre Debs, Songying Fang, James Fearon, Erik Gartzke, Colin Krainin, David Lake, Suzie Caldwell Mulesky, David Shambaugh, Jack Snyder, Marc Trachtenberg, Scott Wolford, and Mingmin Yang. Particular thanks to Bridget Coggins and Brent Strathman for their continued insights and feedback, especially on the regressions. Thanks very much to Bob Kelly for reading successive drafts of various chapters in detail. Victor Cha's feedback was helpful from start to finish, as always. Extra thanks are due to T. J. Pempel and Alice Ba for generously reading the entire manuscript and participating in a manuscript review workshop at the University of Southern California (USC) Korean Studies Institute in November 2016. They provided intensive and extensive comments and were particularly helpful in shaping and sharpening the arguments in this book.

Friends, colleagues, and interlocuters throughout East Asia are far too numerous to mention, but in particular I would like to thank the following people for their help at various stages of this project. In the Philippines, my old friend Frankie Roman was particularly helpful in setting up new meetings, and I thank all the folks at the Asian Institute of Management for their support as well. Thanks also to Herman

Joseph Kraft, Jay Batongbacal, and Tina Clemente at the University of the Philippines, and Charithie Joaquin of the National Defense College, who later made introductions to various military personnel at the Department of National Defense. Renato Cruz de Castro, Aileen Baviera, and Walden Bello were also very insightful, as always, and especially helpful to my RA Xinru Ma when she visited.

In Vietnam, very helpful people are at the Diplomatic Academy of Vietnam, including Dr. Tran Truong Thuy (director of East Sea Institute, Foundation for East Sea Studies), Dr. Ha Anh Tuan, Dr. Viet Nguyen, Dr. Nguyen Duc Thanh, and Dr. Truong Minh Huy Vu (University of Social Sciences and Humanities, Ho Chi Minh City). Dr. Thuy Do provided wonderful feedback on part of the Vietnam chapter and was very helpful in many ways, as well, especially with Xinru.

Parts of this book were presented at the Strategic and Defense Studies Center at the Australian National University; the Asan Institute in Seoul; the annual meetings of the International Studies Association, Atlanta, Georgia, March 18, 2016; the University of Michigan Ford Security Studies Series; the Institute for Korean Studies; the Mershon Center at Ohio State University; the Korea Society (thanks, Stephen Noerper); the Brookings Institute (thanks, Kathy Moon); the University of California, San Diego (thanks, Steph Haggard); the Naval War College, Newport, Rhode Island (thanks, Terry Roehrig); and the USC Center for International Studies.

I would also like to gratefully acknowledge generous funding from two equally important agencies. At various times in this very long process, these agencies were critical in providing the financial support that allowed this project to continue, and I am deeply grateful to them for their support of basic research that has important policy implications. This work was centrally supported by Laboratory Program for Korean Studies through the Ministry of Education of Republic of Korea and Korean Studies Promotion Service of the Academy of Korean Studies (AKS-2015-LAB-2250002), which convened a "manuscript review" at the USC Korean Studies Institute to help review the draft of the book, as well as research support.

I am also extremely grateful to the MacArthur Foundation for its support, without which this research could not have begun and been sustained. MacArthur support early on provided a tremendous impetus for this research and allowed me to conduct a wide range of research activities. The MacArthur grant not only supported field research in Vietnam, the Philippines, China, and Japan, but also made possible a number of meetings and workshops from 2015–2018.

Parts of this book had its genesis in a series of papers that have been written with coauthors in other form with Brad Glosserman, Jiun Bang, Stephanie Kang, and Xinru Ma. Their energy and ideas and far more rigorous thinking have been critical to forming and crafting the argument, and I have tried to make sure they are explicitly noted in the text. Thanks are also due to some outstanding research assistants – Alexis Dale-Huang, Sarah Shear, and Xinru Ma. Amy Dost did some outstanding editing on this book. John Haslam and Lew Bateman were outstanding editors at Cambridge University Press, and I thank them for shepherding this book all along the way.

1 | *Comprehensive East Asian Security*

Comprehensive security is a policy that will secure our national survival or protect our social order... through the combination of diplomacy, national defense, economic and other policy measures.

— Japanese Diplomatic Blue Book, 1981, p. 30

Is East Asia increasingly prosperous and stable? If so, why?

China's share of regional gross domestic product (GDP) grew from 8 percent in 1990 to 51 percent in 2014, while Japan's share fell from 72 percent in 1990 to 22 percent (Figure 1.1).[1] China's share of regional trade grew from 8 percent in 1990 to 39 percent by 2014 (Figure 1.2).

As the region has grown richer and more integrated over the past twenty-five years, and as China has grown richer and more integrated within East Asia itself, East Asian defense spending has steadily declined. The proportion of the economy devoted to defense spending is now roughly half of what it was in 1990 and shows no sign of increasing. Indeed, East Asian military expenditures are now similar to those in Latin America (Figure 1.3).[2] Specifically, the defense spending of the eleven main East Asian states declined from an average of 3.35 percent of GDP in 1990 to an average of 1.84 percent in 2015.

The rest of this book is essentially an effort to explain these three figures – a rich China in a deeply intertwined region that is experiencing long-term declines in defense spending. I argue that these three figures tell an accurate, enduring, and often overlooked story about East Asia: what I am calling the quest for comprehensive security. The region has grown richer. China has already managed a head-spinningly

[1] Figures from the World Bank, World Development Indicators.
[2] East Asia: China, Japan, South Korea, Taiwan, Australia, Singapore, Vietnam, the Philippines, Malaysia, Indonesia, Thailand. Latin America: Mexico, Argentina, Bolivia, Brazil, Chile, Columbia, Ecuador, Peru, Uruguay, and Venezuela.

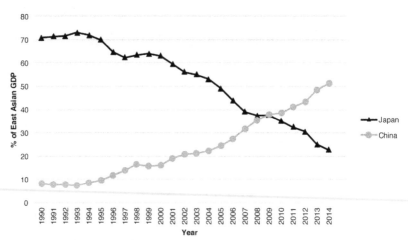

Figure 1.1 Share of total East Asian GDP, 1990–2014 (%).
Countries: China, Japan, South Korea, Taiwan, Vietnam, Philippines,
Singapore, Malaysia, Indonesia, Thailand, and Australia.
Source: World Bank, World Development Indicators.

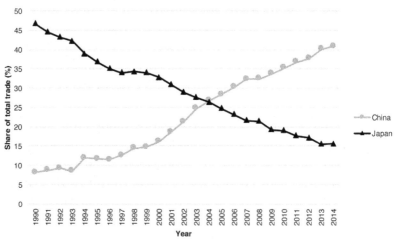

Figure 1.2 Share of East Asian regional trade, 1990–2014 (%).
Source: World Bank, World Development Indicators.

fast regional power transition. Countries are rapidly increasing their
economic ties to China and each other. And, East Asian countries have
steadily reduced their defense spending because they see little need to
arm. There are numerous issues still to be resolved, but countries think

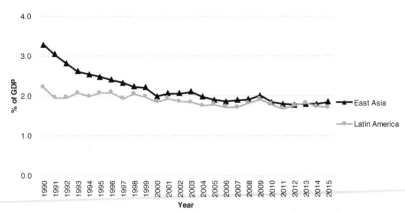

Figure 1.3 East Asian and Latin American defense spending, 1990–2015
(% of GDP). East Asian countries: China, Japan, South Korea, Taiwan,
Vietnam, Philippines, Singapore, Malaysia, Indonesia, Thailand, and
Australia. Latin American countries: Argentina, Bolivia, Brazil, Chile,
Columbia, Ecuador, Peru, Uruguay, Venezuela, and Mexico.
Source: Information from the Stockholm International Peace Research Institute (SIPRI),
www.sipri.org/databases/milex, 2016.

most of those issues are not worth fighting over. All countries in the
region have to coexist with each other – none is picking up and moving somewhere else – and countries are thus dealing with that reality
and seeking diplomatic, not military, solutions with each other.

This East Asian reality runs counter to a largely Western narrative that views China's rise as a threat and the region as increasingly unstable. Indeed, for over a quarter-century, some scholars have
made dire and continued predictions that East Asia is going to experience an arms race, that the regional security dilemma is intensify-
ing, and that dangerous instability driven by China is just around the
corner. In recent years, perceptions of increased Chinese assertiveness, regional fears, and a muscular U.S. rebalancing effort toward
the Pacific have increased concern among some observers that the
region may be drifting toward rivalry and containment blocs.[3] This

---

[3] Avery Goldstein, "First Things First: The Pressing Danger of Crisis Instability
in U.S.–China Relations," *International Security* 37, no. 4 (Spring 2013): 55.
Adam P. Liff and G. John Ikenberry, "Racing Toward Tragedy? China's
Rise, Military Competition in the Asia Pacific, and the Security Dilemma,"
International Security 39, no. 2 (Fall 2014): pp. 52, 88; Ja Ian Chong and

literature sees substantial uncertainty about intentions and goals among East Asian states, with countries rapidly arming themselves, and nationalist publics pushing leaders to stand tough in disputes with neighbors.[4]

However, there is little evidence that East Asian states are engaged in an arms race, and few states are sending costly signals about their resolve to suffer the costs of war. In the scholarly literature, costly signals are actions that a country committed to fighting over an issue would take, but that a country that was bluffing would not take. Almost all countries in East Asia are not sending costly signals to each other in any meaningful manner.

Rather than engaging in military competition, East Asian countries are pursuing *comprehensive security:* a wide range of diplomatic, institutional, and economic strategies – as well as military strategies – in their dealings with each other. This pursuit of comprehensive security is regionwide. Almost all countries in the region view their security

Todd H. Hall, "The Lessons of 1914 for East Asia Today: Missing the Trees for the Forest," *International Security* 39, no. 1 (Summer 2014): 42; Jonathan Holslag, *China's Coming War with Asia* (Cambridge, UK: Polity, 2015); John J. Mearsheimer, "The Gathering Storm: China's Challenge to US Power in Asia," *Chinese Journal of International Politics* 3, no. 4 (2010): 381–96; Dan De Luce and Keith Johnson, "How FP Stumbled into a War with China – and Lost," *Foreign Policy*, January 15, 2016, foreignpolicy.com/2016/01/15/how-fp-stumbled-into-a-war-with-china-and-lost/; Harry J. Kazianis, "Get Ready, America: Are China and Japan Destined for War?" *National Interest*, January 22, 2016, nationalinterest.org/blog/the-buzz/get-ready-america-are-china-japan-destined-war-14991; Aaron Friedberg, "Ripe for Rivalry: Prospects for Peace in a Multipolar Asia," *International Security* 18, no. 3 (Winter 1993/1994): 5–33; Abraham M. Denmark, "Could Tensions in the South China Sea Spark a War?" *National Interest*, May 31, 2014, nationalinterest.org/feature/could-tensions-the-south-china-sea-spark-war-10572; Robert D. Kaplan, "The South China Sea Is the Future of Conflict," *Foreign Policy*, August, 15, 2011, foreignpolicy.com/2011/08/15/the-south-china-sea-is-the-future-of-conflict/; Andrew Browne, "The Specter of an Accidental China–U.S. War," *Wall Street Journal*, August 16, 2016, www.wsj.com/articles/the-specter-of-an-accidental-china-u-s-war-1471360811?tesla=y; and Sebastian Rosato, "Why the United States and China Are on a Collision Course," *Policy Brief* (Cambridge, MA: Belfer Center for Science and International Affairs, May 2015), belfercenter.ksg.harvard.edu/publication/25378/why_the_united_states_and_china_are_on_a_collision_course.html.

[4] Jessica Chen Weiss, "Authoritarian Signaling, Mass Audiences, and Nationalist Protest in China," *International Organization* 67, no. 1 (2013): 1–35; Chong and Hall, "The Lessons of 1914 for East Asia Today," 26; Goldstein, "First Things First," 59; Liff and Ikenberry, "Racing Toward Tragedy?" 88.

environment as relatively benign, particularly compared to a generation ago. China's economic growth, East Asian growth, and increasing
security is a regional phenomenon that has been occurring together.
The intertwined nature and increasing interactions among regional
countries are closely linked. China's rise occurred within a rapidly
integrating region that has been experiencing dramatic economic
growth and prolonged social and political stabilization. Both China
and the region have grown richer and more stable together, and the
policies they have pursued have been, for the most part, mutually reinforcing. The major exception to this argument is North Korea, which
is attempting to convince everyone that it is willing to use force to
achieve its aims.

The explanation for this relatively stable security environment in
East Asia is straightforward: few countries fear for their survival. Even
residual maritime disputes do not threaten their national survival.
Leaders and citizens want economic growth, social integration, and
better regional architecture. Their publics and businesses are oriented
toward openness, trade, and increasing cultural and social interactions
in the region. As Etel Solingen put it, "Leaders in most East Asian
states pivoted their political control on economic performance and
integration into the global economy."[5] Indeed, China threatens the
survival of only one country – Taiwan – and even that relationship
has largely stabilized over the years due to rapid economic integration
between the two sides and an agreement that Taiwan can act like a
country as long as it does not call itself a country.

It is true that China is seen as increasingly aggressive, particularly
in the United States, and the U.S. Pentagon is planning for the possibility of a military strategy in dealing with China. As the administration of recently elected President Trump takes form, Trump and his
key advisers appear to be planning to take a more confrontational
stance toward China. For example, the leader of Trump's National
Trade Council, Peter Navarro, has blamed China for virtually all
American economic and strategic woes, writing that "Over the past
decade, riding tall astride the Trojan Horse of free trade, a 'pred-
atory' China has stolen millions of American manufacturing jobs

---

[5] Etel Solingen, "Pax Asiatica Versus Bella Levantina: The Foundations of War
and Peace in East Asia and the Middle East," *American Political Science Review*
101, no. 4 (November 2007), 757–80, 758.

from under our noses."[6] In January 2017, Trump's secretary of state nominee Rex Tillerson also suggested the United States might engage in a naval blockade of Chinese South China Sea claims. Trump advisers have called for increasing the U.S. navy to 350 ships and suggested levying a 45 percent tariff on Chinese goods.[7] Trump himself has suggested abandoning U.S. alliances with Japan and Korea and that the "one-China policy" was up for reconsideration, and his first official order of business upon taking the presidency in January 2017 was to formally pull out of the Trans-Pacific Partnership economic initiative.

How this U.S.–China dynamic plays out will have an impact on regional security, of course. But if the United States and China increasingly compete directly with each other or engage in a trade war, it is unlikely that East Asian countries will feel the necessity to choose sides. The evidence is fairly clear: regional states want good relations with both the United States and China, and there is little appetite in the region for a containment coalition against China. Put differently, East Asian leaders and peoples share some, but not all, American priorities.

Considering the ample evidence of China's rising power, states in the region could easily have already begun a vigorous counterbalancing strategy against China if that were their intention. It seems reasonable to argue that if states were going to balance against China, they would have begun by now. Those who predict that a containment coalition will rise against China in the future need to explain why this has not already occurred, despite three decades of transparent and rapid Chinese economic, diplomatic, and military growth.[8] Idle speculation about what could happen decades from now provides little insight into the decisions states are making today. If China's neighbors

---

[6] See, for example, Isaac Stone Fish, "Trump's China-Bashing Id," *Slate*, December 22, 2016, www.slate.com/articles/news_and_politics/foreigners/2016/12/peter_navarro_trump_s_trade_czar_embodies_the_china_bashing_id_of_his_campaign.html.

[7] Peter Navarro, "Trump's 45% Tariff on Chinese Goods Is Perfectly Calculated," *Los Angeles Times*, July 21, 2016, www.latimes.com/opinion/op-ed/la-oe-navarro-trump-trade-china-tariffs-20160721-snap-story.html.

[8] See, for example, David C. Gompert, Astrid Cevallos, and Cristina L. Garafola, *War with China: Thinking Through the Unthinkable* (Santa Monica, CA: RAND Corporation, 2016). www.rand.org/pubs/research_reports/RR1140.html.

believed China would be more dangerous in the future, they would have begun preparing for that possibility already.

So What?

The research presented in this book is consistent with a sizable literature that sees East Asia as relatively stable and prosperous.[9] For example, Evelyn Goh identifies both complicity and resistance to U.S. hegemony in East Asia, and carefully charts the changing order in the region that desires to incorporate both China and the United States but that is fundamentally more stable than generally believed.[10] Iain Johnston has argued that China's new assertiveness is neither new nor that assertive.[11] And Amitav Acharya has consistently argued that East Asian countries are building an institutional order that moves far beyond American hegemony.[12]

Accurately understanding East Asian regional perceptions and their grand strategies is central to U.S. policy in East Asia. The key debate is whether to contain China, and whether East Asian countries would go along with a containment policy of China. The outlines of a Trump approach to East Asia are only beginning to become clear and will not fully emerge for some years. Yet, as noted previously, early indications have revealed that a Trump administration will more likely pursue a policy toward China that is more nationalist and confrontational than usual in security issues, and more isolationist and protectionist than usual in economic issues.

Only time will show how East Asian countries will react to a more confrontational United States. Yet if the survival of East Asian

[9] Steve Chan, *Looking for Balance: China, the United States, and Power Balancing in East Asia* (Stanford, CA: Stanford University Press, 2012); Thomas Christensen, *The China Challenge: Shaping the Choices of a Rising Power* (New York: Norton, 2015).

[10] Evelyn Goh, *The Struggle for Order: Hegemony, Hierarchy, and Transition in Post–Cold War East Asia* (Oxford: Oxford University Press, 2013).

[11] Alastair Iain Johnston, "How New and Assertive Is China's New Assertiveness?" *International Security* 37, no. 4 (Spring 2013): 7–48; and Alastair Iain Johnston, "What (If Anything) Does East Asia Tell Us About International Relations Theory?" *Annual Review of Political Science* 15, no. 1 (2012): 53–78.

[12] Amitav Acharya, "The Emerging Regional Architecture of World Politics," *World Politics* 59, no. 4 (2007); and Amitav Acharya, *The End of American World Order* (Oxford: Oxford University Press, 2015).

states is not actually threatened and East Asian countries prefer to use economic, institutional, and diplomatic tools to deal with each other rather than military force, then U.S. policy should emphasize economic and diplomatic engagement with the region. A minimalist U.S. approach – one that avoids getting deeply involved in regional issues where the U.S. has no direct stake – is more likely to promote stability than a maximalist one that blunders in and hopes to perpetuate U.S. primacy for its own sake. The research presented in this book leads to the conclusion that East Asian countries do not want to choose between China and the United States; and that while American presence is welcomed, there is little appetite for a containment strategy against China. Indeed, all countries in the region are increasing their economic, social, and diplomatic relations with China, not limiting them. Within this larger context, it is unlikely that these same countries would then choose to side with the United States against China, especially if their own national survival was not threatened.

Costly Signals and Cheap Talk

How do we know that countries care enough about an issue to fight over it? This book uses the insights of "bargaining theory" as its overall framework. Bargaining theory posits that although bigger countries might be stronger than smaller countries, what is more important is *how much* a country cares about an issue – and that is hard to measure. A small country that cares intensely about an issue could prevail over a much bigger country that doesn't care as much.[13] This approach relies on the central insight that because war is costly, states are better off negotiating than fighting. After all, if it is obvious which side will win a war, then both sides might as well simply agree on the outcome and avoid fighting in the first place.

However, what if the outcome is *not* clear? It is often difficult to determine a country's relative capabilities and how much it cares

---

[13] James D. Fearon, "Rationalist Explanations for War," *International Organization* 49, no. 3 (Summer 1995): 379–414; Robert Powell, "Bargaining Theory and International Conflict," *Annual Review of Political Science* 5 (2002): 1–30; Robert Powell, "War as a Commitment Problem," *International Organization* 60, no. 1 (January 2006): 169–203; David A. Lake, "Two Cheers for Bargaining Theory: Assessing Rationalist Explanations of the Iraq War," *International Security* 35, no. 3 (Winter 2010/2011): 8.

about the issue.[14] States may wish to misrepresent their willingness to use force over a disputed issue to deter potential challengers. Put more simply, states may bluff. Talking tough and exaggerating one's strength and willingness to fight is a classic strategy to deter others or cause them to back down without a fight. The reason wars can start is because of the difficulty in differentiating between a country that is bluffing and a country that truly is willing to go to war.

Years ago, James Fearon argued that *costly signals* from states that are truly willing to fight can set them apart from countries that are engaging in "cheap talk."[15] Costly signals are actions that a committed country would take, but that a country that was bluffing would not take. First and foremost among his examples of costly signals is military expenditures. Investing in the military is costly, but it also directly improves the chances of a country in war. A country that doesn't care that much about an issue may talk tough, but if it is not investing in its military it is probably not serious about its willingness to fight.

This book is organized to use bargaining theory as the key lens through which to assess East Asian countries' security strategies. Chapter 2 introduces the theoretical framework that uses military expenditures as the central and most commonly used indicator of costly signals, security strategies, and intentions in the scholarly literature. Overwhelmingly, scholars exploring costly signals and threat perceptions use military expenditures and preparations as the most common indicator of resolve to fight a war.

A straightforward application of this measure to East Asia would expect states that are preparing for war (or have high threat perceptions) to be spending heavily on their militaries. If East Asia is as unstable and close to war as the pessimists argue, then we should see ample costly signaling in the region. Indeed, the whole point of costly signals is that they clearly communicate one country's intentions to another country. This book examines all types of costly signals, but focuses primarily on military expenditures as a key costly signal for a nation's security perceptions and priorities. And, bargaining theory works in

---

[14] Formally, "asymmetric information." In Fearon's model, there always exists a bargain between two states that is preferable to suffering the costs of war.

[15] Clayton L. Thyne, "Cheap Signals with Costly Consequences: The Effect of Interstate Relations on Civil War," *Journal of Conflict Resolution* 50, no. 6 (December 2006): 937–61.

a straightforward and intuitive manner when applied to contemporary East Asian security dynamics: there is a marked absence of costly signals. Countries in the region are not excessively investing in their militaries or preparing for long-term war. They do not limit economic relations with China, nor do they apply economic sanctions on China. Nor do leaders of East Asian countries make rhetorical statements about a willingness to fight China that put their reputations at stake and create the expectation within their own peoples of forceful action.

At an extreme, costly signaling and rapid increases in defense spending can result in an arms race. After all, an arms race is simply two countries engaging in reciprocal costly signals. As Chapter 3 will explore in more detail, there is almost no evidence of anything approaching an arms race in East Asia. The intuition of an arms race is fairly straightforward, and the widely influential Buzan and Herring definition of an arms race is "two sides going flat out or almost flat out in major competitive investments in military capacity."[16] Perhaps a bit more precisely, Rider, Findley, and Diehl use the "straightforward and replicable" definition of an arms race as 8 percent or more increases in military expenditures by both states over at least three years.[17] However, rather than sending signals that carry "some risk of rejection and war,"[18] East Asian countries indeed appear to be signaling that they do not want to fight. There are no dyads (pairs of countries) in East Asia that come anywhere near to meeting the definitions of an arms race as commonly used by political scientists.

Chapter 3 also compares East Asia with Latin America in their military spending and deployments. This comparison leads to a surprising conclusion: East Asia and Latin America look similar in their military spending and deployments. By some measures, Latin America is even more militarized than East Asia. In short, no matter how it is measured, over the past quarter-century, militarization and military spending in East Asia have been reduced by almost half. This granular measurement of defense spending reveals that states in East Asia are not, in fact, engaging in arms races or sending costly signals.

---

[16] Barry Buzan and Eric Herring, *The Arms Dynamic in World Politics* (Boulder, CO: Lynne Rienner Publishers, 1998), 80.

[17] Toby J. Rider, Michael G. Findley, and Paul F. Diehl, "Just Part of the Game? Arms Races, Rivalry, and War," *Journal of Peace Research* 48, no. 1 (2011): 90.

[18] Fearon, "Rationalist Explanations for War," 396–7.

Chapters 4 through 8 delve into key case studies that examine the lack of costly signals and arms racing in East Asia. Chapter 4, which examines North Korea's military and security strategy, is the conforming "empirical indicator" that clearly and tightly fits the costly signaling that Fearon identified. North Korea has consistently taken actions that show it is willing to fight for its survival, and the North sends a wide range of costly signals to that effect. For its part, South Korea also sends costly signals to North Korea to show it will not back down to Northern pressure. Competition on the Korean peninsula is thus the benchmark by which to compare other East Asian countries. Even more than South Korea, however, North Korea is doing everything it can to signal a willingness to fight for its survival. It spends heavily on its military. It suffers enormous economic costs in order to limit its interactions with its adversaries. It consistently makes rhetorical claims that it is willing to fight. Perhaps most importantly, other countries believe North Korea: it is widely and commonly agreed that North Korea is not bluffing, but is indeed prepared to fight for its survival. In short, this book affirms that costly signals are a useful and identifiable tool. North Korea is an exemplary, textbook case of costly signaling, and in fact is the only clear case of costly signals in the entire East Asian region.

Why Countries Do Not Send Costly Signals

What if a country does *not* send costly signals? The most intuitive and straightforward reason is that it does not intend to fight and is not preparing for war. Bargaining theory argues that if a country does send costly signals, then it must care enough about an issue to be willing to fight. Conversely, if a country does not send costly signals, the issue must not be worth fighting over.[19]

Compared to North Korea, none of the other East Asian countries are using costly signals or preparing for war in dealing with each other and China. Detailed case studies in Chapters 5 through 8 explain East

---

[19] The only two exceptions I have found in the literature are Branislav L. Slantchev, "Feigning Weakness," *International Organization*, Vol. 64, No. 3 (July 2010), pp. 357–88; and Scott Wolford, "Showing Restraint, Signaling Resolve: Coalitions and Crisis Bargaining," *American Journal of Political Science* 58, no. 1 (2014): 144–156, both of which obtain only under explicit scope conditions.

Asian countries' strategies toward the United States, China, and each other. Individually, these case studies reveal a consistent pattern that East Asian countries are not preparing to choose sides or contain China. Taken together, these chapters reveal a consistent, regionwide process of integration, slow learning, and evolution in policies; the use of a wide variety of diplomatic, economic, institutional, and military strategies to manage relations with each other; and a search for comprehensive security.

In Chapter 5, South Korea provides an important contrast case to North Korea. While South Korea does send costly signals to North Korea about its willingness to fight, South Korean relations with China and Japan fit almost none of the standard theories. Most theory predicts that South Korea should fear a rising, powerful, authoritarian China and cleave toward Japan – a capitalist, rich, democracy with a close U.S. alliance. Yet South Korea is far more skeptical of Japan, and less skeptical of China, than many Western analysts expect or desire. South Korea is not militarizing its relations with China, but rather increasing its relations with China economically, diplomatically, and socially. Opinion polls have consistently found that Koreans view Japan as a greater national security threat than China, and this makes perfect sense when viewed from the perspective of Korean history. Korea has lived next to a powerful China for centuries, and its only real threats have come from Japan. This is unlikely to change.

Chapters 6 and 7 are a pairwise comparison of the Philippines and Vietnam, both of which are not using costly signals or preparations for war in their dealings with China. Both these countries are in Southeast Asia, both have maritime disputes with China, and both have deep economic ties to China. The Philippines is a longtime U.S. ally with a mutual defense treaty with the United States, while Vietnam recently fought a war against the United States and only normalized relations in 1995. A granular exploration of their strategies toward both the United States and China reveals that neither the Philippines nor Vietnam is displaying a willingness to go to war with China. Indeed, both countries have steadily reduced their military expenditures and military deployments – even naval deployments – over the past twenty-five years.

Put differently, neither country is pursuing a military strategy of costly signaling in its relations with China. Rather, both countries are pursuing diplomatic and institutional strategies in dealing with China.

The Philippines is pursuing an institutional and multilateral strategy in dealing with China's maritime claims. The Philippines took a dispute to the international tribunal in the Hague. Often overlooked in the Philippines victory in the Hague ruling was that this was an institutional and diplomatic strategy, not a military one. There was little indication that it intended to pursue a military enforcement strategy of its maritime claims. In contrast, Vietnam is pursuing a bilateral diplomatic strategy with both China and the United States. Furthermore, it appears that the United States is chasing Vietnam, rather than the other way around; this is in contrast to theories that predict that Vietnam should be pursuing the United States in an attempt to balance against China. Ultimately, neither country is preparing for war in the South China Sea.

Chapter 8 examines two other pairs of East Asian countries that are pursuing comprehensive security with each other and the great powers. Japan and Australia are U.S. allies, but both have complex relationships with China and neither reveals costly signals. Japan has a set of disputes with China, but Japan also has enduring reluctance to taking a "normal," or even a leadership, role in the region. Japan under Prime Minister Abe has probably reached its high point of international assertiveness, and even under Abe defense spending has remained essentially flat, and revision of Article Nine has not proceeded. In short, if Abe is not able to change Japan's overall trajectory, it is unlikely that any other leader can do so in the short to medium term. As for Australia, this close U.S. ally has measurably positive views of China, views increasing American bellicose strategy toward China skeptically, and has many pressing security concerns near its borders that do not involve either China or the United States. These two stalwart U.S. allies are thus supportive of the United States but highly unlikely to clearly join a containment coalition against China.

Two other important countries – Singapore and Indonesia – have warm and close relations with China, even while they enjoy close relations with the United States. Singaporean leaders have consistently argued that the United States needs to take Chinese goals and attitudes seriously, even while Singapore pursues good relations with both China and the United States (redundant somehow). Indonesian leaders and citizens view the United States more skeptically than most countries in East Asia, both because Indonesia is a heavily Muslim country, and because it does not view China with the same skepticism as many in the U.S. policy-making establishment. Not one of these four countries sends costly signals about its willingness to use military means as their primary strategy for dealing with China.

American Policy to East Asia

The book concludes by examining implications for American grand strategy to the region. Chapter 9 examines U.S. security and economic relations in Asia, emphasizing that there is little evidence that East Asian countries are free-riding on a forward U.S. military commitment to the region. This chapter shows that in fact, the United States has steadily reduced its military commitment to the region over the past half-century and there is good evidence that countries would be careful about too eagerly joining a U.S. containment coalition against China. Rather, these countries have built increasingly complex and plentiful relations with each other, and that American presence, while welcomed, is not nearly as central to the functioning of the region as might be believed. The United States is a powerful patron, but it is not indispensable to the region.

Chapter 10 concludes with general observations about continued East Asian stability, as well as lessons for American grand strategy in the region. These countries have experienced more than a generation of increasing regional integration and spectacular economic growth. Leaders and publics have crafted peaceful, outward-looking foreign policies that attempt to navigate diplomatic, economic, and security issues as a whole. China's rise is intricately interwoven with this larger regional rise, and China's rise is just one element of the increasing economic, diplomatic, and social integration of East Asia. No country appears eager for a containment policy of China. All countries want good relations with both China and the United States. China is not a problem to be solved, but rather an immense, complex, and rapidly changing country that has to be lived with.

Within this situation, then, an American grand strategy that emphasizes a confrontational approach to China is unlikely to attract many Asian participants. Rather, it is more likely that East Asian countries will avoid being caught between the United States and China, and indeed will back slowly away. This chapter thus argues that a *minimalist* U.S. grand strategy – one that emphasizes diplomacy and economic relations, and that avoids entangling the United States in regional issues to the extent possible, is the path most likely to contribute to American interests as well as the continued stability of the region. It argues against a mainstream American view of liberal hegemony that sees America as an indispensable element of regional stability, pointing out that too intrusive American attempts at military-first leadership often make things worse, not better. The decisions the new Trump administration makes can either accelerate the decline of the American-led order or further American leadership and influence the diplomacy and economic relations in the region.

2 | *The Size of the Fight in the Dog: Costly Signals in International Bargaining*

It's not the size of the dog in the fight; it's the size of the fight in the dog.

– Mark Twain

How do we know when a country fears another country? How do we know when a country is willing to use military force to defend its interests? These questions lie at the heart of the international relations discipline, and answering them is a key element of any social scientific argument about the likelihood of war in a particular circumstance. Resolve, the key insight from bargaining theory, moves us beyond simple material calculations of who is stronger. How resolved a country is – how much a country cares about an issue, and whether it cares sufficiently to fight – is far harder to judge than simply which country is bigger or stronger. As history has shown time and again, often smaller countries prevail over more powerful ones, simply because they care more about the issue. Deciding whether a country truly cares enough about an issue to fight, or whether it is simply bluffing, is thus a key task for political leaders.

In its most straightforward application, military expenditures as an indicator of a nation's resolve works quite well: states preparing for war spend heavily on defense, and this is a robust and clear indicator of their resolve to fight if necessary. Indeed, military expenditures are probably the predominant indicator used by scholars and policy analysts in assessing a nation's intentions: more military spending means a country is preparing for war, less spending means it views its environment as more peaceful. Accordingly, this book thus focuses on military expenditures as one of the key elements of a nation's "costly signals" and resolve to fight.

Bargaining theory, and indeed most theories of international conflict, assume that the situation is one of crisis bargaining. In this implicit assumption, two countries are locked in a tense and momentous dispute that requires focused attention and rapid decisions. Implicit in many theories is an example such as the Cuban missile crisis between the United States and the Soviet Union. In that case, both countries did not know the other's intentions and willingness to use force, and war hung in the balance. However, this is quite rare, and theorists tend to be silent on the scope and boundary conditions for when bargaining theory actually applies. In most of the world, disagreements between countries are not crises, but rather unfold slowly, over weeks, years, and even decades. A country's long-term stance on a particular issue is often relatively easy to discern, because military spending is fairly transparent, and a wide variety of other evidence or indicators combine to form a national preference about an issue. In many cases, figuring out a nation's enduring threat perceptions or intentions is not that difficult.

Bargaining Theory and Costly Signals

David Lake calls bargaining theory the "workhorse" theory of war, as it has become the dominant approach for explaining war initiation, escalation, and termination.[1] Central to the theory is the idea of *costly signals*, or threats that are rendered credible given "the act of sending it incurs or creates some cost that the sender would be disinclined to incur or create if he or she were in fact *not* willing to carry out the threat."[2] Because states possess private information about their own preferences, capabilities, and resolve, states need to communicate to avoid costly conflict. Verbal signals are often seen as "cheap talk" because they lack credibility – states can renege on their commitments with little cost. Thus states may resort to sending costly signals to convey their willingness to fight for an issue they care deeply about.

Costly signals differ from other potential signals of intention because senders incur costs or risks that unresolved actors might not be willing to suffer, including "an offer that carries some risk of rejection and war."[3]

---

[1] Lake, "Two Cheers for Bargaining Theory," 8. See also Powell, "Bargaining Theory and International Conflict"; Powell, "War as a Commitment Problem"; Dan Reiter, "Exploring the Bargaining Model of War," *Perspectives on Politics* 1, no. 1 (March 2003): 27–43.
[2] James Fearon, "Signaling Foreign Policy Interests: Tying Hands versus Sinking Costs," *Journal of Conflict Resolution* 41, no. 1 (1997): 68–90.
[3] Powell, "War as a Commitment Problem," 69. See Fearon, "Signaling Foreign Policy Interests," 69.

Costly signals must be different from cheap talk or bluffing. The typical methods of costly signaling that Fearon identified over two decades ago include the following:

... building weapons, mobilizing troops, signing alliance treaties, supporting troops in a foreign land, and creating domestic political costs that would be paid if the announcement proves false ... To be genuinely informative about a state's actual willingness or ability to fight, a signal must be costly in such a way that a state with lesser resolve or capability might not wish to send it.[4]

Fearon further distinguished between two "ideal types" of costly signals: sunk costs, which are *ex ante* commitments, and tying hands, which are *ex post* (Table 2.1). A "hand-tying" signal is not itself costly to send, and the sender pays a cost only if the commitment is not upheld because it creates "*ex post* audience costs for bluffing (usually in the form of public statements)."[5] In contrast, sunk costs "are actions that are costly for the state to take in the first place ... Building arms or mobilizing troops entails costs no matter what the outcome."[6] These indicators – military expenditures, economic sanctions, and military alliances – have been widely used in the scholarly literature and in fact could be called the "default" indicators of costly signaling. One of a myriad of examples is Clayton Thyne's scholarship on cheap talk. Thyne writes, "Examples of costly supportive signals include military alliances and trade ties. Examples of costly hostile signals include troop mobilizations and economic sanctions. Each of these is financially costly and transparent."[7]

Although the bargaining literature is rife with references to costly signals, empirical applications of the bargaining theory that inform when and why we should expect states to send costly signals are limited.[8] According to bargaining theory, states send costly signals

---

[4] Fearon, "Rationalist Explanations for War," 396–7. See also Fearon, "Signaling Foreign Policy Interests," 69; James D. Fearon, "Domestic Political Audiences and the Escalation of International Disputes," *American Political Science Review* 88, no. 3 (1994): 577–92.

[5] Thyne, "Cheap Signals with Costly Consequences," 939.

[6] Fearon, "Signaling Foreign Policy Interests," 70.

[7] Thyne, "Cheap Signals with Costly Consequences," 939.

[8] Thyne, "Cheap Signals with Costly Consequences," 939; Matthew Fuhrmann and Todd S. Sechser, "Signaling Alliance Commitments: Hand-Tying and Sunk Costs in Extended Nuclear Deterrence," *American Journal of Political Science*

Table 2.1. *Types of costly signals*

Type	Tying hands	Sunk costs
Military	• Military alliance treaties • Small "trip-wire" forces	• Defense spending • Troop mobilizations • Building up of arms • Engagement in limited conflicts • Stationing troops on foreign soil • Brinkmanship
Economic		• Economic sanctions against adversary • Increasing trade ties with ally
Diplomatic	• Public statements and claims that create domestic audience costs	

when at least two conditions are met. First, costly signaling occurs when there is large enough asymmetric information about a state's resolve to fight. While uncertainty and miscalculation about intentions or relative power raise the risk of war in a region, uncertainty alone is not enough to cause states to go to war. Rather than a *lack* of information, states may fail to reach mutual bargains due to strategic incentives to withhold or misrepresent private information about their resolve or capabilities.[9] As a result, states may attempt to overcome such uncertainty by credibly signaling their resolve. Second, states send costly signals when the costs of fighting are less than the value of the disputed issue. For signals to be credible, senders must take actions

---

58, no. 4 (October 2014): 920; Branislav L. Slantchev, "Military Coercion in Interstate Crises," *American Political Science Review* 99, no. 4 (November 2005): 535, 545; Branislav L. Slantchev, "Feigning Weakness," *International Organization* 64, no. 3 (July 2010): 359; James D. Fearon, "Signaling Versus the Balance of Power and Interests: An Empirical Test of a Crisis Bargaining Model," *Journal of Conflict Resolution* 38, no. 2 (1994): 236–69.

[9] Fearon, "Rationalist Explanations for War," 393–401. States may go to war, even under complete information, when they cannot credibly commit to a mutual bargain. See Powell, "War as a Commitment Problem," 176.

that an unresolved state – or a state that is bluffing – would be unwilling to take.[10]

If the first condition is not met, then costly signaling will not occur because the relevant states' resolves are known and a settlement preferable to war can be reached. If the second condition does not hold, then costly signaling will not occur because the disputed issue is simply not worth fighting over. In fact, countries that care deeply about an issue and are resolved to fight for the issue are likely to send costly signals regardless of the *ex ante* balance of capabilities.

Military Expenditures as Costly Signals

Military expenditures are the most direct indicator of a nation's security strategy. It is no surprise that the first example of a costly signal in James Fearon's seminal 1995 article was military spending, as noted earlier.[11] Indeed, arms races would then be a particularly acute costly signal, as an arms race is typically defined as two sides mutually increasing military expenditures at far greater than normal levels. If two countries are involved in an arms race, that would imply that at least one side miscalculates its chances in war and is overly optimistic. Chapter 3 will introduce arms race definitions as commonly used in the political science literature in more detail. For our purposes here, it is simply worth noting that arms races and defense spending are the most obvious examples of costly signals as defined in the formal literature.

As with bargaining theory, defense spending is by far the most common indicator used to measure a nation's external threat perceptions, its militarization, and of its intentions in the scholarly literature on international security more generally. In fact, it may seem intuitively clear that military expenditures are often directly linked to the external threats that a country faces, and the greater the external threat, and the more a country is preparing to fight a war, the greater will be its defense spending.[12] If balancing, or the balance of power, is defined

[10] Fearon, "Signaling Foreign Policy Interests," 69.
[11] Fearon, "Rationalist Explanations for War," 396.
[12] For representative scholarship that uses military expenditures as the key indicator of external threat and security strategy, see Paul Collier and Anke Hoeffler, "Unintended Consequences: Does Aid Promote Arms Races?" *Oxford Bulletin of Economics and Statistics* 69, no. 1 (2007): 1–27;

as military preparations to deal with a perceived or potential threat to national security, it follows that a nation's military expenditures would directly respond to its external security environment. Indeed, the most widely accepted measures of balancing behavior are defense expenditures by states to "turn latent power (i.e., economic, technological, social, and natural resources) into military capabilities."[13]

Much of the scholarly literature also uses military expenditures as an indicator for threat perceptions, tensions, and arms races. Ades and Chua, for example, find a link between regional instability, defined as revolutions and coups in neighboring countries, with a higher defense burden and lower economic growth.[14] Maoz finds that a local measure of security environment, the "politically relevant international environment," has a positive influence on military expenditure.[15] Dunne and Perlo-Freeman find that the military expenditures of "potential enemies" was the "most important" explanation of a country's military expenditures.[16] Rider, Findley, and Diehl use the "straightforward and replicable" definition of an arms race as 8 percent or more increases in military expenditures by both states over at least three years.[17]

However, states need not face threats alone – the presence of powerful allies can reduce a state's military expenditures.[18] All things being equal, the more powerful a state's alliance partner, the less incentive a

Charles W. Ostrom, "A Reactive Linkage Model of the U.S. Defense Expenditure Policymaking Process," *American Political Science Review* 72, no. 3 (1978): 941–57; Glenn Palmer, "Alliance Politics and Issue Areas: Determinants of Defense Spending," *American Journal of Political Science* 34, no. 1 (1990): 190–211.

[13] Keir A. Lieber and Gerard Alexander, "Waiting for Balancing: Why the World Is Not Pushing Back," *International Security* 30, no. 1 (2005): 109–39; Campbell Craig, "Rebuttal of John Glenn's 'The Flawed Logic of a MAD Man," *Review of International Studies* 37, no. 4 (2011): 2025–8.

[14] Alberto Ades and Hak B. Chua, "Thy Neighbor's Curse: Regional Instability and Economic Growth," *Journal of Economic Growth* 2, no. 3 (1997): 279–304.

[15] Zeev Maoz, *Domestic Sources of Global Change* (Ann Arbor: University of Michigan Press, 1996).

[16] Paul Dunne and Sam Perlo-Freeman, "The Demand for Military Spending in Developing Countries," *International Review of Applied Economics* 17, no. 1 (2003): 23–48.

[17] Rider, Findley, and Diehl, "Just Part of the Game?" 90.

[18] James D. Morrow, "Arms Versus Allies: Tradeoffs in the Search for Security," *International Organization* 47, no. 2 (1993): 214; Victor D. Cha, *Alignment Despite Antagonism: the US-Korea-Japan Security Triangle* (Stanford: Stanford University Press, 1999).

state has to spend on its own defense, if it can free-ride on a stronger alliance partner.[19] Conversely, states lacking a powerful ally can be expected to feel more threatened than those with powerful ally, and we should be able to observe different levels of military expenditures between the two when facing an external threat. There is also a large literature on the role of economic interdependence in reducing conflict. States that trade with each other might have a lower propensity to fight than those that do not trade with each other, and hence reduce their military expenditures.[20]

Domestic politics can also affect military expenditures. Almost all studies relating political regime to military expenditures conclude that "democracies spend less than autocracies do on defense."[21] Not only are democracies generally considered to be more peaceful than autocracies, and hence need to devote fewer resources to their militaries, they also may be more able to mobilize resources during times of war and to recruit more allies in times of need, thus reducing the need for direct military spending.[22] Economic growth may affect military expenditures, as well, although there is considerable disagreement in the literature. On one hand, countries experiencing economic growth should be able to spend more in absolute terms on defense, even if those military expenditures as a proportion of the overall economy

---

[19] Mancur Olson, Jr., and Richard Zeckhauser, "An Economic Theory of Alliances," *The Review of Economics and Statistics* 48, no. 3 (1966): 266–79.

[20] Erik Gartzke, Quan Li, and Charles Boehmer, "Investing in the Peace: Economic Interdependence and International Conflict," *International Organization* 55, no. 2 (2001): 391–438; Erik Gartzke, "The Capitalist Peace," *American Journal of Political Science* 51, no. 1 (2007): 166–91.

[21] Daniel Albalate, Germa Bel, and Elias Ferran, "Institutional Determinants of Military Spending," *Journal of Comparative Economics* 40, no. 2 (2012): 279; David A. Lake, "Powerful Pacifists: Democratic States and War," *American Political Science Review* 86, no. 1 (1992): 24–37; Julide Yildirim and Selami Sezgin, "Democracy and Military Expenditure: A Cross-Country Evidence," *Transition Studies Review* 12 (2005): 93–100; Collier and Hoeffler, "Unintended Consequences"; Dunne and Perlo-Freeman, "The Demand for Military Expenditure in Developing Countries."

[22] Nordhaus, Oneal, and Russet find that "Highly autocratic regimes spend much more on the military than do democracies or governments with mixed political characteristics ... And, not surprisingly, the level of national output (measured by real GDP) has a powerful effect." William Nordhaus, John R. Oneal, and Bruce Russett, "The Effects of the International Security Environment on National Military Expenditures: A Multicountry Study," *International Organization* 66, no. 3 (2012): 511–12.

decline. A state's capacity to tax and borrow also increases with development, and hence can also be expected to increase military spending.[23] Alternatively, some studies have found that economic growth had no effect on the defense effort; Benoit concluding that, "the distribution of changes in the defense burden was nearly random," while Russett finds that a decline in the economy increases defense spending.[24]

In sum, there are a number of straightforward arguments about the conditions under which states will send costly signals, and the factors that affect the amount of military expenditures in a country.

When Countries Don't Send Costly Signals

What happens when a country does *not* send a costly signal? Why might a country not invest heavily in its military? Arguments about why a country would invest in costly signals is straightforward: it must be resolved to fight. Intuitively, if a country doesn't invest heavily in its military, then it must not care that much about an issue and not be willing to fight over it. Indeed, this is the most straightforward application of bargaining theory, and how most of the literature views costly signals. Differentiating between costly signals and cheap talk make intuitive sense: if there are no costly signals, the country must not be resolved to fight. Thus, Canada does not send costly signals to the United States because it does not fear American invasion. Germany and the United Kingdom a century ago sent costly signals about their willingness to fight, but today neither country sends costly signals to each other because today they do not view each other as potential enemies.[25]

[23] Karen Rasler and William Thompson, "Assessing the Costs of War: A Preliminary Cut," in *The Effects of War on Society*, ed. Gorgio Ausenda (Republic of San Marino: Center for Interdisciplinary Research on Societal Stress, 1992): 245–280.

[24] Emile Benoit, *Defense and Economic Growth in Developing Countries* (Lanham: Lexington, 1973); Bruce Russett, *Controlling the Sword: The Democratic Governance of National Security* (Cambridge: Harvard University Press, 1990); see also Karl DeRouen, Jr., "The Guns-Growth Relationship in Israel," *Journal of Peace Research* 37, no. 1 (2000): 71–83; Collier and Hoeffler, "Unintended Consequences"; Guy D. Whitten and Laron K. Williams, "Buttery Guns and Welfare Hawks: The Politics of Defense Spending in Advanced Industrial Democracies," *American Journal of Political Science* 55, no. 1 (2011): 117–34.

[25] There are limited exceptions to this general result. Slantchev, for example, argues that a powerful country in very particular circumstances might want to

Despite the seemingly straightforward manner in which to apply the theory, however, there are two ad hoc explanations for low military expenditures – an absence of costly signals – that potentially arise. Some scholars argue that a country might be too weak to balance and hence does not prepare to fight, or that country might be "passing the buck" and letting a powerful patron defend it. However, there are numerous theoretical and logical problems with these two common rejoinders. Unfortunately, theory is of little guidance in sorting out when an issue is not important enough to fight over, when a country simply capitulates because it is too small, and when a country is just avoiding the issue by passing the buck to an alliance partner.

These rejoinders are essentially guesses – observationally equivalent but tautological ideas arrived at through backward induction. In ad hoc application, the observer has already decided that a state *must be* fearful, and because there is no evidence of fear, therefore it must have capitulated without fighting. Furthermore, these two rejoinders are mutually contradictory – a country cannot simultaneously be capitulating because it is too small to balance and also not capitulating because it is buck passing to a powerful external ally. And most significantly, both are intuitively less compelling than the explanation that there the country simply might not be resolved enough about the issue to fight over it.

Too Small to Balance and Costly Signals

Some scholars argue that East Asian states are simply "too small to balance" against China and, thus, are unwilling to send costly signals because the difference in power is too large to overcome.[26] Intuitively, it is highly unlikely that a state cares deeply about an issue but simply gives up. When states are resolved and willing to fight for it, then even much smaller countries facing an unfavorable balance of power will send costly signals to demonstrate that resolve. And the weight

conceal its intentions in order to gain a tactical advantage over an adversary through surprise attack. But these exceptions are rare and occur only under restrictive scope conditions. Branislav Slantchev, "Feigning Weakness," *International Organization* 64 (Summer 2010): 357–88.

[26] Robert S. Ross, "Balance of Power Politics and the Rise of China: Accommodation and Balancing in East Asia," *Security Studies* 15, no. 3 (September 2006): 355–95.

of theoretical scholarship and historical and contemporary evidence from East Asia reveals that even the small Asian minnows can and do send costly signals to regional and global behemoths when they truly care about an issue. If states are faced with challenges such as national survival, then states will send costly signals.

Although it may seem intuitive that larger powers can push around smaller powers, what is often overlooked is the intensity of resolve between the two parties. Sometimes, small states simply care more about an issue than a larger adversary. In this way, "too small to balance" emphasizes the relative capabilities of two sides but ignores the key theoretical contribution of bargaining theory. It is precisely the intensity of a country's resolve that lies at the heart of the bargaining theory of war.[27] One of the most important contributions of bargaining theory was recognition that it is not simply the relative capabilities of two sides, but rather the intensity of resolve, that is key for understanding the contours and dynamics of international disputes. As Todd Sechser points out, asymmetric compellent threats (that is, a big bully trying to push a smaller country around) rarely succeed, because "an abundance of military power can be self-defeating in coercive diplomacy … Even when a challenger's threats are completely credible, the balance of capabilities is publicly known, and settlements are enforceable, fears about a challenger's future intentions can motivate rational targets to fight losing wars to deter further aggression."[28]

In fact, history is full of examples of small countries that did not capitulate to larger powers. Art and Cronin find that U.S. compellence was successful in less than 30 percent of cases, while Blechman and Kaplan find that U.S. compellence worked only 19 percent of the time.[29] In 1941, Japanese naval commanders in particular argued that a war against the United States was futile. Yet even so, Japan started a war it knew it would lose, and Scott Sagan notes that the "Tokyo government found itself in a desperate position in which starting a war

---

[27] Fearon, "Rationalist Explanations for War," 393–5.
[28] Todd Sechser, "Goliath's Curse: Coercive Threats and Asymmetric Power," *International Organization* 64, no. 4 (2010): 627–60.
[29] Robert J. Art and Patrick M. Cronin, *The United States and Coercive Diplomacy* (Washington, DC: United States Institute of Peace Press, 2003); Barry M. Blechman and Stephen S. Kaplan, *Force Without War: U.S. Armed Forces as a Political Instrument* (Washington, DC: Brookings Institution, 1978).

that all agreed was not likely to end in victory was considered the least repugnant alternative."[30]

Vietnam spent much of the twentieth century fighting countries far larger than itself: France, the United States, and China. In 1965, when the United States entered the war, it was widely expected that Vietnam would simply capitulate in the face of overwhelming American power. We often forget how confident American policy makers were in the mid-1960s: Stanley Karnow reports that American intelligence experts were "almost certain" that the U.S. air strikes against North Vietnam would deter the enemy. "The CIA estimated that the Communists, though they would exploit the chaos in Saigon, would 'probably avoid actions' that might bring 'the great weight of U.S. weaponry' down on them."[31] As David Levy notes:

A little show of force, they [U.S. decision makers] assumed, a few promises of subsequent American aid, a concession or two at some bargaining table, and America's opponents would see reason. Once Ho Chi Minh "sobers up and unloads his pistol," as Johnson put it, the whole thing would end with the public amply satisfied by the resolute stance against communism.[32]

However, Vietnam clearly was prepared to suffer incredible costs during its war with the United States, and its resolve was much greater than American resolve. Despite a massive power differential, Vietnam not only endured but managed to achieve essentially all its war aims by 1975. No balance of power theory could possibly have predicted that outcome – another reason that bargaining theory and its emphasis on resolve is such an important contribution to our understanding of international relations. Small countries that are resolved can often prevail.

In fact, the case of Vietnam over the decades easily conforms to the expectations of bargaining theory: when Vietnam was preparing to fight and valued the issue intensely, such as its independence, the country spent heavily on its military and suffered enormous costs. As recently as the mid-1980s, Vietnam devoted more than 18 percent

---

[30] Scott D. Sagan, "The Origins of the Pacific War," *Journal of Interdisciplinary History* 18, no. 4 (Spring 1988): 895.

[31] Stanley Karnow, *Vietnam: A History* (New York: Penguin, 1991), 417.

[32] David W. Levy, *The Debate over Vietnam* (Baltimore: Johns Hopkins University Press, 1991), 128.

of its GDP to defense and engaged in regular border skirmishes with Chinese troops.[33] That it does not spend nearly so heavily today is thus *prima facie* evidence that it does not have the same intensity of threat perceptions as it did three decades ago. Chapter 7 will show that Vietnam today is not undertaking the same militarization and not sending the same costly signals that it did a few decades ago, leading to the conclusion that Vietnam cared much more about national survival and the integrity of its land borders in the 1970s than it does about maritime disputes in the South China Sea in the 2010s. Clearly, Vietnam did not simply capitulate thirty years ago, and it is implausible that Vietnam today has suddenly become "too small to balance." It is far more likely that Vietnam does not value the issues at stake today with the same intensity as it did about national survival thirty years ago.

Perhaps most relevant for contemporary regional security is the case of North Korea. As will be shown in Chapter 4, North Korea is certainly not "too small to balance." Despite being far smaller than its adversaries, North Korea has clearly sent costly signals about its resolve, and continually demonstrates its willingness to use military force to defend its interests. In short, there is little theoretical or empirical evidence small countries capitulate in the face of greater power. If small countries care deeply about an issue, such as their survival, they will often endure tremendous costs. The key contribution of bargaining theory is precisely to point out that the intensity of resolve can often be more decisive than simply which side is bigger.

Alliances and Costly Signals

Almost all theory assumes that small countries want alliances more than big countries. Thus, a second common rejoinder when faced with an absence of costly signals could be that states "must be" passing the buck to a more powerful patron, who will send costly signals on their behalf. After all, why should small states pick a fight if a more powerful patron will do it for them? Yet as with "too small to balance," even a superficial glance at the scholarly literature reveals the causal complexity involved in making such a claim. There exists ample

---

[33] Carlyle A. Thayer and Ramses Amer, eds., *Vietnamese Foreign Policy in Transition* (Singapore: Institute of Southeast Asian Studies, 1999); Paul Quinn-Judge, "Borderline Cases," *Far Eastern Economic Review*, June 21, 1984, 26.

theoretical justification for believing that there should be wide variation in states' interactions with a powerful patron.[34] All things being
equal, the more powerful a state's alliance partner, the less incentive a
state has to spend on its own defense, if it can free-ride on a stronger
alliance partner.[35] Conversely, states lacking a powerful ally can be
expected to feel more threatened than those with a powerful ally, and
we should be able to observe different levels of military expenditures
between the two when facing an external threat. If this is the case, we
would look for clear costly signals on the part of the patron for when
it would defend an ally. The clearer the signal, the more likely the
patron will defend the small state.

But will the powerful patron actually come to the protégé's aid when
the time comes? Small countries are always aware that a more powerful country might abandon it; and this possibility of abandonment
has formed one of the key elements of alliance theory.[36] Thus, there
are good theoretical reasons to believe that a powerful patron would
not want to be entrapped into a war, hence not want the small state
to make costly signals.[37] The small state would want to send a costly
signal because it would lock in the patron. The more the small state
believes the patron will support it, the more reason it has to make a

[34] Brett Ashley Leeds, "Do Alliances Deter Aggression? The Influence of Military
Alliances on the Initiation of Militarized Interstate Disputes," *American
Journal of Political Science* 47, no. 3 (2003): 427–39; Brett V. Benson,
Constructing International Security: Alliances, Deterrence, and Moral Hazard
(New York: Cambridge University Press, 2012); Brett V. Benson, Patrick B.
Bentley, and James Lee Ray, "Ally Provocateur: Why Allies Do Not Always
Behave," *Journal of Peace Research* 50, no. 2 (2012): 47–58; Songying Fang,
Jesse C. Johnson, and Brett Ashley Leeds, "To Concede or to Resist? The
Restraining Effect of Military Alliances," *International Organization* 68, no. 4
(2014): 775–809.
[35] Olson and Zeckhauser, *An Economic Theory of Alliances*; Morrow, "Arms
Versus Allies," 214; Cha, *Alignment Despite Antagonism*.
[36] Thomas J. Christensen and Jack Snyder, "Chain Gangs and Passed
Bucks: Predicting Alliance Patterns in Multipolarity," *International
Organization* 44, no. 2 (1990): 137–68; Glenn H. Snyder, *Alliance Politics*
(Ithaca: Cornell University Press, 1997); Alastair Smith, "To Intervene
or Not to Intervene: A Biased Decision," *Journal of Conflict Resolution*
40, no. 1 (1996): 16–40; Michael Beckley, "The Myth of Entangling
Alliances: Reassessing the Security Risks of U.S. Defense Pacts," *International
Security* 39, no. 4 (2015): 7–48.
[37] Snyder, *Alliance Politics*; Smith, "To Intervene or Not to Intervene"; Victor D.
Cha, "Powerplay: Origins of the U.S. Alliance System in Asia," *International
Security* 34, no. 3 (Winter 2009/2010), 158–96.

costly signal. The more unsure, the less likely the costly signal because it could be abandoned. Or, the logic could work in the opposite direction: the more unsure the small state, the more it must hedge against the possibility of abandonment and thus should be sending costly signals or at least investing in its own military. The surer the small state is of a patron's support, the less it needs to send a costly signal or build its own military. In short, the theoretical literature as it stands today provides poor guidance.

Unpacking the theoretical predictions for when a country cares about an issue enough to fight and when it does not; when a small state will believe a powerful patron, and when it will not; and when a small states capitulates and when it does not, is key to making systematic claims about when countries send costly signals. While bargaining theory is still useful for explaining state behavior during crises, an empirical application of the theory reveals that it is difficult to predict when states will send costly signals over an issue they care deeply about, and to determine why states are not sending costly signals even if they are resolved.

In short, the weight of theoretical and empirical literature leads to the conclusion that there is probably more justification to expect that when a state cares about an issue, it will fight, no matter what the difference in the balance of power. What the theoretical literature lacks is a causal hypothesis that *ex ante* can differentiate between small states that capitulate and small states that simply do not care enough to fight. Absent that hypothesis, any argument about too small to balance is backward induction and tautological: the state must be too small to balance because it did not balance.

These competing hypotheses lead to observationally equivalent outcomes. Formal theory and indeed theories of arms races are both of little guidance for adjudicating these competing claims. When this happens, the only way to adjudicate between competing hypotheses is through careful empirical research in a particular country that can provide evidence to help decide that particular country's perceptions, intentions, resolve, and strategies.

Conclusion: Most Countries Are "Playing Poker with the Cards Exposed"

This book will show that costly signals do work, and they are generally quite easily identifiable. To focus on the intensity of a country's resolve, rather than simply looking at its capabilities and the balance of power, is a major step forward in understanding the sources of international conflict. Applying the theory to empirical cases should also be straightforward. After all, the point of bargaining theory is that costly signals should be clear and aimed at communicating and bargaining between countries. The way to differentiate between competing hypotheses is to conduct detailed and careful qualitative research about the country in question. This book is based on careful, nuanced, and extensive research about East Asian countries' resolves, intentions, and beliefs about other countries' resolve and intentions. Situating the security domain alongside economic and social domains of interaction among countries is important for creating a full analysis of a state's priorities in a particular region, or with a particular other state. In sum, this book will use the concepts of costly signals and military expenditures as indicators of a country's resolve to fight as a guide to explaining East Asian security dynamics. But it will be sensitive to the broad and multifaceted situation within which military expenditures and costly signals appear.

This book also turns the arguments of Erik Gartzke on his head: he wrote that "What Fearon in effect asks us to imagine is a poker game in which each player is permanently assigned a particular set of cards. Players would soon identify which players had which hands."[38] Yet most of the time, both states and researchers actually *do* know a state's goals and intentions. Communicating preferences and intentions is actually more straightforward than the formal literature suggests. Most international interactions are like "playing poker with the cards turned up." Indeed, the vast majority of states and issues do a very competent job of both communicating their preferences and intentions, and also interpreting other states' preferences and goals. This is especially true because countries observe each other's costly signals, grand strategies, and intentions closely and slowly, over years and years, through a wide variety of means. This nuanced, subtle, comprehensive, and multifaceted judgment about another country is rarely simply the result of one action or indicator, but rather accumulates slowly and by a wide variety of evidence and indicators.

[38] Erik Gartzke, "War Is in the Error Term," *International Organization* 53, no. 3 (Summer 1999): 570.

3 | No Arms Race: Military Expenditures in East Asia and Latin America

Latin America is generally considered to be relatively more peaceful but less wealthy than East Asia. Conversely, East Asia is widely considered to be less stable but richer. Yet by almost any measure, East Asian defense spending and Latin American defense spending have become similar. Significantly, East Asian military expenditures have steadily declined over the past three decades as a proportion of their economies, and are now virtually indistinguishable from those in Latin America.[1]

This chapter measures militaries and military expenditures in East Asia, using Latin America as a useful comparison. There are numerous ways to measure militaries – such as examining changes in absolute defense spending or looking at specific types of procurements, platforms, and the distribution of effort between different services. This chapter measures military expenditures using those indicators, as well as measuring naval and coast guard procurement and planning. The goal is to be as specific and careful as possible in measuring what and how East Asian countries devote resources to their militaries.

As was briefly noted in Chapter 1, the data reveal that the East Asian defense effort in 2015 was almost half of what it was in 1990. With rapid economic growth outpacing other regions of the world over the past generation, East Asian absolute expenditures on defense have increased. Yet East Asian increases have been, on average, smaller than Latin American increases even accounting for the differences in economic growth between the two regions.

Put differently, three decades of leaders in East Asian countries have seen China's military and economic growth, and have decided year

---

[1] East Asia: China, Japan, South Korea, Taiwan, Australia, Singapore, Vietnam, the Philippines, Malaysia, Indonesia, and Thailand. Latin America: Mexico, Argentina, Bolivia, Brazil, Chile, Columbia, Ecuador, Peru, Uruguay, and Venezuela.

after year not to contest that growth and not to prepare their militaries for war. It is probably unrealistic to argue that the United States and East Asian governments have been so myopic that a generation of their foreign policy, political, and military leaders have been unable to see China's growth as a potential challenger to the United States and as a dominant East Asian actor. In short, while "just wait" for East Asian costly signals to China might have been a reasonable prediction in the mid-1980s or even the 1990s, by 2017 the regional power transition is now complete. There is no more question about which country will be the most powerful and the largest economy. Rather, the only question in the region is how big the gap between China and its neighbors will become. If East Asian states were going to compete with China and attempt to keep up, they would have started long ago.

No Arms Races in East Asia

The standard way in which security scholars measure a country's militarization is to measure the "defense effort" or the "defense burden," that is, the ratio of defense expenditures to GDP.[2] The defense effort serves as a proxy for both balancing behavior and domestic politics. The share of its economy that a nation devotes to the military reflects a nation's priorities and is a proxy measure for the trade-offs the country chooses to make. When countries perceive a significant external threat, military priorities take precedence over domestic priorities such as education or social services. In times of relative peace, countries are more willing to devote a greater share of their economy to domestic priorities – perhaps the best example of this was the ephemeral "peace dividend" following the Cold War.

By this most widely used measure of external threat and arms races, data on the East Asian defense effort reveal that East Asian military expenditures have declined fairly significantly over the past quarter-century. The data presented in Chapter 1 bear repeating here. The eleven major East Asian countries (including China) devoted an average of 3.35 percent of their economies to military expenditures in

---

[2] Benjamin Goldsmith, "Defense Effort and Institutional Theories of Democratic Peace and Victory," *Security Studies* 16, no. 2 (2007): 189–222; Dan Reiter and Allan C. Stam III, *Democracies at War* (Princeton: Princeton University Press, 2002).

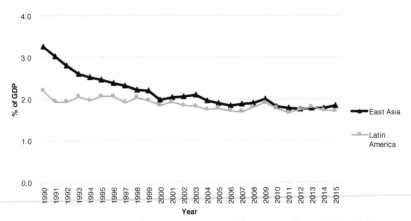

Figure 3.1 East Asian and Latin American defense spending, 1990–2015 (% of GDP).
Countries: China, Japan, South Korea, Taiwan, Vietnam, Philippines, Singapore, Malaysia, Indonesia, Thailand, Australia.
Latin America: Argentina, Bolivia, Brazil, Chile, Columbia, Ecuador, Peru, Uruguay, and Venezuela.
Source: Information from the Stockholm International Peace Research Institute (SIPRI), www.sipri.org/databases/milex, 2016.

1990, but by 2015 that average was 1.84 percent of GDP (Figure 3.1).[3] Furthermore, the gap between East Asian and Latin American spending has narrowed considerably. In 2015, Latin American countries devoted an average of 1.70 percent of their economies to the military.

Even measured in absolute terms, Japanese defense expenditures rose only 27 percent over twenty-five years when adjusted for inflation, and Japanese Prime Minister Abe's proposed increases will total only 5 percent by 2018 (Figure 3.2).

The level of military expenditures may be similar between the two regions, but what about the changes in expenditures? Although examining changes in absolute defense spending may provide insights, we should be cautious about inferring too much from these data. As Benjamin Goldsmith notes, "The price paid in analytical power is high. Measuring only changes in defense spending does not distinguish between countries with relatively high or low levels of spending – obviously a serious drawback if we are interested in the determinants

---

[3] Stockholm International Peace Research Institute (SIPRI), 2014.

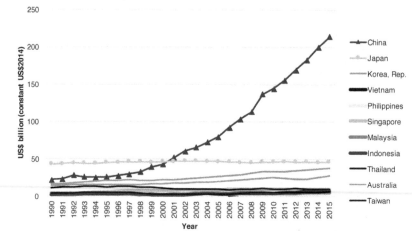

Figure 3.2 East Asian defense expenditures, 1990–2015 (constant U.S.$ 2014).
Source: SIPRI 2016.

of such levels."[4] Over a twenty-five-year period (1990–2015), absolute spending in East Asia increased by an average of 207 percent, while Latin American countries averaged increases of 246 percent (Table 3.1). The exception is China: since 1990, Chinese military spending has increased 973 percent in real terms.

Perhaps these long-term trends mask more recent concerns about China. However, average annual changes in absolute spending between 2002 and 2015 are also more similar than difference between the two regions, with Latin America actually averaging greater annual increases than East Asia. Adjusted for inflation, East Asian states (excluding China) increased their absolute military expenditures an annual average of 4.3 percent between 2002 and 2015, while Latin American countries averaged annual increases of 4.7 percent.

Defense spending may result in an arms race, and indeed, defense spending is the single most often used indicator of an arms race in the scholarly literature.[5] As Andrew Kydd points out, whether arising from

---

[4] Benjamin Goldsmith, "Bearing the Defense Burden, 1886–1989: Why Spend More?" *Journal of Conflict Resolution* 47, no. 5 (2003): 551–73.
[5] There is considerable disagreement in the literature over whether, empirically, arms races exist. Albalate et al. conclude that "Arms race models based on bilateral relationships have proved unsuccessful in explaining the determinants of military expenditures," while Ido Oren finds that in the

Table 3.1. *Change in absolute military spending (constant U.S.$ 2014)*

Country	Average annual change (%), 2002–2015	Change in absolute expenditures (%), 1990–2015
China	10.7	973.8
Indonesia	11.4	327.6
Japan	–0.1	108.3
South Korea	3.9	232.3
Malaysia	4.5	293
Philippines	4.4	184.4
Singapore	1.8	250.3
Taiwan	0.1	89.6
Thailand	4.8	156.3
Vietnam	8.8	235.2
Australia	3.4	194.4
East Asia average	**4.9**	**276.8**
East Asia average (except China)	**4.3**	**207.1**
Argentina	9.4	265.7
Bolivia	3.2	167.1
Brazil	2.2	193.8
Chile	3.7	240.8
Colombia	5.0	486.6
Ecuador	10.6	474.7
Peru	5.9	177.5
Uruguay	1.5	97.7
Venezuela	0.2	39.6
Mexico	5.5	323.2
Latin America average	**4.7**	**246.7**

Source: Calculated from SIPRI 2016.

case of India–Pakistan, "statistical findings reported by studies of the Indo–Pakistani arms race are as contradictory and inconsistent as the results generated by analyses of the superpowers' arms race. Virtually every hypothesis with regard to the sign of India and Pakistan's arms reaction coefficient receives some support." Daniel Albate, Germa Bel, and Ferran Elias. "Institutional Determinants of Military Spending," *Journal of Comparative Economics* 40, no. 2 (2012): 281; Ido Oren, "The Indo-Pakistani Arms Competition: A Deductive and Statistical Analysis," *Journal of Conflict Resolution* 38, no. 2 (1994): 190. See also Charles L. Glaser, "When Are Arms Races Dangerous? Rational Versus Suboptimal Arming," *International Security* 28, no. 4 (2004): 44–84.

a security dilemma in which a spiral of mutual fears cause two peaceful states to arm, or a prisoner's dilemma in which both sides have incentive to defect, arms races are "self-reinforcing cycles of mutual fear."[6] Buzan and Herring's definition is worth repeating here: "actors going flat out or almost flat out in major competitive investments in military capability."[7] As Buzan and Herring point out, routine, or even enhanced modernization of military forces, does not constitute an arms race; intensive qualitative and quantitative measures aimed at an opponent are the key. There is no agreed threshold at which regular modernization becomes competitive or when upgrading becomes an arms race. Simple quantitative measures of military spending need to be supplemented with qualitative discussion of the types of military spending and weapons procurement.[8]

However, even understanding these caveats, a key element of any definition of an arms race is above normal mutual investments in military forces aimed at an adversary. Colin Grey and Grant Hammond point out that an arms race involves more than simple increases in military expenditures. Rather, the "key factor is bilateral reactions in which both sides specifically designate the other to be an adversary, and where each party's military/political planning is *directly* based on the capabilities and intentions of the other party."[9] As was pointed out also in Chapter 1, Rider, Findley, and Diehl use the "straightforward and replicable" definition of an arms race as 8 percent or more increases in military expenditures by both states over at least three years.[10] By this criterion, there are no dyads in East Asia that have a three-year period of 8 percent of more increases in military expenditures in the last twenty-five years.

In East Asia, it appears that regional military expenditures are positively correlated with a home country's expenditures, but given that the East Asian regional defense burden is declining, this would imply that the region is becoming more stable compared to the 1980s. In

---

[6] Andrew Kydd, "Arms Races and Arms Control: Modeling the Hawk Perspective," *American Journal of Political Science* 44, no. 2 (2000): 222–38.

[7] Buzan and Herring, *The Arms Dynamic in World Politics*, p. 80.

[8] Joseph Maiolo, introduction in Thomas Mahnken, Joseph Maiolo, and David Stevenson, eds., *Arms Races in International Politics: From the Nineteenth to the Twenty-First Century* (Oxford: Oxford University Press, 2016).

[9] Richard A. Bitzinger, "A New Arms Race? Explaining Recent Southeast Asian Military Acquisitions," *Contemporary Southeast Asia* 32, no. 1 (2010): 60.

[10] Rider, Findley, and Diehl, "Just Part of the Game?" 90.

short, rather than arms races, the long term trend in East Asia appears to suggest an emulation or neighborhood dynamic in which reductions by some may have led to reductions by others.

Economic Growth and Military Expenditures

Does economic growth allow for greater military expenditures? The data show that although East Asia's economies experienced higher average growth than those in Latin America over both the past quarter-century (measured in constant terms), East Asian increases in defense spending in both cases were smaller than those in Latin America (excluding China; Table 3.2).

Excluding China from the East Asian figures increases this gap even further – East Asia, in short, shows almost no response to China's economic and military growth. While China, Indonesia, and Vietnam have increased their military expenditures at a higher rate than their economic growth over the past twelve years, no other country in East Asia has done so. Indonesia has the highest average annual increase in military expenditures after 2002 (11.4 percent annually), yet its overall military expenditures remain below 1 percent of GDP as of 2016. As Goldsmith cautioned, the absolute levels of military expenditures in these countries are so vastly different that it is difficult to draw any firm conclusions: Vietnam's absolute spending on defense in 2015 was US$4.5 billion (2.3 percent of GDP), Indonesia's was $7.6 billion (0.9 percent of GDP), and China's was $214.7 billion (1.9 percent of GDP). Put differently, on average and measured in constant terms, Latin American countries are increasing their military spending at a greater rate than are East Asian countries, despite lower economic growth. Richer countries have the capacity to spend more on defense, but at least in East Asia they appear to be choosing not to do so, at least compared to what is widely considered to be a more peaceful Latin American region.

Restating the data from graphically and adding regional trendlines is also revealing (Figure 3.3). Although we have reason to believe that increasing threats lead to increasing military expenditures, the trend lines in East Asia from 2002 to 2015 are actually declining, meaning that, on average, increases measured in constant terms are growing smaller over time.

Looking within East Asia, the four most likely rivals of China (Japan, Taiwan, Vietnam, and the Philippines) actually had lower

Table 3.2. *Average annual change in military expenditures and economic growth, 1990–2015 (constant U.S.$ 2014)*

	Average annual economic growth (%), 1990–2014	Average annual military expenditure growth (%), 1990–2015
PRC	9.8	9.7
Indonesia	5.1	6.5
Japan	1.1	0.5
Korea, South	5.3	3.5
Malaysia	6.0	5.4
Philippines	4.1	2.6
Singapore	6.3	4.3
Taiwan	5.1	−0.1
Thailand	4.6	2.4
Vietnam	6.8	4.4
Australia	3.1	2.7
East Asia average	**5.2**	**3.8**
East Asia average (ex. China)	**4.8**	**3.2**
Argentina	3.9	3
Bolivia	4.1	4.1
Brazil	2.8	2.6
Chile	5.0	3.4
Colombia	3.8	7.5
Ecuador	3.5	7.6
Uruguay	3.3	0.4
Venezuela	2.8	−0.2
Mexico	2.9	5.0
Latin America average	**3.6**	**3.7**

For World Bank data, annual percentage growth rate of GDP at market prices is based on constant local currency. Aggregates are based on constant 2005 U.S. dollars.

Source: Calculated from SIPRI 2016, World Bank 2015, and National Statistics of Republic of China (Taiwan) 2016.

average military expenditures growth than nonrivals (Table 3.3). The statistical analysis in the appendix confirms this finding with results showing that the four most likely opponents of China are actually less likely to spend on their militaries than other states.

Finally, to put China's defense spending in perspective, it is useful to compare it with the United States. From 1990 to 2015, the United

Table 3.3. *Rivals and nonrivals*

	Average annual economic growth, 1990–2014 (%)	Average annual military expenditure growth, 1990–2015 (%)	Average annual military expenditure growth, 2002–2015 (%)
Rivals	4.3	1.9	3.3
Nonrivals	5.1	4.1	5.0

Rivals: Japan, Vietnam, Philippines, Taiwan.

Nonrivals: Korea, Malaysia, Singapore, Thailand, Indonesia, Australia.

Source: Calculated from SIPRI 2016, World Bank 2015, and National Statistics of Republic of China (Taiwan) 2016.

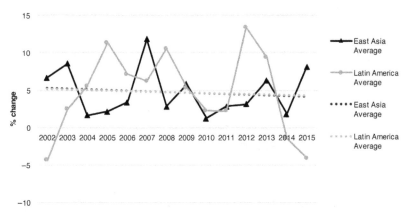

Figure 3.3 Average annual change in military expenditures, 2002–2015 (constant U.S.$ 2014).
Source: Calculated from SIPRI 2016.

States has always devoted a greater share of its economy to the military than has China, and has always spent at least twice as much on its military than China (Figures 3.4 and 3.5). China's military expenditures may dwarf those of any East Asian country, but American military expenditures dwarf those of China, no matter how they are measured.

Naval Forces as Costly Signals

The data in this book lead to the conclusion that no East Asian state appears to be sending a costly signal to China about its willingness

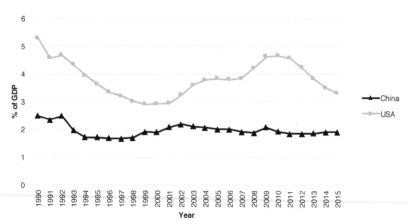

Figure 3.4 U.S. and PRC military expenditures, 1990–2015 (% of GDP).
Source: SIPRI 2016.

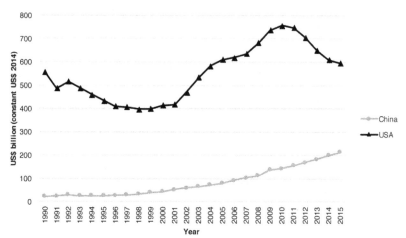

Figure 3.5 U.S. and PRC military expenditures, 1990–2015 (constant
U.S.$ 2014).
Source: SIPRI 2016.

to fight over maritime disputes. The opportunity cost of every year
spent not modernizing or expanding the military is a year falling
further behind in relative terms. This is especially true when the
potential rival has annual economic and military growth of almost
10 percent. Examining naval forces in Latin America and East Asia
tells a story similar to that of overall military expenditures – there

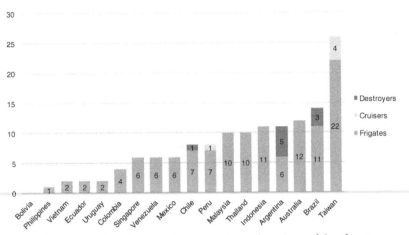

Figure 3.6 Principal surface combatants in Latin America and Southeast Asia, 2016.
Source: International Institute for Strategic Studies (IISS), *The Military Balance*, 2016.

is no discernible difference between the two regions. Brazil (fourteen) and Argentina (eleven) have more principal surface combatants than any Association of Southeast Asian Nations (ASEAN) member (Figure 3.6). Venezuela, Chile, and Argentina have more naval personnel than Australia and Malaysia; Colombia, Mexico, and Brazil have more naval personnel than either Taiwan or Vietnam (Figure 3.7). Peru (six submarines) has as many submarines as any Southeast Asian country, as well as nine principal surface combatants, including one cruiser (Figure 3.8). The total naval personnel in Latin American navies are roughly equivalent to those in Southeast Asia, and there is no discernable pattern.

The Philippine navy has only one active surface combatant, the *Rajah Humabon*, a World War II-era U.S. frigate built in 1942 and one of the oldest active warships in the world. Vietnam currently has two modern Russian-built frigates completed in 2007, with orders for two more. In short, while some countries may be modernizing and expanding their navies, the rate and scale at which this is occurring is so small as to make no realistic difference in a maritime dispute with China. Waiting is itself a costly signal in the face of a rapidly growing potential adversary. Vietnam has ordered six Kilo-class submarines from Russia, which have begun to arrive. They will replace two older

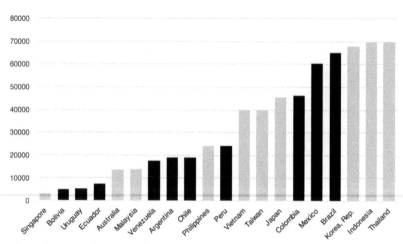

Figure 3.7 Naval personnel in Latin America and East Asia, 2016.
Source: IISS, *The Military Balance*, 2016.

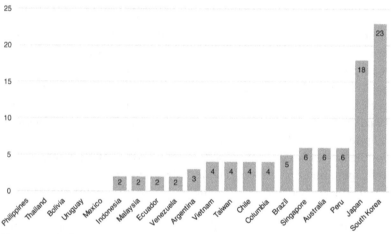

Figure 3.8 Submarines in Latin America and East Asia, 2016.
Source: IISS, *The Military Balance*, 2016.

submarines that were built in the Democratic People's Republic of Korea (DPRK).[11] However, as Carl Thayer points out:

[11] Carlyle Thayer, "Southeast Asian States Deploy Conventional Submarines," *The Diplomat*, January 3, 2014, thediplomat.com/2014/01/southeast-asian-states-deploy-conventional-submarines/.

Regional naval analysts argue that the Vietnamese People's Army (VPA) Navy, as it is currently structured and organized, is incapable of effectively operating a fleet of six Kilo-class submarines in the future. Further, Vietnam has yet to master the revolution in military affairs and create truly joint naval-air operational groups...Analysts say much depends on sustained Russia and India support over the coming years for Vietnam to develop a truly modern submarine fleet.[12]

All countries in the region are upgrading the capabilities of their aircraft, naval, and ground forces. At issue is whether this represents a normal process of modernization as economies grow and old platforms become outdated, or whether there are any extra expenditures aimed at potential adversaries. It would not be surprising, for example, if military forces in 2016 were vastly superior to those from the mid-1980s simply because of normal modernization and increases in technology. Ooi Tjin-Ka argues that current military expenditures in Southeast Asia are "part of an ongoing and expected process of modernization that ensures each state's conventional deterrence remains relevant and effective."[13] Richard Bitzinger calls Southeast Asian military expenditures an "arms dynamic," – that is, "a regional arms competition that falls somewhere short of a true arms race, but which is more extensive than 'mere' modernization."[14]

Many regional analysts argue that East Asian navies – particularly in Southeast Asia – are either old or designed for dealing with piracy, smuggling, and local concerns. Koh Swee Lean Collin writes that "ASEAN navies are deemed small, 'light' fleets optimized for littoral surveillance and defense with sealift capabilities relegated to secondary importance. They comprise mainly patrol vessels and fast attack craft save for a handful of frigates."[15] It is likely that newer forces will be more powerful than their older counterparts, resulting in higher

---

[12] Carlyle Thayer, "Vietnam's Maritime Forces," presentation at the Conference on Recent Trends in the South China Sea and U.S. Policy (Washington, DC: Center for Strategic and International Studies, 2014), 7–8.

[13] Major Ooi Tjin-Kai, "Interpreting Recent Military Modernizations in Southeast Asia: Cause for Alarm or Business as Usual?" *Pointer: Journal of the Singapore Armed Forces* 38, no. 1 (2012): 13–31.

[14] Bitzinger, "A New Arms Race?" 51.

[15] Koh Swee Lean Collin, "Typhoon Haiyan and ASEAN's Naval Effort," *The Diplomat*, December 6, 2013, thediplomat.com/2013/12/typhoon-haiyan-and-aseans-naval-effort/.

quality with lower quantity. However, in light of the decrease in overall military expenditures as a proportion of the economy over the past
twenty-five years, it seems fair to conclude that many countries have
shown they were willing to devote a larger share of their budgets to
their militaries in the past, and they could be spending far more today.
De Koning and Lipscy point out that Japan's personnel costs are so
great that the brunt of savings have come from procurement, with a
decline of 20 percent in procurement budgets for Japan's military since
2002. They point out that "Japan's focus has shifted from acquisition
to preservation, and maintenance costs have skyrocketed: at the end of
the Cold War, maintenance spending was roughly 45 percent the size
of procurement expenditures; it is now 150 percent."[16]

Coast Guards Are Not Navies

Some have argued that while military expenditures may appear low,
in reality this is not the case because coast guards are becoming more
militarized than ever before. Richard Samuels makes this argument
most forcefully, arguing that the Japanese Coast Guard (JCG) represents a "second Japanese navy."[17] It is most certainly true that the
majority – indeed, almost all – of confrontations over maritime disputes in the region are between coast guards and fishermen. The most
recent death from maritime disputes came when the Philippine coast
guard killed two Taiwanese fishermen in 2013, while a Chinese fisherman stabbed and killed a member of the Japanese coast guard in
2012. The most recent crisis in the region concerned the placement
of a Chinese oil rig in 2014 and Vietnamese and Chinese coast guard
attempts to resolve the standoff.[18]

[16] Philippe De Koning and Phillip Y. Lipscy, "Land of the Sinking Sun: Is Japan's
Military Weakness Putting America in Danger?" *Foreign Policy*, July 30, 2013,
www.foreignpolicy.com/articles/2013/07/30/the_land_of_the_sinking_sun_
japan_military_weakness.
[17] Richard Samuels, "New Fighting Power! Japan's Growing Maritime
Capabilities and East Asian Security," *International Security* 32, no. 3
(2007): 99.
[18] Jethro Mullen, "Relations Sour between Taiwan and Philippines over
Fisherman's Death," *CNN*, May 17, 2013, www.cnn.com/2013/05/17/world/
asia/philippines-taiwan-dispute/; An Dien, "China's Oil Rig Withdrawal from
Vietnam Waters: Retreat or Tactical Feint?" *Thanh Nien News*, July 21, 2014,
www.thanhniennews.com/politics/chinas-oil-rig-withdrawal-from-vietnam-
waters-retreat-or-tactical-feint-28895.html.

However, regional coast guards are considerably less powerful and much smaller than navies, whether measured by size, spending, or armaments. In all countries for which data are available, the personnel and budgets of East Asian coast guard forces are far smaller than their respective navies. The JCG's 2013 budget was a miniscule 3.4 percent of the total Japanese military budget, and the JCG's personnel was only 27 percent of that of the Japanese navy, or MSDF. For its part, the Philippine coast guard budget is only 4.8 percent of the total military budget, and the Philippine coast guard personnel were 28.1 percent of total naval personnel. Singapore's coast guard is 29 percent of the military budget and 11.1 percent of the naval personnel.

Furthermore, the signal sent by using coast guards instead of navies is that states are not yet willing to use force or militarize the dispute. As Chin-hao Huang and Avery Simmons conclude, "The increasing deployment of the CCG shifts the onus to other claimant states to either double down or retreat from confronting a civilian law enforcement agency, even as the use of force and costly military deployments are restrained to assert China's territorial claims."[19] As long as the disputes remain mostly contested with coast guards and other paramilitary or commercial entities, actual war is unlikely. And states are consciously keeping their navies from confronting each other. As Carl Thayer noted in May 2014 about Vietnam–China clashes in the Paracel Islands, "Vietnam has also kept its Navy warships and submarines in port or well away from the area of the current confrontation."[20] Use of navies would be a clear escalation and signal that states are willing to fight over the issue. That they explicitly keep their navies away is a clear signal that states do *not* want escalation.

While ramming ships and using water cannon are undoubtedly coercive, the distinction between coast guards and navies is also important because inadvertent escalation or miscalculation is less likely. All coast guards in East Asia are patrol ships, lightly armed vessels with small caliber weapons. The most heavily armed Japanese coast guard vessel is the Hida-class Large Patrol Vessel, which carries anti-air radar

[19] Chin-hao Huang and Avery Simmons "The China Coast Guard: A New Maritime Power?" manuscript, Yale-NUS College, January 3, 2017, p. 3.
[20] Carlyle Thayer, "Vietnam Mulling New Strategies to Deter China," *The Diplomat*, May 28, 2014, http://thediplomat.com/2014/05/vietnam-mulling-new-strategies-to-deter-china/.

and Oerlikon 35 mm twin cannons. Vietnam's largest coast guard vessel is a 1960s-era Soviet vessel armed with four rudimentary homing ability or straight-run-only torpedo tubes. The Philippines' most heavily armed coast guard vessel is the San Juan class, armed with 2 by 12.7 mm heavy machine guns. While confrontations might occur, escalation is less likely.

If the goal were escalation dominance, why would countries not use their navies, which are more clearly designed for fighting and far more powerful, rather than coast guards, which are trained and equipped for a number of activities, including coastal defense, smuggling, piracy, search and rescue, and other humanitarian goals? Put differently, the choice to use coast guards represents a conscious decision not to escalate tensions beyond a certain point.

Rather than sending costly signals that risk rejection and war, or making "take it or leave it" propositions, states appear to be signaling that they do not want to fight. In short, there is little evidence that states are sending costly signals, and ample evidence that they are signaling the wish to continue negotiating rather than fight. East Asian states are not excessively investing in their militaries or preparing for long-term war. They do not limit economic relations with China nor do they apply economic sanctions on China. And they actively keep their militaries from the areas of dispute.

Maritime Disputes in East Asia

Although subsequent chapters will deal with individual cases in more detail, this section will provide an overview of maritime disputes in East Asia. Particularly important is to provide some sense of scale or scope. That is, there is one maritime dispute in which the contending parties engage in all the forms of signaling and commitment that the bargaining theory of war identifies: North and South Korean disputes over the Northern Limit Line. Navies, not coast guards, regularly engage in armed clashes. As will be shown in more detail in Chapter 4, the extent of military and civilian casualties in the North–South skirmishing dwarfs any of the other maritime disputes in the region. Compared to North and South Korea dispute, the other East Asian maritime disputes are less militarized, less tense, and far less violent. This perspective is important to being able to properly explain the range of disputes and their valence.

Table 3.4. *Maritime disputes in East Asia*

Country	Disputed maritime claims
Japan	• China/Taiwan: Senkaku/Daioyu (Japan controls the islands) • Russia: Kurile/Northern Territories (Russia controls the territory) • North and South Korea: Dokdo/Takeshima (Korea controls the territory)
China and Taiwan*	• Numerous: South China Seas • Japan: Senkaku/Daioyu
Russia	• Japan: Kurile/Northern Territories
Korea	• Japan: Dokdo/Takeshima
Vietnam	• South China Seas
Philippines	• South China Seas
Malaysia	• South China Seas

* Taiwan makes territorial claims identical to those of China.

East Asian maritime disputes exist throughout the region and are the result of a century of unclear and incompletely applied border demarcations in areas under a Western, Westphalian international set of rules and institutions that had never been used in East Asia before. China is neither the cause of the maritime disputes nor even its most deeply involved participant. Japan has maritime disputes with every single country that it could have disputes with: Russia and Japan have never reconciled their dispute over the Kurile Islands/Northern Territories; Japan and both Koreas disagree on ownership of the Dokdo/Takeshima islets; and Taiwan, China, and Japan all disagree on ownership of the Senkaku/Diaoyu islands (Table 3.4). Thus far, American concern has focused on China, but Korea and China are just as focused on Japanese claims that are also outside of international law. Over six major countries claim islands in the South China Seas (SCS), for example, and all of them have engaged in land reclamation, airfield building, and competitive diplomacy. China is the most recent and perhaps the most aggressive, but it is not by any means the only active claimant attempting to change the facts on the ground.

Not only do all countries have claims and have occupied some territory, all countries are reclaiming land (Table 3.5). For example, between 2014 and 2016, Vietnam itself reclaimed 120 acres of

Table 3.5. *South China Sea maritime disputes*

	Islands claimed	Hectares reclaimed	Airfield built	Airfield size (m)	Location	Fighter/bomber capable
Vietnam	48	32	1976, refurbished 2004	550	Spratly	No/no
Philippines	8	6	1978	1,000	Thitu	Yes/no
Malaysia	5	28	1983	1,368	Swallow Reef	Yes/no
Taiwan	1	3	2006	1,195	Ita Aba	Yes/no
China	8	1,295	2014	3,000	Fiery Cross	Yes/yes

Sources: Compiled from Raul Pedrozo and James Kraska, "Will China Decide to Reduce Tension in the South China Sea?" *Straits Times,* May 31, 2016, http://www.straitstimes.com/opinion/will-china-decide-to-reduce-tension-in-the-south-china-sea; statement of David Shear, Assistant Secretary of Defense for Asian and Pacific Security Affairs, before the Senate Committee on Foreign Relations, May 13, 2015; and Center for Strategic and International Studies (CSIS) Asia Maritime Initiative, "Airpower in the South China Sea," amti.csis.org/airstrips-scs/.

new land.[21] Vietnam has also ignored American calls to halt its island building. This point needs to be emphasized: China is not alone in reclaiming land. In June 2015, Vietnamese Minister of National Defense General Phung Quang Thanh acknowledged that Vietnam had conducted land reclamation on nine "floating islands" and twelve "submerged islands," or a total of twenty-one features, but defended the actions, saying, "On the floating islands, we conducted embankment (consolidation) to prevent them from waves and erosion, to ensure safety for the people and the soldiers stationed on the islands." Thanh argued that, "The scope and characteristic of our work is purely civilian,"[22] although this is exactly what China claims, as well.

For its part, Japan is actively attempting to regrow the coral reef around Okinotorishima, which is eroding and sinking. Article 121 of the United Nations Convention on the Law of the Seas (UNCLOS) defines an island as a "naturally formed area of land," while a rock cannot "sustain human habitation or economic life on [its] own." However, these definitions are difficult to sustain in the case of Okinotori. The Japanese government has spent over $600 million to cultivate coral, erect breakwaters, and build concrete walls on Okinotori.[23] "There is no clear definition of rocks in UNCLOS – this is the government of Japan's stance," argues Hideaki Kaneda of the Okazaki Institute in Japan.[24]

Japan thus hopes to define one rock as an island that can sustain its own exclusive economic zone in Okinotori while simultaneously denying China's claim that its rocks are islands and can sustain an

[21] Asia Maritime Transparency Initiative (AMTI), "Vietnam's Island Building: Double Standard or Drop in the Bucket?," Center for Strategic and International Studies, April 15, 2016, https://amti.csis.org/vietnams-island-building/; Alice D. Ba, "Staking Claims and Making Waves in the South China Sea: How Troubled Are the Waters?," *Contemporary Southeast Asia* 33, no. 3 (December 2011): 269–91.

[22] David Alexander, "Vietnam, U.S. Discuss Land Reclamation in South China Sea," *Reuters*, June 1, 2015, uk.reuters.com/article/2015/06/01/uk-vietnam-usa-defense-idUKKBN0OH1L320150601.

[23] T. Y. Wang, "Japan Is Building Tiny Islands in the Philippine Sea. Here's Why," *Monkey Cage (Washington Post)*, May 20, 2016, www.washingtonpost.com/news/monkey-cage/wp/2016/05/20/the-japanese-islet-of-okinotori-is-the-size-of-a-tokyo-bedroom-but-the-basis-of-a-big-claim/.

[24] Robin Harding, "Japan Grows an Island to Check China's Territorial Ambitions," *Financial Times*, December 26, 2015, www.ft.com/content/e31054d8-9c88-11e5-b45d-4812f209f861.

exclusive economic zone (EEZ) in the South China Seas. As T. Y. Wang points out, "Yes, there is a double standard." The Japanese declaration of an EEZ is a unilateral declaration, because both South Korea and China challenged Japan's claim in 2008, and the UN Commission on the Law of the Seas has thus far declined to rule on the matter. In other words, Japan's claim is not recognized by UNCLOS. Jeffrey Hornung notes: "In the same way that Washington's nonsignatory status of UNCLOS remains a blight on its credibility to take others to task for convention-related issues, Okinotorishima stands as the Achilles' heel in Tokyo's credibility to take a harder position against China in the South China Sea. It is simply too hard to ignore the hypocrisy: Japan criticizes China for claiming islands out of low-tide elevations or rocks while Tokyo itself is doing the same thing in Okinotorishima."[25] As Wang points out:

While Tokyo's island-building activities on Okinotori are not as extensive as Beijing's effort, the unilateral declaration of a Japanese EEZ to circumvent international law and arbitrary detention of Taiwanese fishing vessels around the islet are problematic. Beijing is likely to exploit the obvious double standard in Tokyo's position on Okinotori to defend its own activities in the South China Sea.[26]

Vietnamese, Taiwanese, Philippine, and Japanese reclamation efforts make it harder for the United States to pursue an "international norm" against reclamation and apply it to China.[27] U.S. Assistant Secretary of Defense David Shear testified that as of May 2015, Vietnam claimed forty-eight outposts in the Spratly Islands, the Philippines eight, China eighth, Malaysia five, and Taiwan one. Shear also noted the following:

Between 2009 and 2014, Vietnam was the most active claimant in terms of outpost upgrades and land reclamation, reclaiming approximately 60 acres. All territorial claimants, with the exception of China and Brunei, have also

---

[25] Quoted in Jesse Johnson, "After South China Sea Ruling, Could Tiny Okinotorishima Be the Next Flash Point?" *Japan Times*, July 14, 2016, www.japantimes.co.jp/news/2016/07/13/national/south-china-sea-ruling-tiny-okinotorishima-next-flash- point/?utm_source=feedburner&utm_medium=feed&utm_campaign=Feed%3A+japantimes+%28The+Japan+Times%3A+All+Stories%29.

[26] Wang, "Japan Is Building Tiny Islands in the Philippine Sea."

[27] AMTI, "Vietnam's Island Building."

already built airstrips of varying sizes and functionality on disputed features of the Spratlys. These efforts by claimants have resulted in a tit-for-tat dynamic which continues to date ... While other claimants have upgraded their South China Sea outposts over the years, China's land reclamation activity vastly exceeds those of the other claimants' activities. Since 2014, China has reclaimed 2,000 acres – more than all other claimants combined over the history of their claims.[28]

China is also not the first, nor the only, country to build airfields (Tables 3.5 and 3.6). Vietnam built an airfield in 1974 and refurbished it in 1990, and the Philippines, Malaysia, and Taiwan have all built substantial airfields capable of landing military craft. In sum, decades before China decided to act, other regional claimants had made substantial moves to reclaim land and build up their maritime claims. China is, however, the most aggressive and assertive. As Michael Chase and Ben Purser write, "Beijing's activities are on a scale that vastly exceeds what any of its rival claimants are capable of doing."[29]

China is, however, the most aggressive participant in these disputes. After engaging in almost no island building for years, in 2014 China began a rapid acceleration of reclamation. China's actions over the decades to consolidate its maritime claims can be characterized as a sophisticated long-run strategy – if it can get what it wants without fighting, why not incrementally push forward? However, this begs the question of why other countries have not yet responded in any meaningful manner. If China is making incremental, "sausage tactics" progress in consolidating its maritime claims, why have its opponents not decided to show resolve and resist for reputational reasons? As Sechser points out, "when a target capitulates to a compellent threat, it reveals information about the limits of its resolve ... fears about a challenger's future intentions can motivate rational targets to fight losing wars to deter further aggression."[30]

---

[28] Statement of David Shear, Assistant Secretary of Defense for Asian and Pacific Security Affairs, before the Senate Committee on Foreign Relations, May 13, 2015.

[29] Michael Chase and Ben Purser, "China's Airfield Construction at Fiery Cross Reef in Context: Catch-Up or Coercion?" *AMTI Brief*, July 29, 2015, amti.csis.org/chinas-airfield-construction-at-fiery-cross-reef-in-context-catch-up-or-coercion/.

[30] Sechser, "Goliath's Curse," 629.

Table 3.6. *Major events in the South China Sea*

Date	Country	Event
1972	Philippines	Philippines legislature declares 53 islands as formally part of Palawan province
1976	Vietnam	Builds 550 meter airfield on Spratly Island
1978	Philippines	Builds 1,000 meter airfield on Thitu (Pagasa) Island
1988	Vietnam–China	Johnson South Reef incident, 64 Vietnamese deaths
1983	Malaysia	Malaysia builds 1,368 meter Layang-Layang Airport on Swallow Reef
1995	China	Takes control of Mischief Reef
1999	Philippines	Purposely grounded the naval ship Sierra Madre at the Second Thomas Shoal
2004	Vietnam	Begins rebuilding an airfield on Big Spratly that had been abandoned since it had served the South Vietnamese in the 1970s
2006	Taiwan	Begins work on airfield 1,195 meters in length on Taiping Island (Itu Aba)
2014	China	Begins massive land reclamation project in South China Seas (20,000 acres)
2014	China	Builds 3,000 meter airfield on Fiery Cross Reef
2016	China–Philippines	International tribunal in the Hague rules largely against China, declares "nine-dash line" has no legal standing, clarifies definitions

One country did challenge China, but through institutional and diplomatic means. In 2013, the Philippines brought a case against China to the Permanent Court of Arbitration in the Hague, prompted by Chinese island-building on Scarborough Shoal, which both the Philippines and China claim. On July 12, 2016, the court issued a unanimous decision that was a sharp rebuke to Chinese claims. The court declared that China's expansive "9-dash line" had no basis in law outside of the ordinary UNCLOS provisions, and that most of the features in the South China Seas were too small to sustain any legal claims.

The aftermath of that decision is still playing out, but the decision to go to the Hague has a number of implications. First, the Philippines made clear it was not planning to use military options to enforce the ruling, but rather was going to use diplomatic and other means to advance its claim and devise a long-term solution to its relations with China.[31] Second, although at the time the Hague ruling received intense media coverage, especially about how China would respond, in the immediate aftermath China did nothing other than publicly denounce the ruling. Sometimes "crises" are nothing of the sort – the maritime disputes have played out over decades, and China's response could come soon, or it could come years from now. Singaporean diplomat Bilahari Kausikan is worth quoting at length:

Even with regard to FON (Freedom of Navigation) there may be less difference between US and Chinese interests than immediately meets the eye. China says that is has not and will never impede FON in the SCS. This is credible in so far as the merchant marine is concerned because China too is a trading nation. The US riposte is that there is a difference between FON granted by the leave and favor of a major power and FON as a right enshrined in international law. This is true. But the US is not a party to UNCLOS and says it considers UNCLOS, or at least parts of the regime, customary international law and abides by it on that basis. It does not take an extreme skeptic to consider this another way of saying that the US too grants FON by its leave and favor, particularly when some American interpretations of FON have been questionable, for example when it tried to assert the right to stop and search vessels on the high seas under the Proliferation Security Initiative after 9/11. One may have more trust in one major power's leave and favor than another's, but that is a matter of political choice and not international law.[32]

The United States continually points out that it takes no stance on sovereignty, and that the question of sovereignty is to be worked out by the disputants. The United States calls for peaceful resolution but will not impose sovereignty, and the United States particularly will not make claims based on UNCLOS, a treaty it has not ratified and only selectively follows.[33]

---

[31] "Philippines' Duterte to China: Let's Talk on South China Sea Claims," *Straits Times*, July 5, 2016, www.straitstimes.com/asia/se-asia/philippines-duterte-to-china-lets-talk-on-south-china-sea-claims.

[32] Bilahari Kausikan, "Security Challenges in Asia," speech, Policy Forum toward the G-7 Ise-Shima Summit, Ise-Shima, Japan, May 12, 2016.

[33] Jeremy Page, "China's Defiance of International Court Has Precedent – U.S. Defiance," *Wall Street Journal*, July 7, 2016, www.wsj.com/articles/chinas-defiance-of-international-court-has-precedentu-s-defiance-1467919982.

There is in fact considerable complexity in sorting out competing claims. For example, if the United States starts supporting Japan's claim instead of China's claim in the East China Seas using the principle that Japan is the country that currently administers the Senkaku Islands, then it will end up supporting Korea's claim against Japan over the Dokdo islets, because Korea currently administers those islands. Japan has in fact put all three disputed territories (also the Russia dispute over the Kuriles) under the same management system, thus making it impossible for the United States to take sides. Furthermore, Taiwan has perhaps the strongest historical claim to the Senkakus/Daioyu, but Taiwan is not recognized as a nation-state and thus exists outside much international law. Taiwan makes identical claims to the Senkakus, as does China; if the United States recognizes Japan as rightful owner of the Senkaku/Daioyu, it undercuts Taiwan's continued existence.[34]

There have been increasing calls, such as from Ely Ratner, for the U.S. to drop "its position of neutrality" and start militarizing its own stance in the South China Seas in order to "stop China's advance."[35] But this would be problematic at best – after all, Ratner identifies Taiwan-controlled Taiping island as one possible U.S. military base. But while China claims Taiping, so too do the Philippines and Vietnam. To simply decide that whichever country administers the disputes currently has sovereignty would put the United States in the awkward position of choosing against at least one of its own allies. One reason sorting out claims in the South China Seas has been so difficult is that the various claimants cannot agree among themselves how to proceed, and thus do not present a unified front towards China. Hackers linked to the Vietnamese government, for example, have reportedly hacked Philippine government agencies related to maritime disputes, and Malaysia regularly arrests Vietnamese fishermen for illegal intrusions into Malaysia's claimed waters.[36] Furthermore, the rationale for

---

[34] Alexis Dudden first made these points informally.

[35] Ely Ratner, "Course Correction: How to stop China in the South China Seas," *Foreign Affairs* 96, no. 4 (July/August 2017), 64.

[36] Karen Lema, "Vietnam-linked hackers likely targeting Philippines over South China Sea Dispute: FireEye," *Reuters* May 25, 2017, http://www.reuters .com/article/us-cyber-philippines-southchinasea-idUSKBN18L1MR?utm_ content=buffere8a14&utm_medium=social&utm_source=twitter.com&utm_ campaign=buffer; n.a., "Vietnamese embassy verifies reported arrest of fishermen in Malaysia," *Vietnam.net* May 22, 2017, http://english.vietnamnet .vn/fms/government/178958/vietnamese-embassy-verifies-reported-arrest-of- fishermen-in-malaysia.html.

a massive increase in U.S. military presence in the region, and taking sides in sovereignty, appears to be simply that China wants it. Chapter 10 will directly address the question of whether it is wise to pursue American primacy for its own sake, rather than the means to an end, but calls such as Ratner's certainly raise questions as to the rationale and the utility of doing so.

Conclusion

In sum, the data reveal that, measured as a proportion of their economy, the East Asian defense effort in 2016 was almost half of what it was in 1990. With rapid economic growth outpacing other regions of the world over the past generation, East Asian absolute expenditures on defense have increased. Yet East Asian increases are, on average, smaller than Latin American increases measured from both 1990 and 2002. Economic growth is linked to military expenditures, but the key finding is that East Asian governments appear to have chosen to increase their expenditures at a lower rate than Latin America, despite achieving higher economic growth. The real surprise in the data, however, is the lack of response by China's regional neighbors. In short, by almost any measure, East Asia looks like Latin America in terms of military expenditures.

Military expenditures are commonly viewed as the most obvious of costly signals a country can send about its willingness to use force in disputes. In East Asia, the evidence overwhelmingly leads to the conclusion that most countries are not using costly signals in their dealings with each other, and they are not resolved to use force against each other. East Asia actually looks very much like Latin America – a region in which countries spend around 2 percent of their economies on the military, a baseline that provides border protection and control, but is not "war footing."

Appendix: Statistical Analysis of Military Expenditures

It is possible to test a number of the ideas listed in this book using standard ordinary least squares (OLS) using the following model:[37]

---

[37] Albalate et al. ("Institutional Determinants of Military Spending," 285) use pooled OLS and reject using a fixed effects model because "of the lack

$$MX_{it} = f(WBgrwt\_1_{it} + GDPPC\_IMF_{it} + Tra\_ratio_{it\text{-}1} + Regime_{it} + USally_{it} + Region_{it} + Neighborhood_{it} + War\_45_{it} + China\_rival_{it})$$

where:

- MX_{it} is military expenditures, measured by the *level* of military spending in country i at time t.[38]
- $WBgrwt\_1_{it}$ is a lagged measure of economic growth during previous year t-1, measured as the percentage change. Data come from the World Bank, World Development Indicators.
- $GDPPC\_IMF\_log_{it}$ is the log of per capita GDP.
- $Tra\_ratio_{it\text{-}1}$ is total trade with China (exports and imports) as a percentage of a country i's total trade in year t. Data from the International Monetary Fund (IMF), "annual direction of trade statistics," with data for Taiwan taken from the Republic of China (ROC) "National Statistics."
- $Regime_{it}$ uses the twenty-one-point Polity IV score in country i at time t.
- $USally_{it}$ is a dummy variable for the presence of a U.S. military alliance with country i in year t. The list of U.S. military alliances is taken from the U.S. Department of State, "U.S. Collective Defense Arrangements."
- $Region_{it}$ is a dummy variable for East Asia and Latin America.
- $Neighborhood_{it}$ is a measure of military spending of regional countries as a proxy for potential threat. Threat is measured by absolute military expenditures by neighbors as a share of home GDP.[39]

---

of variation over time of key institutional variables of the analysis makes impossible the use of the within estimator due to time invariant covariates. Therefore, fixed effects does not seem to be the right estimator." Because many of the key variables – U.S. alliances, region, and Chinese rivalry – do not change, a panel fixed effects model will not capture the results.

[38] Collier and Hoeffler ("Unintended Consequences," 4) note that "because absolute levels of military spending are highly correlated with the level of development, it is more revealing to define the dependent variable as the share of military spending in GDP."

[39] "There are neighborhood arms race effects, which turn military spending into a regional public 'bad,' inflicting negative externalities across borders ... empirically, the behavior of neighbors is important." Collier and Hoeffler, "Unintended Consequences," pp. 2, 8. Dunne and Perlo-Freeman ("The Demand for Military spending in Developing Countries") find that the military expenditures of "potential enemies" was the "most important" explanation of a country's military expenditures.

- *War_45*$_{it}$ is a dummy variable that measures the risk of participation in international war based on whether the country had been involved in a war after 1945.[40]
- *China_rival*$_{it}$ is a dummy variable for countries with known rivalries with China. 1 = Philippines, Taiwan, Japan, and Vietnam; 0 = all other countries.

Variable	Operationalization	Expected influence on military expenditures
MX	Annual percentage change in absolute constant U.S.$	DV
WBgrwt_1$_{it}$	Annual percentage change in GDP at t-1	+
GDPPC_IMF	Logged per capita GDP	+
Tra_ratio	Percentage of a country's total trade with China	−
Regime	Polity IV scores (most democratic = 10; most authoritarian = −10)	−
U.S. ally	Dummy: ally = 1	−
Region	Dummy: Latin America = 1	+
Neighborhood	Regional MX divided by home country's GDP	+
War_45	Involved in a war since 1945 (dummy)	+
China_rival	Four known countries with rivalries with China (dummy)	+

Table 3.7 presents the results of the OLS regressions for two models of military spending. Model 1 is standard OLS; model 2 clusters standard errors by country. Model 1 reveals that economic variables have by far the largest effects on military expenditures. Economic growth in the previous year (*WBgrwt_1*) increases military expenditures (4.039), while trade reduces military expenditures (−2.557). The level

[40] Collier and Hoeffler ("Unintended Consequences," 6) argue that, "the risk of participation in international warfare ... one potential indicator of the current risk of such participation [in international war] is the history of participation ... We measure the previous history of participation by a dummy variable if the country has been involved in a war since WWII."

Table 3.7. Regression – military expenditures in East Asia and Latin America

DV: MX/GDP	Coef.	Model 1	Model 2*
		P	P
WBgrwt_1	4.03981	0.001	0.022
GDPPC_IMF	0.00031	0.000	0.091
Tra_ratio	−2.55743	0.004	0.136
Regime	−0.03268	0.012	0.312
USally	0.03025	0.817	0.956
Region	−0.154106	0.310	0.807
Neighborhood	0.25516	0.000	0.036
War_45	0.48097	0.000	0.356
China_rival	−0.24257	0.093	0.702
Constant	1.50340	0.000	0.090
F(9,449)	19.69		F(9,19) = 5.32
Prob > F	0.000		0.0011
R-squared	0.2830		
Adjusted R-squared	0.2686		

* Clustered standard errors by country.

of wealth (GDPPC_IMF) has a miniscule effect (0.0000315). Being a U.S. ally has a small but positive effect on military expenditures (0.0302), while democratization decreases expenditures (−0.0326). The various "threat" variables play a small role: neighborhood is positive (0.2551), having fought a war since 1945 is positive (0.4809). Perhaps most interestingly, the dummy variable for four China rivals (Philippines, Japan, Taiwan, and Vietnam) is negative (−0.2425). While the level and direction of the independent variables are interesting, striking is that neither U.S. alliances ($p > 0.817$) nor region ($p > 0.31$) are statistically significant.

However, looking more closely at the country effects provides more insight. Model 2 clusters standard errors by country to isolate country effects. Using clustered standard errors instead of fixed effects allows the model to isolate much of the domestic politics, which are most likely very important for military expenditures but not directly related to external threats. Most notably, the entire model becomes far less significant than in the previous model – indicating that explanation for military expenditures resides in country-specific factors and not generalizable external factors. For example, previously statistically significant independent variables that become insignificant include trade with China ($p > 0.136$); democracy ($p > 0.312$); war since 1945 ($p > 0.356$); rivalry with China ($p > 0.702$); and level of wealth ($p > 0.091$). The F also drops from 19.69 in Model 1 to 5.32 in Model 2.

In short, almost none of the hypothesized factors – political regime, U.S. alliances, or a variety of external threat variables – are significant in explaining military expenditures in either East Asia or Latin America. Economic growth remains the most significant factor. This lends credence to the possibility that the real explanation for decisions about military expenditures lies in perceptions that the regions are not in fact experiencing significant external threats.

4 | *North Korea: Going Down Swinging*

Three years ago the baptism of retaliatory fire was limited to Yeonpyeong, but next time the presidential Blue House and all headquarters of the puppet regime will be targeted. If the South recklessly provokes us again, the sea of fire at Yeonpyeong will turn into a sea of fire at the Blue House.

– North Korean People's Army, November 22, 2013

We begin the case studies in this book in what may appear at first glance to be an odd place: the Korean peninsula. Yet the Korean peninsula is a textbook example of resolved countries sending costly signals to each other about their willingness to fight a war. National survival is at stake for both North and South Korea, and they respond accordingly. Both South and North Korea sink costs. Both countries tie their hands. Both build arms, deploy their military, and engage in economic competition with each other. Both sides make clear and repeated diplomatic and rhetorical pronouncements about their willingness to use force to defend themselves. In short, both Koreas use all the examples identified in the theoretical literature about costly signals, and the risk of major war on the Korean peninsula is higher than anywhere else in East Asia.

There is little ambiguity about North Korean costly signals and its willingness to fight. The North Korean case demonstrates what costly signals look like empirically, and North Korea's actions are consistent with theoretical predictions that only a resolved state is willing to bear the high costs needed to send credible threats to potential challengers. North Korea continues to attempt to convince the rest of the world that it still cares about deterrence and is willing to fight. New leaders, a deteriorating economy, and varying political considerations occasionally raise doubts about North Korean resolve. Yet North Korea consistently signals its resolve and its willingness to fight.

North Korea is a particularly important case not only because it sends a constant barrage of costly signals, but also because its adversaries believe those signals. There is almost unanimous agreement in scholarly and policy-making circles about the interpretation of North Korean actions. U.S. officials involved in extensive planning for contingencies on the Korean peninsula have consistently and overwhelmingly believed that North Korea would fight back if attacked, and indeed would probably respond with devastating force. General Gary Luck, commander of the U.S. forces in Korea in the early 1990s, told the National Security Council in 1994 that a wargame showed that the United States and South Korea would win a war, but with an estimated 300,000 to 750,000 casualties just among military personnel, and excluded civilian casualties and industrial damage. Wit, Poneman, and Galliuci note that in 1994:

The overwhelming majority of American officials ... believed Pyongyang could well respond to a preemptive strike with a full-scale assault. As General Luck told Poneman during his Washington visit, "If we pull an Osirak, they will be coming south."[1]

A decade later, those assessments of North Korean willingness to fight were still widely accepted in Washington. Even at the height of the neocon interventionism of the early 2000s, the George W. Bush administration carefully assessed the options and concluded that North Korea would fight, and that the war would be devastating for both sides. Mike Chinoy points out that in 2004:

It was evident even to the most extreme hard-liners that a military strike against the North carried enormous risks ... The mainstream view [in Washington] was "If any kind of military strike starts against North Korea, the North Koreans will invade South Korea, and they will cause enormous destruction of Seoul. And we are not prepared to handle all this."[2]

In 2017, with the advent of the Trump presidency, such questions were raised again. Yet the Trump administration also concluded that North Korea would not back down, and despite the usual tough

---

[1] Joel Wit, Daniel Poneman, and Robert Gallucci, *Going Critical: The First North Korean Nuclear Crisis* (Washington, DC: Brooking Institution Press, 2004), 104.

[2] Michael Pillsbury, quoted in Mike Chinoy, *Meltdown: The Inside Story of the North Korean Nuclear Crisis* (New York: St. Martin's Press, 2008), 161.

rhetoric from both sides, neither chose to escalate to actual fighting. In June 2017, for example, Secretary of Defense, James Mattis, told a House committee that although the U.S. would win a war with North Korea, it would come "at great cost...If this goes to a military solution, it's going to be tragic on an unbelievable scale...it will be a war more serious in terms of human suffering than anything we've seen since 1953. It will involve the massive shelling of an ally's capital, which is one of the most densely packed cities on earth."[3]

War is clearly a possibility on the Korean peninsula, and the costs for all sides would be devastating. The North Korean case is thus an important starting point for examining the variety of security strategies that exist in East Asia. It is a textbook case of costly signaling – the case against which all other cases must be compared. Because North Korea so clearly exemplifies costly signals, subsequent chapters are a stark contrast, because other East Asian cases exhibit so few costly signals.

Military Costly Signals

North and South Korea – and South Korea's main ally, the United States – regularly exchange gunfire that kills both civilian and military personnel; their navies have attacked each other three times since 2000; and both sides constantly provoke each other with military posturing, forces, tough rhetoric, and threats.[4] North Korea also often mobilizes its military, has forward deployed military units, and pursues nuclear weapon and intercontinental missile programs. North Korea is also far smaller than South Korea by many measures – population, economy, and modern weapons (Table 4.1). Yet North Korea's puny size compared to South Korea has not caused North Korea to capitulate or give up, as some theorists have suggested might happen when a smaller power faces a more powerful adversary. Rather, the weaker that North Korea has become relative to South Korea, the harder it has worked to send costly signals about its resolve.

---

[3] Ryan Pickrell, "Mattis Gives Congress a Sobering View of What War with North Korea Would Look Like," *The Daily Caller*, June 16, 2017, http://dailycaller.com/2017/06/16/mattis-gives-congress-a-sobering-view-of-what-war-with-north-korea-would-look-like/.

[4] Terence Roehrig, "North Korea and the Northern Limit Line," *North Korea Review* 5, no. 1 (Fall 2009): 8–22.

Table 4.1. *North Korea versus South Korea capabilities*

	North Korea	South Korea
Population (million)	24.8	49.0
GDP ($billion)	44	1,660
GDP per capita (US$)	1,800	33,200
Military expenditures (% of GDP)	10–25	2.6
Military expenditures (US$ billion)	5–10 (estimated)	31.8
Nuclear weapons	8–16 (estimated)	0
Military forces	1,190,000	639,000
Modern aircraft	35 (MiG-29)	226 (F-15K, F-16)

Sources: ca.reuters.com/article/topNews/idCATRE70H1BW20110118. IISS Military Balance; CIA World Factbook.

Although data on North Korea are unreliable, it is estimated that North Korea devotes between 10 and 25 percent of its GDP to its military. This is in stark contrast to defense spending of every other country in the region, including even China and Taiwan, both of which have dramatically reduced their military spending as a proportion of the economy over the past generation. North Korea prioritizes military spending over any social or economic services the government might provide, despite the enormous cost its citizens have borne.[5]

It is estimated that the North Korean military has around 1.2 million men in uniform, out of a total North Korean population of 25 million. This makes North Korea one of the most militarized countries on earth. This military has 21,000 artillery pieces and 3,500 main battle tanks. The air force is equipped with 560 combat aircraft, and the navy has 72 submarines. However, these general numbers far overstate North Korea's strength. Although North Korea superficially has thousands of artillery, planes, and tanks, the reality is that they are ancient. Most of North Korea's main battle tanks are Russian-made T-34 and T-54 type that date literally from World War II or the Korean War. The air force has mostly Soviet-era MiG-21 (introduced in 1959), or ten regiments of Chinese-made J-5 and J-6 jets, that also date from the 1950s. The most advanced fighters in the North Korean military are one regiment of MiG-29, introduced in 1983.

[5] Sandra Fahy, *Marching Through Suffering: Loss and Survival in North Korea* (New York: Columbia University Press, 2015).

North Korea's military is thus very large, but also very poorly trained, malnourished, and supplied with poor weapons. North Korea's military equipment is so old because it is too poor to buy new weapons. This is a result of decisions North Korean leaders have made that have isolated the country economically. However, it is also a testament to the seriousness with which North Korea intends to conduct a war that it has amassed such large numbers of weapons and keeps such a massive fighting force in uniform despite being so poor. This is a military that is far larger on a relative basis than any military in the region. As a costly signal, and as an indicator of the regime's willingness to fight, the resources devoted to the military are quite clear.

North Korea also sends costly signals by engaging in repeated skir-mishing that risks sparking a wider war. The most recent round of inci-dents began in November 2009, when a South Korean naval ship badly damaged a North Korean naval ship and killed an unspecified number of North Korean sailors.[6] North Korea "vowed revenge," and four months later, in March 2010, North Korea torpedoed and sank South Korean naval corvette *Cheonan*, killing forty-six sailors.[7] In response, South Korea conducted live fire exercises within viewing distance of the North Korean shore, which prompted a North Korean shelling of Yeonpyeong Island, killing two soldiers and eighteen civilians. Between 1999 and 2015, there were dozens of deaths on both sides (Table 4.2). Skirmishes between the two have regularly occurred ever since the end of the Korean War in 1953, with the largest number of casualties occurring in the 1960s.[8]

Perhaps more important than even these exchanges of fire between military units are North Korea's aggressive nuclear weapons and mis-sile programs. The North Korean nuclear issue has been one of the most pressing national security issues for South Korea and the United States over the past generation.[9] It is estimated that North Korea has

---

[6] Choe Sang-hun, "North Korea Warns South After Naval Clash," *New York Times*, November 11, 2009, www.nytimes.com/2009/11/12/world/asia/12korea.html.

[7] "North Korean torpedo sank *Cheonan*, South Korea claims," *The Guardian*, April 22, 2010, www.theguardian.com/world/2010/apr/22/north-korea-cheonan-sinking-torpedo.

[8] Dick K. Nanto, *North Korea: Chronology of Provocations, 1950–2003* (CRS Report No. RL30004) (Washington, DC: Congressional Research Service, 2003), www.au.af.mil/au/awc/awcgate/crs/rl30004.pdf.

[9] Victor D. Cha and David C. Kang, *Nuclear North Korea: A Debate on Engagement Strategies* (New York: Columbia University Press, 2003);

Table 4.2. *North Korea and South Korea casualties, 1999–2015*

Year	Incident	ROK casualties	ROK	DPRK casualties	DPRK
1999	First battle of Yeonpyeong	9 wounded	1 corvette slightly damaged	17–30 (perhaps 100) sailors killed	1 torpedo boat sunk, 3 patrol boats severely damaged
2002	Second battle of Yeonpyeong	6 killed, 19 wounded	1 patrol boat sunk	13 killed, 25 wounded	1 patrol boat severely damaged
2009				1 sailor killed, 3 wounded	Patrol boat "engulfed in flames"
2010	Cheonan sinking	46 killed 56 wounded 1 corvette sunk			
2010	Yeonpyeong shelling	2 dead 19 wounded 2 civilians killed 3 civilians wounded		5–10 killed and 30 wounded	
	Totals	54 killed, 103 wounded, 2 civilians killed, 3 civilians wounded		~36–124 killed, 58 wounded	

between eight and sixteen nuclear weapons.[10] Indeed, one likely rationale for North Korea's nuclear weapons program is precisely to counter the threat it feels it faces from South Korea and the United States.[11]

Economic and Diplomatic Costly Signals

In addition to military preparations for war, North Korea also repeatedly sends clear and costly economic signals that it is willing to bear
significant costs in its rivalry with South Korea. North Korea is one of
the most heavily sanctioned countries in the world and remains largely
isolated from the global economy. The United Nations has passed
sanctions against North Korea eight times, the most recent coming in
2016.[12] The United States prohibits almost all economic relations with
North Korea, including export and investment of any kind.[13] South
Korea prohibits economic relations with North Korea except under
specific and exceptional terms. Furthermore, South Korea still retains
a National Security Law that is broad in scope and often used to pun-
ish South Korean citizens who work with the North. These sanctions
appear to have had no impact on North Korea's foreign policy, and
North Korean statements regularly denounce them.[14] Despite the fact
that decades of economic sanctions have not changed North Korean

Leon Sigal, *Disarming Strangers: Nuclear Diplomacy with North Korea*
(Princeton, NJ: Princeton University Press, 1998).

[10] Arms Control Association, "Arms Control and Proliferation Profile: North
Korea," January 16, 2016, www.armscontrol.org/factsheets/northkoreaprofile.

[11] Sigal, *Disarming Strangers*, "The Clinton Administration Ties Itself in
Knots," 52–90.

[12] Rick Gladstone and David E. Sanger, "New Sanctions on North Korea Pass in
Unified U.N. Vote," *New York Times*, March 7, 2013, www.nytimes.com/2013/
03/08/world/asia/north-korea-warns-of-pre-emptive-nuclear-attack.html.

[13] U.S. Department of Treasury, *North Korea Sanctions Program* (Washington,
DC: Office of Foreign Assets Control, 2015), www.treasury.gov/resource-
center/sanctions/Programs/Documents/nkorea.pdf. See also U.S. Census
Bureau, Foreign Trade, "Trade in Goods with Korea, North," U.S. Department
of Commerce, 2015, www.census.gov/foreign-trade/balance/c5790.html.

[14] Colum Lynch, "Is There Anything Left to sanction in North Korea?" *Foreign
Policy*, February 13, 2013, foreignpolicy.com/2013/02/13/is-there-anything-
left-to-sanction-in-north-korea/; Edith Lederer, "UN Experts: North Korea
Continues to Evade UN Sanctions," *Salon*, February 9, 2016, www.salon
.com/2016/02/10/un_experts_north_korea_continues_to_evade_un_sanctions/;
Joseph DeThomas, *Sanctions' Role in Dealing with the North Korean Problem*
(Washington, DC: US-Korea Institute at the School of Advanced International
Studies, 2016).

behavior, some observers argue that more sanctions might be punishing enough to change North Korean behavior.[15] Yet the evidence appears to lead to the conclusion that North Korea is clearly willing to suffer the opportunity costs of economic isolation.

Perhaps most vividly, in 2013 North Korea closed the Kaesong Industrial Complex, a joint economic zone it shares with South Korea. This complex was widely viewed as safe from North Korean interference precisely because its economic benefits to North Korea were so substantial, approaching $100 million annually and employing over fifty thousand North Korean workers at its height in 2013. However, as Stephan Haggard argued, this is precisely why North Korea closed the zone – the North was sending a message that nothing was more important to it than its political goals. When North Korea closed the economic zone and withdrew all its workers in April 2013, Haggard wrote: "In any contest of resolve, weaker parties seek to show they can bear costs. If that signal was missed by anyone over the last several weeks, Kim Jong Un has just delivered it again."[16] The closing of Kaesong is a prime example of costly signaling: cutting off a profitable business enterprise is an act that is purely one of *signaling*, since it does not increase North Korea's war fighting capability.

Furthermore, the North Korean regime continually – and clearly – makes explicit public statements that vow to use force against South Korea and the United States. These statements are not meant to tie its hands with respect to its own citizens, but rather are aimed squarely at the United States and South Korea.[17] Much of the literature on bargaining theory sees rhetoric as creating domestic audience costs for the leader who makes claims – costs he will pay if he backs down from claims. However, in the North Korean case, these rhetorical claims are clearly aimed at its adversaries. What is often overlooked when

[15] Bruce Klingner, "Debunking Six Myths About North Korean Sanctions," *Korea Chair Platform* (Washington, DC: Center for Strategic and International Studies, 2014), www.csis.org/analysis/debunking-six-myths-about-north-korean-sanctions.

[16] Stephan Haggard, "Kaesong Blues," *North Korea: Witness to Transformation* (Washington, DC: Peterson Institute for International Economics, April 10, 2013), blogs.piie.com/nk/?p=9982.

[17] "North Korea Threatens to Turn South into a 'Sea of Fire' After Activists Use Balloons to Send Propaganda Leaflets over the Border," *Daily Mail*, August 14, 2015, www.dailymail.co.uk/news/article-3198893/North-Korea-threatens-turn-South-sea-fire.html.

outside observers remark on North Korean rhetoric is that this rhetoric is almost completely defense and reactive in nature. The quotation that begins this chapter is simply one example of that pattern. That is, North Korean rhetoric almost never promises an unprovoked attack, but consistently emphasizes that if the United States or South Korea attacks first, North Korea will respond with force. For example, in 2016, the United States flew nuclear-capable B-2 bombers over South Korea in a show of force toward the North. In response, North Korean Foreign Minister Ri Yong Ho said:

Only a couple of days ago, the United States has again threatened the DPRK by flying the strategic bombers "B-1B" over the military demarcation line on the Korean peninsula and landing in South Korea. We will never remain onlookers at it and the United States will have to face tremendous consequences beyond imagination.[18]

Whether the North truly feels it is being provoked is not the point – the point is that the North issues rhetorical statements consistently that threaten to fight back if provoked. While these undoubtedly do not tie the leader's hands in North Korea, they certainly do communicate to the outside world that North Korea is not intending to back down. More importantly, these threats are taken seriously by the leadership in the United States and South Korea.

Not only has the North Korean leadership made public threats to turn Seoul into a "sea of fire," Pyongyang has also taken costly actions, such as canceling family reunions and using escalatory rhetoric, to limit diplomatic relations with the South in order to signal its resolve.[19] North Korea's use of public threats to demonstrate its willingness to fight stands in stark contrast with the public statements of leaders in East Asia who advocate peaceful resolution of maritime disputes in the South China Sea.

---

[18] Nicole Gaouette, "North Korea at UN: US Faces 'Consequences Beyond Imagination'," *CNN*, September 23, 2016, www.cnn.com/2016/09/22/politics/north-korea-un-asean/.

[19] Madison Park, "North Korea Blames South, Cancels Family Reunions," *CNN*, September 21, 2013, www.cnn.com/2013/09/21/world/asia/korea-family-reunions-cancel/; Christine Kim and Joyce Lee, "North Korea Warns Foreigners to Leave South Amid New Threats of War," *Reuters*, April 9, 2013, www.reuters.com/article/us-korea-north-idUSBRE93408020130409.

No Capitulation or Free Ride on Chinese Support

The North Korean case also provides insight into the two ad hoc arguments about why a country might not send a costly signal: free-riding on an alliance or capitulating to overwhelming power. Clearly, North Korea is not simply giving up in the face of the overwhelming power of its adversaries, and North Korea is not too small to balance. North Korea shows that small but intensely resolved countries do not simply capitulate. North Korea is far smaller and weaker than South Korea and the United States, but that has not caused it to back down. North Korea is almost an exemplary case of a small power with intense resolve that is preparing to fight and is sending costly signals and searches for ways to deter its adversaries, despite being far weaker.

Furthermore, North Korea is also not free-riding on the Chinese commitment to its survival, either. China–North Korea relations exemplify these complex causal dynamics of interpreting a lack of costly signals or the presence of costly signals as inferring anything about the strength of an alliance. China has come under continual criticism for its continued support of North Korea, but this has not led North Korea to substantially reduce its military expenditures or engage in any other visible free-riding on China. Yet the North Korea–China relationship is a precise fit for the general theory about free riding: a much smaller country, backed by a powerful patron, faces an enduring dispute against a much more powerful potential rival.

China as a powerful patron of North Korea highlights the difficulty in assuming that alliances work ineluctably and seamlessly. China has its own national interests on the Korean peninsula, and for those national interests it is widely agreed that China will not tolerate a pro-U.S. unified Korea.[20] Scholars also widely agree that China is opposed to a regime change in North Korea, because collapse or change could trigger massive unrest along the China–North Korea border, unleashing as many as perhaps 2 million refugees from North Korea into China.[21] China even opposes putting pressure on North Korea to

---

[20] Yinhong Shi, "China and the North Korean Nuclear Issue: Competing interests and Persistent Policy Dilemmas," *Korean Journal of Defense Analysis* 21, no. 1 (2009): 33–47; Pacific Forum CSIS Young Leaders, "Kim Jong-Un-Prepared: Allied Contingency Plans for Korean Peninsula Unification," *Issues & Insights* 14, no. 5 (September 2013): 1–63.

[21] Victor D. Cha and David C. Kang, eds., "Challenges for Korean Unification Planning: Justice, Markets, Health, Refugees, and Civil-Military Transitions,"

moderate or change its ways – China is widely condemned by the United States and other countries because it only grudgingly agrees to sanctions against North Korea and, even when it agrees to sanctions, it does not enforce them, rendering sanctions virtually meaningless.

China has also made repeatedly clear that it will not tolerate U.S. troops along the Yalu.[22] China intervened to protect the Korean peninsula from foreign domination during the 1950 Korean War, and as far back as Hideyoshi's invasion of 1592, China sent one hundred thousand troops to support Choson Korea.[23] In short, there is widespread empirical evidence that China will defend North Korea and keep it from falling to a U.S.-backed South Korea.

Despite very clear evidence that China will not willingly abandon North Korea, and indeed despite clear evidence that China – in its own interests – will support the North Korean regime, North Korea is hardly free-riding on China and assuming that its survival is guaranteed by China. North Korea does not simply engage in external balancing by relying on China. North Korea does not assume that China will protect it. As James Person points out, "American observers may have exaggerated the docility of North Korea toward China from the beginning, according to the diplomatic record of Sino–North Korean relations during the Cold War."[24] Yet the North Korean case is evidence that a smaller protégé rarely free-rides on a more powerful patron. After all, North Korea clearly distrusts China as well as relying on China – and North Korean leaders are quite aware that China will make decisions in China's best interests, not in North Korea's best interests. So at any time, North Korean leaders are vulnerable to a Chinese decision to abandon or change their policy toward the

An Interim Report of the USC-CSIS Joint Study, The Korea Project: Planning for the Long Term (Washington, DC: Center for Strategic and International Studies, 2011), csis.org/files/publication/111221_Cha_ChallengesKorea_WEB. pdf.

[22] See, for example, Scott Snyder, "Where China and the United States Disagree on North Korea," *Asia Unbound* (Washington, DC: Council on Foreign Relations, 2016), blogs.cfr.org/asia/2016/01/08/where-china-and-the-united-states-disagree-on-north-korea/.

[23] David C. Kang, *East Asia Before the West: Five Centuries of Trade and Tribute* (New York: Columbia University Press, 2010).

[24] James Person, "On North Korea, US Policymakers Misunderstand the History Between Beijing and Pyongyang," *The Diplomat*, February 12, 2016, thediplomat.com/2016/02/on-north-korea-us-policymakers-misunderstand-the-history-between-beijing-and-pyongyang/.

peninsula. These fears of abandonment are far greater than the incentive to free-ride on a Chinese commitment. This suspicion of Chinese motives exists despite China's clear support of North Korea. In short, free rides are far less attractive than commonly believed in the theoretical literature.

Conclusion: North Korea as a Case of Costly Signals

North Korea is a key case study because it illustrates so many of the dynamics examined in this book. North Korea sends costly signals. It spends heavily on its military. It suffers enormous economic costs by limiting relations with its adversaries. But North Korea also shows how weak and ad hoc are the hypotheses about free rides on powerful patrons, and how quickly small states will capitulate in the face of greater power. North Korea is also clearly not "too small to balance," and yet it continues to defy enormous international and direct pressure on itself. North Korea is weaker, tiny indeed, compared to its main adversary, South Korea. Yet North Korea has not crumbled, does not give up, and indeed shows no signs of collapsing despite decades of predictions that collapse was "just around the corner."[25] North Korea has a powerful patron – China – yet it clearly is not free-riding on a Chinese defense umbrella. In short, many of the causal dynamics that might be expected to be in play with other countries in East Asia facing China are just as present with North Korea and its dealings with South Korea and the United States. Compared to the barrage of costly signals being sent on the Korean peninsula, the following chapters will show that it appears safe to conclude that countries dealing with China's rise are sending almost no costly signals.

[25] Byung-joon Ahn, "The Man Who Would Be Kim," *Foreign Affairs*, November 1994, www.foreignaffairs.com/articles/asia/1994-11-01/man-who-would-be-kim.

5 | South Korea: An Independent Grand Strategy

President Xi brought up the 'Chinese dream' as a national vision and it has much in common with my idea of the South Korean dream which aims to build a new era of hope and national happiness. I think the two dreams share the same ultimate goal and it's an important reason why the two countries should enhance cooperation.

– South Korean President Park Geun-hye, speaking in Chinese at Tsinghua University in Beijing, June 2013

Why might a country *not* send a costly signal? A straightforward explanation from bargaining theory is that an absence of costly signals means that a country is not resolved to fight over the issue at hand. South Korea is the first of a series of case studies where there is a notable absence of costly signals. While North Korea is the prototypical case of a resolved country that sends costly signals about its willingness to fight for its survival, South Korea is an important case study precisely because it does not engage in similar costly signaling to China.

The South Korean case is important because South Korea certainly sends clear costly signals to North Korea about its resolve. This makes the absence of costly signals toward China even more clear. Explaining a non-event can be harder than explaining events. Indeed, South Korea has confounded several expectations, the first of which concerns China. There have been predictions that Seoul would (or should) fear a rapidly growing, geographically and demographically massive, authoritarian and communist China that sits on its border.[1] There have also

---

[1] For example, see Lee Chung Min, "Recalibrating the Rebalance: A View from South Korea," *Special Forum* (Seoul: Asan Forum, April 9, 2015), www.theasanforum.org/recalibrating-the-rebalance-a-view-from-south-korea; Yoshihide Soeya, "The Future of U.S.-Japan-ROK Trilateral Cooperation: A Japanese Perspective," National Bureau of Asian Research (NBR), March 25, 2016, nbr.org/research/activity.aspx?id=659.

been calls for greater Korea–Japan security cooperation, and indeed perhaps even an alliance.[2] After all, not only does China already have the military capability to threaten the peninsula, but the power disparity between China and South Korea is huge and widening. Yet South Korea has rapidly become China's largest trade partner; it focuses its military more on contingencies with North Korea than on China, and its diplomatic relations are more tense with Japan than they are with China.

This has led to claims that Seoul may be misguidedly accommodating Beijing or that it is "tilting" toward China and has entered its orbit or sphere of influence.[3] Partly, South Korea's willingness to have good relations with China arises from instrumental South Korean attempts to affect the foreign policy of North Korea's closest supporter. After all, North Korea has been South Korea's main external threat since 1945. Yet this pragmatism does not change the reality that South Korea has drawn closer to China over the past three decades, not farther away.

In contrast, relations with Japan have not been smooth for well over a century. South Korea has had endemic friction with Japan, even though Japan shares with South Korean the traits of a capitalist market economy, a democratic political regime, and an alliance with the United States. Indeed, there are voices in South Korea that appear to be more worried about Japanese militarization than fearful of Chinese armaments.[4]

Korea's relations with China and Japan, and its reluctance to fully embrace its position in the tripartite U.S.–Japan–South Korea alliance, has often vexed American observers. For example, in 2015, Wendy Sherman – the U.S. under secretary of state for political affairs – stated in a speech that such issues as the Koreans and Chinese being "sensitive to changes in Japan's defense policy," along with the fact that

---

[2] McDaniel Wicker, "America's Next Move in Asia: A Japan–South Korea Alliance," *National Interest*, February 24, 2016, nationalinterest.org/feature/americas-next-move-asia-japan-south-korea-alliance-15301.

[3] For instance, see Julia Oh, "An Interview with Evans Revere: Trilateral Development in Northeast Asia: South Korea, Japan, and China," National Bureau of Asian Research, December 15, 2015, nbr.org/downloads/pdfs/psa/Revere_interview_121515.pdf.

[4] Seok-min Oh, "Japan's Greater Military Role Double-Edged Sword for S. Korea," *Yonhap News Agency*, April 28, 2015, english.yonhapnews.co.kr/national/2015/04/28/92/0301000000AEN20150428008400315F.html.

the two have "quarreled" with Japan over the comfort women issue, are all "understandable, but it can also be frustrating."[5] Implying that South Koreans did not understand their own strategic interests as well as she did, Sherman added that "nationalist feelings can still be exploited, and it's not hard for a political leader anywhere to earn cheap applause by vilifying a former enemy." South Koreans immediately reacted negatively to her speech, which in essence blamed Korea for its behavior toward Japan (the "former enemy").[6]

Yet these enduring South Korean traits are not simply superficial nationalist feelings exploited by cynical politicians, as Sherman claims. The lack of costly signals about resolve to fight China, and suspicion of Japanese motives and occasional costly signals about South Korean willingness to challenge Japan over certain disputes, do not arise from naivete, nor do they arise from South Koreas' inability to identify its own national interests, as Sherman implied. Rather, they reflect a deeper, stable, and fundamental Korean strategic culture. As Iain Johnston writes, strategic culture "is an integrated system of symbols that acts to establish pervasive and long-lasting grand strategic preferences by formulating concepts of the role and efficacy of military force in interstate political affairs, and by clothing these conceptions with such an aura of factuality that the strategic preferences seem uniquely realistic and efficacious."[7] This chapter seeks to explore the perhaps puzzling nature of Korea's foreign policy choices by tracing the sources of South Korea's strategic culture. In doing so, it bridges the historical foundations of Korea's strategic culture and the more contemporary sources.

---

[5] The speech was to commemorate the seventieth anniversary of the end of World War II. See Wendy R. Sherman, "Remarks on Northeast Asia," speech, Carnegie Endowment for International Peace, Washington, DC, February 27, 2015, www.state.gov/p/us/rm/2015/238035.htm.

[6] For instance, see "[EDITORIAL] Toeing Japan's Line," *Korea Herald*, March 4, 2015, www.koreaherald.com/view.php?ud=20150304000752&mod=skb; and "Japanese PM Needs to Show Courage to Admit Japan's Past Wrongdoings," *Dong-A Ilbo*, March 2, 2015, english.donga.com/List/3/all/26/410196/1. While secretary of state, Hillary Clinton chastized South Koreans for not fully supporting American policy initiatives, saying that South Koreans had "historical amnesia" and had forgotten what America did for South Korea during the Korean War. See "Hillary Clinton Accuses S. Korea of 'Historical Amnesia'," *One Free Korea*, October 26, 2005, freekorea.us/2005/10/26/hillary-clinton-accuses-s-kore a-of-historical-amnesia-2/.

[7] Alastair Iain Johnston, *Cultural Realism: Strategic Culture and Grand Strategy in Chinese History* (Princeton, N.J.: Princeton University Press, 1998), 37.

While the former greatly informs South Korea's assumptions about its adversaries and its overall threat perception, the latter facilitates its confidence about its ability to manage such threats. While history and historiography will involve a discussion about the enduring impacts of Japanese colonialism and the Korean War, the analysis goes much further back to the premodern period of tributary system of international relations; examining Korea's relations and its position in that particular context informs our understanding of why a proud Korea may be less worried about an assertive China than it is about an assertive Japan. Meanwhile, the complications that come with a compressed process of modernization and democratization have seriously tested South Korea's mettle and self-confidence, reinforcing the value and appeal of a relatively autonomous and independent foreign policy. Furthermore, although the United States is South Korea's chief ally and most important security partner, South Korea has always had a more complicated and independent relationship with its patron than Japan has had with the United States.

No Korean Costly Signals to China

On the whole, South Korea has defied expectations for how China's closest neighbors would react to its increasing capabilities. South Korea is not sending costly signals to China. Indeed, South Korean military expenditures have steadily contracted over the past three decades as a proportion of South Korea's overall economy (Figure 5.1). While Korea devoted over 4.5 percent of its GDP to the military in the late 1980s, by 2010 that proportion had dropped to under 3 percent of GDP, and it appears unlikely to increase any time soon. In short, South Korea has not responded to China's rise with any measurable increase in its own military capabilities. Furthermore, as was shown in Chapter 4, South Korea's military is overwhelmingly focused on preparing for the possibility of a war with the North, not for contingencies with China.

All regional countries are rapidly increasing their economic relations with China, and South Korea is perhaps one of the most vivid cases of that increasing economic relationship. Far from limiting their economic relations, South Korea and China seem to be embracing economic interactions. China overtook the United States as the destination for South Korean exports in 2003, and by 2007 China also overtook Japan as the number one market for imports (Figure 5.2).

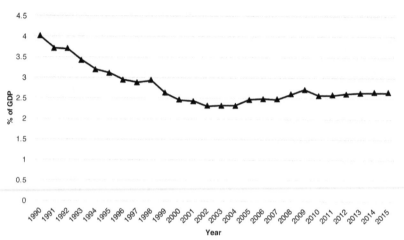

Figure 5.1 South Korean military expenditures, 1990–2015 (% of GDP).
Source: SIPRI 2016.

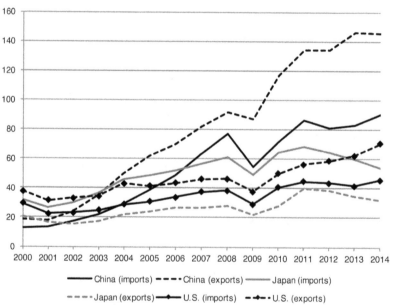

Figure 5.2 Major origins and destinations of South Korea's imports and exports, 2000–2014 (U.S.$ in billions).
Source: International Monetary Fund (IMF) E-library Data, Direction of Trade Statistics.

Needless to say, the speed with which China outpaced other major partners – particularly as South Korea's destination for exports – is significant. Although the net value of imports and exports started off roughly similar in 2000, by 2014 there is clear divergence in the dominance of China as South Korea's major trading partner. Moreover, the South Korean government announced in March 2016 that roughly nine out of ten foreigners who had obtained residency visas through investing in public development projects in South Korea (the "immigrant investor program") originated from China.[8]

The South Korean Ministry of Justice (MOJ) announced that as of February 2016, not only did the highest percent of registered foreigners in South Korea come from China at 946,895 (51 percent) followed by the United States at 139,868 (7.5 percent), but also 59.2 percent of those students studying in South Korea came from China.[9] To some extent, then, considering the basic asymmetry between Korea and China in sheer human capital, there seems to be relative reciprocity in the way that the two publics are becoming enmeshed into each other's society.

South Koreans themselves have also had relatively stable views about their neighbors over time – and this stability is more confirmation of a strategic culture in South Korea. Indeed, the South Korean public holds views that put it squarely within the mainstream of East Asian countries. The recent 2015 Pew opinion poll on global attitudes found that more South Koreans think that China will eventually replace the United States as the world's greatest superpower than thinking that China will never replace the United States (59 to 40 percent), joining India, Australia, and Malaysia. In terms of favorable and unfavorable views of China, South Korea was also well within the Asian mainstream (61 percent favorable, 37 unfavorable), joining the Philippines (54 to 43 percent), Indonesia (63 to 22 percent), and India (41 to 32 percent), among others.[10] It is for this reason that South Korea and

[8] "9 out of 10 Immigrant Investors in Public Business Are from China," *Yonhap News Agency*, March 28, 2016, english.yonhapnews.co.kr/news/2016/03/28/0200000000AEN20160328002600315.html.

[9] "Chool-ip-guk, waegukin jeongchaek tongae wolbo" [Policy and Monthly Statistics on Immigration and Foreigners], Ministry of Justice, Korea Immigration Service, February 2016, 4.

[10] Richard Wike, Bruce Stokes, and Jacob Poushter, "Views of China and the Global Balance of Power," Pew Research Center, June 23, 2015, www.pewglobal.org/2015/06/23/2-views-of-china-and-the-global-balance-of-power.

Table 5.1. *What is the most pressing issue for South Korea's foreign policy?*

Improving South–North relations	55
Strengthening the U.S.–ROK alliance	21
Strengthening ROK–China military cooperation	17
Improving Korea–Japan relations	7

Source: "Survey on America's Role in the Asia-Pacific," Asian Research Network, University of Sydney, Australia, June 2016.

its strategic culture can provide such insights about the complexity of regional relations in general, not just about the Korean peninsula.[11] Furthermore, while 21 percent of Koreans view improving the U.S.-ROK alliance as the "most pressing issue for South Korea's foreign policy," 17 percent see "strengthening ROK–China military cooperation" as the most pressing issue. Both views, however, pale beside the 55 percent who view improving South–North relations as the most pressing issue (Table 5.1).

In contrast to generally stable relations between China and Korea, Japan–South Korea relations have almost never been smooth. This is despite the fact that there are several shared features between South Korea and Japan that should theoretically make it a likely case for cooperation. Both South Korea and Japan are liberal democracies and highly interconnected in terms of trade.[12] Moreover, they are treaty allies with a common great power patron (the United States), which according to the network analysis discourse, should be a key element in catalyzing cooperative ties between otherwise distant actors.[13] To

[11] See also Tom Switzer, "Asia's Confidence in America Is Fraying," *Wall Street Journal*, June 9, 2016, www.wsj.com/articles/ asias-confidence-in-america-is-fraying-1465494886.

[12] For more on their trade connections, see Charles A. Kupchan, *How Enemies Become Friends: The Sources of Stable Peace* (Princeton, NJ: Princeton University Press, 2010); John M. Owen, "How Liberalism Produces Democratic Peace," *International Security* 19, no. 2 (1994): 87–125; and Bruce Russett, *Grasping the Democratic Peace: Principles for a Post–Cold War Peace* (Princeton, NJ: Princeton University Press, 1993).

[13] See Duncan J. Watts, "Networks, Dynamics, and the Small-World Phenomenon," *American Journal of Sociology* 105, no. 2 (1999): 493–527; Zeev Maoz, "Preferential Attachment, Homophily, and the Structure of International Networks, 1816–2003," *Conflict Management and Peace Science* 29, no. 3 (2012): 341–69; Brandon J. Kinne, "Network Dynamics and the Evolution of International Cooperation," *American Political Science Review* 107, no. 4 (2013): 766–85.

a third party, the antagonism that exists between the two has been rather confusing, especially when North Korea provides a clear common threat and the subsequent expectation that this should serve as glue rather than a wedge for bilateral ties.

The Seoul–Tokyo bilateral relationship has continually been puzzling to outside observers. South Korean president Park Geun-hye only met Japanese Prime Minister Abe Shinzo once during her first four years in office, during a November 2015 summit. This coolness toward Japan is not new. The Japanese newspaper *Asahi Shimbun* and Korean newspaper *Dong-A Ilbo* have conducted joint public opinion surveys in both countries since the 1980s, which provide telling insights on how sentiments between the two publics have shifted over time (Figures 5.3 and 5.4). Most notably, the data reveal that there has been a consistent South Korean dislike for Japan. In 1984, 38.9 percent of South Koreans "disliked" Japan, while an historical high of 22 percent "liked Japan." Those numbers have stayed roughly the same: like for Japan fell to a low of 5.4 percent in 1990, even lower than 2015's 6 percent. Dislike for Japan peaked in 1995 at 69 percent, and in 2015 was 50 percent. As for Japan, the predominant feeling is one of apathy or uncertainty, with a large percentage since the 1980s responding as having no particular feelings toward South Korea one way or the other. Japanese "like" for South Korea peaked in 2001 at 21 percent, but by 2015 was only 10 percent; "don't know" peaked in 1997 at 75 percent, and in 2015 was 64 percent. Relatively speaking then, the negative sentiments seem to flow in one direction from South Korea to Japan, although neither country particularly likes the other.

After all, it is hard to entirely exclude the role that the experience of colonization has had in shaping Korea's conception of itself and its attitudes toward Japan. Yet Korean sentiment, and strategic culture, it is not simply a result of history both recent and ancient. History may serve as a source of nationalism and strategic culture, but the way in which that nationalist narrative is propagated and sustained has as much to do with the momentum provided by the everyday consumption and reproduction of that nationalism in the neoliberal marketplace – for instance, the buying, consuming, and living of nationalism that we see through paraphernalia related to territorial sovereignty. For example, in South Korea it is possible to buy "Dokdo" ramen, and in Japan one can purchase "Takeshima" manju. It is no wonder then that there is a relatively high level of awareness and consciousness by the

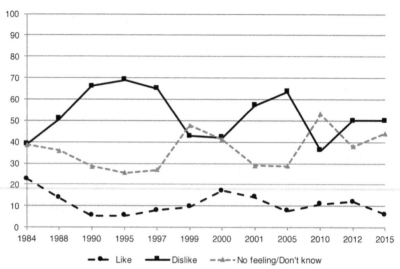

Figure 5.3 Survey results of South Korean sentiments toward Japan, 1984–2015.

Source: *Dong-A Ilbo* and *Asahi Shimbun* Joint Surveys (1984–2015).

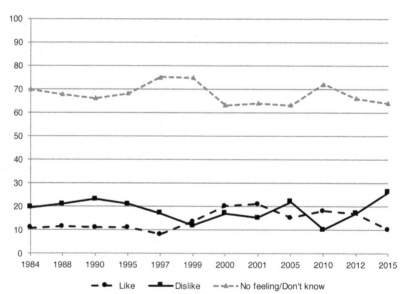

Figure 5.4 Survey results of Japanese sentiments toward South Korea, 1984–2015.

Source: *Dong-A Ilbo* and *Asahi Shimbun* Joint Surveys (1984–2015).

respective publics toward the other, even if this understanding may at times be too one-dimensional or distorted.

The Historical Roots of Korea's Relations with Its Neighbors

Why does South Korea so clearly not send costly signals to China? Why does South Korea have a relatively benign view of South Korea–China relations? Part of the answer lies in a long historical relationship between the two countries. It might seem intuitively obvious that historical relations can affect the present. Is it true that history, culture, language, religion, and context have any bearing on how East Asian leaders and peoples view and interact with one another and the rest of the world? It might be that distinctive cultures, memories, patterns, or beliefs have an effect on contemporary East Asian international relations, and acknowledging this may help our explanations and force us to consider whether we can truly explain contemporary East Asia without reference to its own culture and history.

Like many countries, actual Korean history is not the same as the story about Korean history that emerged from the twentieth century. Nonetheless, this more recent narrative is a nationalist Korean historiography that enjoys wide consensus in Korea, indeed approaching a strategic culture of conventional wisdom. Demonstrably those widely accepted historical facts are wrong, although the enduring traits of this Korean narrative fit – however roughly – the actual cause of events. For example, contemporary Koreans do not question that during their ancient history, Korea suffered serial invasions, mostly from Japan, to the point that "Korea has endured over 900 invasions throughout its history" is repeated often and without qualification.[14] John Duncan notes that a dominant strand of Korean identity consists of a "master narrative" depicting the Korean experience as "one of almost incessant foreign incursions."[15] This meme is, however, a recent perspective and

---

[14] For more discussion about the twentieth-century invention of history by nationalist states throughout East Asia, see David Kang, "Lessons: History Forward and Backward," chapter 8 in *East Asia Before the West: Five Centuries of Trade and Tribute* (New York: Columbia University Press, 2010).

[15] John Duncan, "The Uses of Confucianism in Modern Korea," in Benjamin A. Elman, John B. Duncan, and Herman Ooms, eds., *Rethinking Confucianism: Past and Present in China, Japan, Korea, and Vietnam* (Los Angeles: Asia Institute, University of California, Los Angeles, 2002), 432.

arose during the twentieth-century Great Power land grab over Korea. Indeed, the key point of that meme is not that Korea suffered invasions, but that Korea suffered invasions from Japan. Koreans do not view Chinese relations the same way. For instance, a common word for "pirate" in Korean is *Waegu*, which means literally "invaders from Japan."

More important for today's strategic culture are enduring patterns in the Korean history of regional relations. Historically, Korea has had a confident view of itself as one of the most civilized countries in the known world, and its relations with China were stable. Korea was ranked more highly than Japan by virtue of its relations to China and its more thorough adoption of Chinese ideas, Korea in particular being seen as a "model" tributary.[16] Korea was unquestionably near the top of the hierarchy of the international system at the time. Chosŏn–Ming relations were close, with Korea annually dispatching three embassies to China during the fifteenth century, and with Korean elites "eagerly importing Chinese books and ideas."[17] Ki-baek Lee concludes that the Chosŏn "relationship with Ming China on the whole [was] proceeding satisfactorily."[18] This stable relationship continued under the Qing, and Hevia notes that "... Korea emerges in Qing court records as the loyal domain par excellence. In the *Comprehensive Rites*, Korea appears first among the other domains, and imperial envoys dispatched to the Korean court are always of a higher rank."[19]

Just as important for contemporary strategic culture is the enduring idea that China, while a civilizational influence, was not the threat that the Japanese were. The extraordinary longevity of the Chosŏn dynasty (1392–1910) is itself *prima facie* evidence of Korea's stable international environment. Indeed, rather than the meme of "incessant invasions," between 1368 and 1895 – a period of over five hundred years – Korea experienced pirate (*waegu*) raids in nineteen years,

[16] So-Ja Choi, *Myeongchong sidae Chunghan kwanggyesa yeongu* [Study on Sino–Korean Relations During Ming-Qing Periods] (Seoul: Ewha Womans University Press, 1997).

[17] John E. Wills, Jr., "South and Southeast Asia, Near East, Japan, and Korea," in Grandi Opere Einaudi and Maurizio Scapari, eds., *The Chinese Civilization from Its Origins to Contemporary Times*, Vol. II (forthcoming), 18.

[18] Ki-baek Lee, *A New History of Korea* (Seoul: Ilchokak, 1984), 189.

[19] James Louis Hevia, *Cherishing Men from Afar: Qing Guest Ritual and the Macartney Embassy of 1793* (Durham, NC: Duke University Press, 1995), 50.

skirmishes along its northern border in only twenty-five years, and actual wars in only sixteen years.[20] In short, Korea experienced astonishing stability during five centuries of existence as a single political entity. While Chosŏn Korea clearly needed to manage its relations with China, relations with China did not involve much loss of independence, as these states were largely free to run their domestic affairs as they saw fit, and could also conduct foreign policy independently from China.[21] Gari Ledyard notes that:

While the Koreans had to play the hand they were dealt, they repeatedly prevailed in diplomacy and argument … and convinced China to retreat from an aggressive position. In other words, the tributary system did provide for effective communication, and Chinese and Korean officialdom spoke from a common Confucian vocabulary. In that front, the relationship was equal, if not at times actually in Korea's favor.[22]

In practical terms, the Chinese Song and Korean Koryo formally demarcated their border at the Amnok (Yalu) River in 1034, and that border has remained, essentially unchanged, to the present day. Korea must live with China, and it does not necessarily like dealing with China. But it has no choice, and indeed it has lived with China for literally centuries. The result of this long-standing and stable relationship between Korea and China was that not only did Koreans view Japan with more skepticism and as less civilized, Koreans also have less fear of China than many expect.

In contrast, premodern Korea–Japan relations were distant at best, and singularly marked by the Japanese invasion of Korea in 1592. That war, lasting six years and involving Ming Chinese troops, Jurchens, and Koreans and Japanese, was a vicious war that devastated the

---

[20] Figures taken from David C. Kang, Ronan Tse-min Fu, and Meredith Shaw, "Measuring War in Early Modern East Asia: Introducing Chinese and Korean Language Sources," *International Studies Quarterly* 60, no. 4 (December 2016), pp. 766–77.

[21] Son Seung-chol, ed., *Kangjwa Hanilgwangye-sa* [Lectures on Korea–Japan Relations] (Seoul: Hyonumsa, 1994); Etsuko Kang, *Diplomacy and Ideology in Japanese–Korean Relations: From the Fifteenth to the Eighteenth Century* (New York: St. Martin's Press, 1997), 6–9.

[22] Gari Ledyard in Mark Peterson, "China 'Control' over Choson," *Korean Studies Portal*, March 21, 2006, koreanstudies.com/pipermail/koreanstudies_ koreanstudies.com/2006-March/017808.html

peninsula and reinforced a Korean image of Japan that was violent, untrustworthy, and uncivilized. In the centuries both before and after the invasion, Japan had limited and only sporadic diplomatic interactions with Korea, and indeed the rest of East Asia. There were vibrant trade relations between Japan and Korea throughout the entire premodern era, but trade was heavily regulated and did not ever widen to become a true cultural relationship.[23] Although Japan invaded Korea only once before the modern era, it was the unpredictability and intensity of that invasion that most framed Korean views of Japan.

Events of the twentieth century reinforced Korea's premodern strategic culture. When Japan responded to the arrival of Western imperial powers in the late-nineteenth century, the results for Korea were disastrous. If stability and a focus on China had characterized the previous five hundred years, chaos and Japan dominated the twentieth century. In short, Korea's strategic culture has historically viewed China as a major power to be dealt with, and Japan as a threat to be defended against. That basic interpretation of the world holds today.

Within this larger structural change, the two most important events of the twentieth century that affected Korea's enduring strategic views of itself and the world were Japanese colonization and the Korean War. Japanese colonization in the twentieth century was not only harsh but particularly galling for Koreans. Thirty-five years of increasingly oppressive colonization resulted by the 1930s with the official outlawing of the Korean language and the prohibition on the use of Korean names had left a deep imprint on Korean strategic culture. Japan was clearly not the country to be trusted. Two invasions, spaced three hundred years apart, reinforced a historical lesson that Japan is a barbarous and violent country that is to be feared, contained, and ignored as much as possible.

Just as searing was the division of Korea into two parts, after more than eleven centuries as a unified country. With independence from Japan came the immediate U.S. and Soviet military occupation of the peninsula; brief bickering between the two superpowers resulted in the creation of two governments, both claiming to be the only legitimate Korean state and both claiming to represent the entire Korean people. The focus of Korea instantly became inward,

---

[23] James B. Lewis, *Frontier Contact Between Chosŏn Korea and Tokugawa Japan* (London: RoutledgeCurzon, 2003).

to the peninsula, rather than beyond. Every external relationship was viewed through the lens of how it would affect North–South relations. The horrific war from 1950 to 1953 devastated the peninsula, and essentially froze in place the two sides. South Korea began to focus on the United States for its survival, and more deeply, for its intellectual and strategic leadership. The United States became a focus for national security and economic development; but even during the Cold War, when South Korea was utterly dependent on the United States for its survival, Korean leaders were often viewed by Washington as unreliable and difficult.[24]

The Korean War, and its own interpretation and historical memory in Korea, demonstrates how differently Korea views its own strategic situation. China is directly implicated in the continuing division of the peninsula through its immense military support of the northern Kim regime – Mao's own son was killed in action in Korea, and it is estimated that the People's Liberation Army (PLA) suffered 150,000 to 180,000 battle fatalities. Despite China being a major cause of the survival of North Korea, it is notable that China does not figure prominently in either memorial about the war, nor does the war play into contemporary Korean views of Chinese intentions. Koreans do not blame China nearly as much as they blame the United States and Russia for the division. Furthermore, it is not China that Koreans fear today, but Japan. In short, historical memory is born out of strategic culture: different events are interpreted differently; the way in which the Korean War is remembered and portrayed in contemporary Korea shows again how enduring are its conceptions of its neighbors.

In sum, there are clearly long-enduring strands of Korean strategic culture that have their roots deep in history. A confidence, a seeking for independence, an ability to deal with a powerful China, and a suspicion of a less Confucianized Japan – all these traits were simply intensified during the twentieth century. The arrival of the Americans and the focus on the West did not fundamentally alter these traits, although they did modify them.

[24] See, for example, Jung-en Woo, *Race to the Swift: State and Finance in Korean Industrialization* (New York: Columbia University Press, 1991), especially chapter 3, "A Method to His Madness: The Political Economy of Import-Substitution Industrialization Under Rhee's Korea."

Contemporary Korea's Foreign Policy Choices

Although the U.S.–ROK alliance is currently very strong, it was only a decade ago that the alliance was considered by many to be in deep disarray, threatened by chronic anti-American sentiment within South Korea. Hillary Clinton herself accused South Koreans of "historical amnesia," because they did not sufficiently acknowledge U.S. support for South Korea during the Korean War (1950–1953).[25] From support of brutal dictator Chun Doo-hwan in the 1980s, to tepid support for Korean economic troubles during the aptly named "IMF crisis" of 1997–1998, to disagreements about how best to deal with North Korea during the Roh Moo-hyun years, there is a strand of South Korean people and politicians who are deeply skeptical of American influence and goals. While the alliance is currently quite stable, other strands in South Korean domestic politics exist and have not gone away. There are still a large percentage of Koreans who believe that *Cheonan* was sunk not by North Korea, for example.[26]

South Korea is also a key rebuttal to the idea that countries simply free-ride on powerful patrons. Some Americans believe that South Korea–Japan disputes can only exist under the umbrella of a U.S. military commitment that allows these allies to behave foolishly. The lack of costly signals from South Korea and a willingness to confront Japan lead some to think that South Korea is free-riding on a solid U.S. military commitment to its survival. Thus, respected U.S. observers such as Stephen Walt have called Japanese and Korean disputes over history and territory "indulgent squabbles," arguing that "the continued territorial dispute between South Korea and Japan, and the domestic uproar in South Korea ... derailed a useful intelligence cooperation agreement with Tokyo."[27] Ralph Cossa has proclaimed that "enough is enough," and South Korea–Japan territorial disputes are "'issues left over from history,'" which are increasing tensions to a level that

---

[25] "Hillary Clinton Bemoans 'Historical Amnesia' in Korea," *Chosun Ilbo*, October 26, 2005, english.chosun.com/site/data/html_dir/2005/10/26/2005102661015.html.

[26] Cho Jong Ik, "3 in 10 Don't Trust Cheonan Result," *Daily NK*, March 24, 2011, dailynk.com/english/read_print.php?catald=nk03700&num=7496.

[27] Stephen Walt, "The Goldilocks Problem in East Asia," *Foreign Policy*, September 3, 2012, foreignpolicy.com/2012/09/03/the-goldilocks-problem-in-east-asia.

could get out of control and are already damaging South Korea's – and Japan's and even America's – national security interests."[28] Clearly those purported national security interests are the ones that the United States thinks are more important, such as China's threat. But the point is that for South Korea, the territorial dispute *is precisely its national security interest*. An influential U.S. think tank released a report imploring Japanese and South Korean leaders to "reexamine their bilateral ties through a realpolitik lens," because it remains baffling to many Americans that these countries have more important priorities than dealing with an ostensible Chinese threat.[29] Yet far more South Koreans see Japan's military expansion as a serious threat to South Korean national security than Chinese military expansion. Indeed, only 5 percent of South Koreans see China's military expansion as a threat; and a large majority sees the most important threat as from North Korea (Table 5.2).

The debate surrounding the Terminal High Altitude Air Defense (THAAD) involves an alternative perspective about power. While the issue involves the controversial decision by South Korea to whether or not host THAAD on its soil as supplied by the United States, it has quickly morphed into a debate about whether the deployment is simply leverage against China or if it is indeed meant to counter North Korea's threat of missiles. Some in Korea are baffled at why China is not more annoyed at the North, which, after all, was the provocateur and should feel the brunt of any postlaunch repercussions. The fact is that even before the critical North Korean missile launch in February 2016, Korea watchers in the United States were proposing that Seoul "exercise its sovereign right to defend the country and its citizens against the North Korean threat brought on, in part, by Beijing's unwillingness to confront its belligerent ally."[30] The problem – at least from where

[28] Ralph A. Cossa, "Korea–Japan: Enough Is Enough!" *PacNet* no. 56, (Honolulu: Pacific Forum CSIS, 2012), csis.org/publication/pacnet-56-korea-japan-enough-enough.

[29] Richard Armitage and Joseph S. Nye, *The U.S.–Japan Alliance: Anchoring Stability in Asia* (Washington, DC: Center for Strategic and International Studies, August 2012), csis.org/files/publication/120810_Armitage_USJapanAlliance_Web.pdf.

[30] Bruce Klingner, "South Korea Needs THAAD Missile Defense," *Backgrounder* no. 3024 (Washington, DC: Heritage Foundation, June 12, 2015), www.heritage.org/research/reports/2015/06/south-korea-needs-thaad-missile-defense.

Table 5.2. *What is the most serious threat to South Korea's national security?*

North Korea's nuclear weapons development	64
Japan's military expansion	16
U.S.–China tension in Northeast Asia	10
Territorial disputes among neighboring countries	5
China's military expansion	5

Source: "Survey on America's Role in the Asia-Pacific," Asian Research Network, University of Sydney, Australia, June 2016.

South Korea stands – is that the North Korean issue has increasingly become tied to the larger U.S.–China strategic rivalry. Instead of necessarily seeing greater coleadership, then, Seoul is again sensing its lack of agency and control in its foreign policy. No matter what the South Korean leadership ultimately decides about THAAD, the point is that a seemingly obvious decision – to some outside observers – provoked such an extensive round of introspection in South Korea itself.

This is not the first time where South Korean leaders have felt the need to carve out their own independent path. Back in February 2001, then–South Korean President Kim Dae-jung had hosted a bilateral summit with Russian President Vladimir Putin, which resulted in a joint communique that was interpreted as Seoul criticizing U.S. plans for a national missile defense system (such a system would potentially require a modification or U.S. withdrawal from the 1972 Anti-Ballistic Missile Treaty). This move was viewed to be a "Russia tilt" on the part of North Korea.[31] In context, President Putin had visited North Korea in July 2000 – the first of its kind by a leader from Moscow – and there was hope that Seoul could enlist Russia's help in dealing with the North Korean threat. Immediately after the Seoul–Moscow announcement, U.S. officials pressed Seoul for a clarification of the joint statement, at which point the South Korean Ministry of Foreign Affairs made a semantic distinction between endorsing the ABM Treaty as a "cornerstone of strategic stability" and necessarily opposing national

---

[31] Patrick E. Tyler, "South Korea's New Best Friend?" *New York Times*, March 1, 2001, www.nytimes.com/2001/03/01/world/south-korea-s-new-best-friend .html.

Table 5.3. *Which country is indispensable for Korea's unification?*

China	49
United States	44
Japan	1
Russia	1
Other	5

Source: "Survey on America's Role in the Asia-Pacific," Asian Research Network (University of Sydney, Australia, June 2016).

missile defense on grounds of violating the treaty;[32] Seoul had meant to communicate the former rather than the latter. Soon thereafter, in March 2001, President Kim Dae-jung met with U.S. President George W. Bush in Washington, where the main item on the agenda was North Korea. Thus, crafting a policy toward the North has often become subsumed under a larger geopolitical rivalry, which leaves Seoul with the rather tricky situation of having to manage any fallout as a result of pursuing its own national interests that happen to give off the semblance of "taking sides." Indeed, 49 percent of South Koreans views China as the most indispensable country for Korea's unification, edging out the 44 percent who view the United States as most indispensable (Table 5.3).

There were similar elements of this delicate balancing act in question of whether South Korea would join the Asian Infrastructure Investment Bank (AIIB). The AIIB officially opened for business on January 16, 2016, with Jin Liqun as its head (a former vice-minister of finance in China) to address, among other things, the shortage of infrastructural capital in Asia. Significantly, one of its five vice-presidents is Dr. Kyttack Hong, the chair and CEO of the Korea Development Bank (KDB).[33] Even before its launch, the AIIB had attracted considerable media attention, as the very provenance of the AIIB was viewed to be

[32] Don Kirk, "South Korea Now Pulls Back from Russia on Missile Shield," *New York Times*, March 2, 2001, www.nytimes.com/2001/03/02/world/south-korea-now-pulls-back-from-russia-on-missile-shield.html.

[33] "Asian Infrastructure Investment Bank Appoints 5 Vice-Presidents," Asian Infrastructure Bank, February 5, 2016, www.aiib.org/html/2016/NEWS_0205/91.html.

a blow to U.S. economic leadership and influence in the region, given the decision by many of its key transatlantic and transpacific allies to join the institution.[34] The continued narrative about U.S. hostility to this Chinese-led effort elicited a response by U.S. President Barack Obama, who had to explain that the United States was not opposed to the idea, but that "Our simple point to everybody in these conversations around the Asian infrastructure bank is, let's just make sure that we're running it based on best practices."[35]

Nevertheless, the debate about the AIIB continued to be framed as an oppositional story of China's rising influence against a somewhat frustrated United States. What is worse was that there was a belief that the United States had brought this all upon itself, citing domestic partisanship such as the Republican refusal to approve reforms within the International Monetary Fund (IMF),[36] which purportedly encouraged China to go look for an alternative in the form of the AIIB. There are more moderate views that argue against this stark zero-sum view,[37] but it is difficult to disentangle actions that have been inspired by national interests from actions taken because of the U.S.–China strategic rivalry. In this sense, South Korea's participation in the AIIB is similarly complicated by the larger geopolitical structure. There is no reason to equate South Korea's decision to join the AIIB as siding with China (or against the United States). Instead, surveying the changes in economic and trade relations will highlight that the region has continued to evolve and morph over the past two decades in ways that make the region more focused on itself and less focused simply

---

[34] For instance, see Nicholas Watt, Paul Lewis, and Tania Branigan, "U.S. Anger at Britain Joining Chinese-led Investment Bank AIIB," *Guardian*, March 13, 2015, www.theguardian.com/us-news/2015/mar/13/white-house-pointedly-asks-uk-to-use-its-voice-as-part-of-chinese-led-bank.

[35] Ian Talley, "Obama: We're All for the Asian Infrastructure Investment Bank," *Wall Street Journal*, April 28, 2015, blogs.wsj.com/economics/2015/04/28/obama-were-all-for-the-asian-infrastructure-investment-bank.

[36] Moisés Naím, "America's Self-Inflicted Wounds," *The Atlantic*, May 20, 2015, www.theatlantic.com/international/archive/2015/05/united-states-economy-power/393650/.

[37] For an example of such moderate views, see Erik Voeten, "Why the U.S. Effort to Curb the Asian Infrastructure Investment Bank Is Doomed to Fail (and Why It Doesn't Matter All That Much)," Monkey Cage (*Washington Post*), March 19, 2015, www.washingtonpost.com/blogs/monkey-cage/wp/2015/03/19/why-the-u-s-effort-to-curb-the-asian-infrastructure-investment-bank-is-doomed-to-fail-and-why-it-doesnt-matter-all-that-much.

on the United States. This tracks with South Korea's own strategic culture of its commitment to be, most of all, autonomous and pro-Korea rather than pro-China or pro-U.S.

Conclusion

South Korea is a key case study for this book: it is one of the richest and biggest countries in East Asia, and it has good relations with both China and the United States. In fact, South Korea's pursuit of its own national interests are increasingly being coopted into the larger U.S.–China strategic rivalry, thereby generating misinterpretation about Korea's behavior and the likelihood of "taking sides." Perhaps the most important lesson to take away is that South Korea will probably never have the strategic priorities that Americans may expect. South Korea is an advanced capitalist democracy, with a vibrant civil society and clearly defined enduring interests and strategic goals. It has embraced the U.S.–ROK alliance, and even more so it has embraced the contemporary American-led international order and its institutions. But it just as often has chosen to make decisions that sometimes avoid cleaving too closely to the United States, and this is unlikely to change in the future. South Korea has an enduring and close relationship with the United States. It also desires good relations with its regional neighbors, particularly China. Seoul–Tokyo relations will probably never be as warm as Americans wish, and the cause is not myopia or naiveté on the part of South Koreans but rather arise from a deep and enduring worldview.

The evidence is consistent and broad that South Koreans do not hold China with the same skepticism that do either Japanese or Americans. This is not simply a recent function of a few incidents, but rather an enduring element of Korean strategic culture. It is not likely that one or two negative incidents with China will swing South Korean attitudes and approaches to China away from a generally positive view. South Koreans frame many foreign relations with China in commercial, not strategic terms, Korea has pushed back against a massive China for centuries while retaining its own independent national identity, and that is not likely to change. Perhaps most importantly, South Koreans feel far less threat from China than perhaps other peoples in other countries. In this context, Park Geun-hye's attendance at the seventieth anniversary of the end of World War II in Beijing, attended by Xi Jinping and Vladimir

Putin, was not a mistake or a miscalculation on her part. Nor was it an instrumental strategic visit, made with hopes of gaining Chinese support with North Korea. Rather, it was made because South Korea and China share many similar views about the war, the consequences, and the impact of the Pacific War on their two countries.

Similarly, the South Korean decision to finally deploy THAAD, and the muted Chinese reaction to it, are other evidence of a complex and relatively mature relationship between the two sides. South Korea and China might not be close, but they know how to deal with each other. Beijing largely knew and accepted that Korea would deploy THAAD, although the timing was perhaps sooner than Beijing had expected. And, despite rhetorical denunciation of the deployment, deep down South Korea knows that China would too prefer to disaggregate politics and economics and limit any spillovers from the former to the latter. This does not of course, stop Beijing from doing its best to express its displeasure with the deal on a diplomatic level: apparently, recent efforts in August 2016 by the United Nations Security Council (UNSC) to adopt a statement that denounced North Korea's ballistic missile tests were thwarted by Beijing's demand to include in the statement its opposition to the decision by Seoul to host THAAD.[38]

More directly, often overlooked as Western observers try to make sense of Korea's relatively workmanlike relations with China is that both South Korea and China share very similar viewpoints on a number of key issues. Both China and South Korea interpret the first half of the twentieth century the same way – as times of victimhood. Both see Japan as the key cause of the tumult of the twentieth century. Both see Japanese ostensible intransigence on issues of history as the key roadblock to better regional relations, and both have enduring maritime disputes with Japan that date from the Japanese imperial period. In short, on many issues China and Korea see the world similarly. It is no surprise then that an event commemorating the end of the Pacific War might have a Korean attendee, but not a Japanese.

[38] "(LEAD) China's THAAD Objection Thwarts UNSC's Push to Denounce N. Korea's Missile Launches," *Yonhap News Agency*, August 10, 2016, english. yonhapnews.co.kr/news/2016/08/10/0200000000AEN20160810005651315. html.

6 | The Philippines: Cheap Talk About a Free Ride

I will not allow it [joint U.S.-Philippine patrols] because I do not want my country to be involved in a hostile act ... I do not want to ride gung-ho style there with China or with America.

– Philippine President Rodrigo Duterte, September 13, 2016[1]

In 1991, the Philippine Senate voted not to renew a treaty allowing the United States to maintain military bases in the Philippines, ending decades of a permanent U.S. military presence in the Philippines that dated back to 1947. Subic Bay Naval Base and Clark Air Force Base were closed and turned over to the Philippines. Subic was the largest naval base in the world outside of the United States, over 262 square miles in size – about the size of Singapore. At its height during the Vietnam War, Subic hosted over 200 ships per month and employed over 36,000 Filipinos. In 1990, 13,863 U.S. military personnel were stationed in the Philippines; by 2000, there were only 79 U.S. military personnel, and as of September 2016 there were a total of 36 U.S. military personnel stationed in the Philippines.[2] Since 1992, no Philippine president has attempted to bring back permanent American military bases.

This chapter examines Philippine security strategy, particularly as it relates to the United States and China. The Philippines – like South Korea – is another East Asian country that sends few costly signals and gives little indication of experiencing a severe external threat. The Philippine military has long been considered one of the weakest in Asia and has focused primarily on internal insurgencies and border

[1] Pia Ranada, "Duterte Wants to Stop Joint Patrols in West PH Sea," *Rappler*, September 13, 2016, www.rappler.com/nation/146103-duterte-stops-joint-patrols-south-china-sea.

[2] Figures from the Department of Defense, Defense Manpower Data Center (DMDC), "DoD Personnel, Workforce Reports & Publications," November 2016, www.dmdc.osd.mil/appj/dwp/index.jsp.

control throughout its history. This focus has not changed over time, despite the increased sparring with China over maritime claims in the South China Seas.

This chapter pays particular attention to the administration of Benigno Aquino, president of the Philippines from 2010 to 2016. Largely considered one of the most pro-U.S. presidents in modern Philippine history, Aquino's administration is important because it was the most skeptical of China and the most welcoming of U.S. influence. Yet even President Aquino pursed a comprehensive approach to security that emphasized institutional, diplomatic, and economic elements. Even President Aquino did not pursue any measurable attempt to increase military expenditures or change the basic structure and focus of the Philippine military, nor did Aquino engage in key moves that would indicate costly signals or a determination to pursue a military solution to its dispute with China. What was often overlooked in the torrent of commentary about the International Tribunal in the Hague's July 2016 ruling about the South China Seas was that it was a *diplomatic* and institutional strategy on the part of the Aquino administration, not a military strategy.[3]

The most common explanation for this absence of a muscular stance is to guess that the Philippines must be free-riding on its U.S. alliance and engaging in external balancing. Almost all international relations theories of alliances overwhelmingly assume that the smaller protégé will desire closer relations with a more powerful patron; but this is only an assumption. However, as with both the Philippines and, as we will see later, with Vietnam, conventional arguments often overlook the more straightforward and obvious alternative explanation: that a small protégé may not feel an external threat, and hence may not pursue external balancing vigorously. Bargaining theory is clear in this

---

[3] For example, Robert Beckhusen implies that the Philippines will enforce the ruling through force by arguing that "The Philippines is not capable of building a navy to stand up to China in a war. But it is forming a naval force which can fight, and that might be enough to deter Chinese intrusions to a limited extent." Beckhusen, "The Philippines' Biggest South China Sea Problem: It Has Almost No Navy," *National Interest*, July 27, 2016, nationalinterest. org/blog/the-buzz/the-philippines-biggest-south-china-sea-problem-it-has-17139; Antonio T. Carpio, "How the Philippines Can Enforce the South China Sea Verdict," *Wall Street Journal*, July 17, 2016, www.wsj.com/articles/how-the-philippines-can-enforce-the-south-china-sea-verdict-1468774415.

regard: resolved countries send costly signals; countries not resolved do not send costly signals.

In fact, the Philippines reveals little evidence of external balancing with the United States, and even under President Aquino there was no possibility of allowing the United States to return to permanent military bases in the Philippines. The reluctance of any Philippine president to allow a permanent American military facility should be *prima facie* evidence that the Philippines is not free-riding. After all, the easiest way to entrap or ensnare a powerful patron is to allow that ally a permanent military presence on the protégé's land. If the Philippines is engaging in external balancing or attempting to hide behind the U.S. military, it should be doing everything possible to reestablish a permanent American military base in the Philippines in order to both deter China and also more fully ensure that America would be involved in any military clash that took place. Instead, the Philippines has reduced joint naval patrols it conducts with the United States navy; it is calling for a reduced U.S. military presence in the Philippines, and President Duterte, elected in 2016, said that he would reduce annual joint military exercises with the United States. The evidence leads to the conclusion that the Philippines desires a reduced military relationship with the United States, not an increased one that would allow a free ride.

Low Philippine Military Expenditures

Over the past thirty years, funding for the AFP (Armed Forces of the Philippines) has been steadily reduced. Furthermore, the AFP has consistently prioritized internal security over territorial defense. The reluctance of consecutive Philippine presidents to pursue military-first strategies in their foreign policy is reflected in Philippine defense spending. Even President Aquino continued a three-decade trend of reducing spending on the military. As a proportion of government spending, the Philippines reduced its military expenditures from 10 percent of the budget in 1993 to 6 percent in 2016 (Figure 6.1). As a share of the entire economy, the Philippines has kept military expenditures below 2 percent of GDP ever since the early 1990s, and that proportion has steadily declined since then (Figure 6.2). The Philippines devoted 2.5 percent of its economy to military expenditures in 1990, but by 2015 that proportion had dropped to 1.3 percent of GDP.

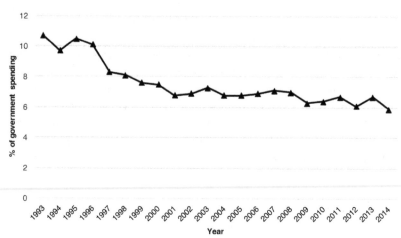

Figure 6.1 Philippines military expenditures, 1993–2014 (% of government spending).
Source: SIPRI 2016.

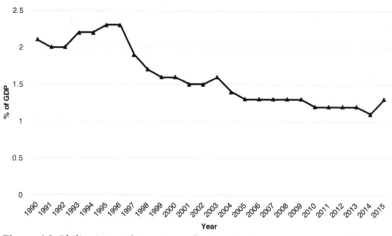

Figure 6.2 Philippines military expenditures, 1990–2015 (% of GDP).
Source: SIPRI 2016.

Over time, the Philippine navy has steadily reduced the number of principal surface combatants it deploys. In the 1980s, the Philippines had seven principal surface combatants. As these ships aged, they were not replaced. The Philippines has no plans to create a blue-water navy capable of conducting naval operations. Thus, while the

Table 6.1. *Principal surface combatants, 2000–2015 (China and the Philippines)*

	1987	2000	2005	2010	2015	Change, 1987–2015
China	53	60	63	80	71	+18
Philippines	7	1	1	1	1	–6

Source: IISS, *The Military Balance*, various years.

navy has announced plans for increases in its overall naval deployments, even if these increases actually occur, it will only return the Philippines to where it was two decades ago (Table 6.1). In January 2016, the Philippine navy commissioned its first new naval hull in two decades: an Indonesian-made landing platform dock, BRP *Tarlac*, the first of four ships ordered. The Philippine coast guard is buying small coastal patrol boats from France and Japan to join the current six patrol boats, but these will be useful mainly for issues such as piracy, smuggling, and humanitarian aid and disaster relief.

So clearly does the Philippines not prioritize the military that it is written into the constitution. Article II, Section 17 of the constitution categorically states that the state places the military below other sectors, such as education, and sets the policy that in the allocation of resources, social development is prioritized over military spending. The article reads: "The State shall give priority to education, science and technology, arts, culture, and sports to foster patriotism and nationalism, accelerate social progress, and promote total human liberation and development."

Despite more muscular rhetoric during President Aquino's term, a more direct measure of the Philippine threat perception is the military expenditure allocated for different branches of the Armed Forces of the Philippines. An examination of the General Appropriations Acts of the Philippines from 1993 to 2016 reveals that there has been little substantive change to Philippine defense policy over the past three decades. The budget allocated for the Armed Forces of the Philippines from 1993 to 2016 in fact shows a *decrease* in the percentage of total budget allocated for the navy or air force (Figure 6.3). Moreover, the gap between the budget allocated for the army, which focuses on internal security operations, and that of the navy or air force, which emphasizes external territorial security, has increasingly widened, a trend that continued until at least 2017. In 1993, the army took 49.6 percent

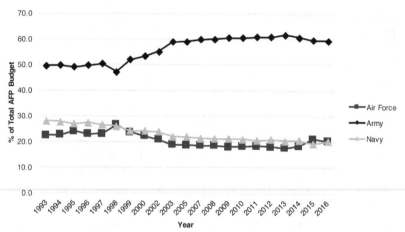

Figure 6.3 Army, navy, and air force budget, 1993–2016 (% of total AFP budget).
Note: Total AFP budget is calculated as the sum of army, navy, and air force.
Source: General Appropriations Act of the Philippines (1993–2016).

of the total AFP budget, but by 2016, that proportion had grown to 59.9 percent. Conversely, the navy took 28 percent of the AFP budget in 1993, yet by 2016 the navy's share of the budget had fallen to 20.5 percent of the budget. The Aquino administration was part of this trend: in 2010, the navy took 21.1 percent of the total AFP budget; by 2016 that amount had fallen slightly, to 20.5 percent. Even Aquino's rhetoric about meeting challenges in the West Philippine Sea was not matched by actual changes in its military expenditures.

Even more revealing is that military modernization plans have often spectacularly failed. The real question is whether there exists the political will to sustain a long-term focus on military modernization. For example, the AFP Modernization Act of 1995 allocated PHP 331 billion total funding to modernize the military over the next fifteen years. However, by the time when the law expired in 2010, the AFP had received only a total of PHP 28.9 billion, or only *9 percent of the planned total funding*.[4] The law "ran the full length of its

---

[4] "National Government Expenditures, Obligation Basis, by Sector, as a Percentage of GDP, 1993–2012 (in Percent; Data Series for the Period 1983–2012 Is Based on 2000 Prices)," *Fiscal Statistics Handbook from 1983 to 2012* (Manila: Philippine Department of Budget and Management, 2013), tables II.B.2 and II.B.3.

implementing period and expired (in December 2011) without any significant progress."[5] In sum, fifteen years of planned modernization was barely funded. Domestic politics got in the way.

Implementation problems began almost as soon as the modernization law was passed. For example, in 1995, since the AFP was reluctant to submit the AFP's Table of Organization and Equipment for the next fifteen years, the execution of the plan was delayed for another year, until 1996. By the time the Congress eventually approved the plan with the promulgation of Joint Resolution No. 28 (JR 28) in December 1996, although the Congress approved the previously proposed amount of PHP 331 billion, it broke the amount into two sub programs to cushion the expense: the core program, with an allocated budget of PHP 164.55 billion, and the ancillary program, with an allocated amount of 167 billion pesos. Consequently, JR 28 trimmed the total operational budget of AFP modernization program to a mere PHP 165 billion.

On February 25, 1998, the Philippine National Police (PNP) Reform and Reorganization Act (RA 8551) was passed, and transferred the primary responsibility of counterinsurgency from the PNP to the AFP, which reoriented the priority list of projects in JR 28 back to internal security operations. In mid-1998, at the height of the Asian financial crisis, President Estrada further postponed the implementation of the AFP modernization "for a better time when the financial crisis is over." The first appropriation from the Philippine Congress amounting to 5 billion pesos only came in 2002, six years after the plan was approved by the Congress. In its 2010 report on the AFP General Headquarters, the Commission on Audit said that fifteen years after the modernization program was established, the AFP had only implemented

---

[5] Vincent Cabreza, "Philippine Defense Secretary Admits AFP Upgrade Plan a Dud," *Philippine Inquirer*, February 18, 2012, sg.news.yahoo.com/philippine-defense-secretary-admits-afp-upgrade-plan-dud-055005371.html. A Department of National Defense White Paper found that, "While the AFPMP required a total of 332 Billion Pesos to fully realize the envisioned capabilities for naval, air, ground, and joint command and control communications and information systems, only *33.9 Billion Pesos* was provided up to the end of 2010." Department of National Defense, "Transforming the Department of National Defense to Effectively Meet the Defense and Security Challenges of the 21st Century: A White Paper on Philippine National Defense Transformation" (Quezon City, Camp General Emilio Aguinaldo, July 2012), 7.

55 percent – or 278 projects out of the programmed 504 – under the first modernization law.

This lack of focus on military modernization is likely to continue under President Duterte. Malcolm Cook observes that "Duterte clearly identifies the Moro Islamic insurgency in western Mindanao and the nation-spanning but less threatening communist insurgency as the greatest threats to Philippine security. Adding to his lack of support for military modernization is his ambivalence about the benefits to the Philippines of the alliance with the United States."[6] In sum, Philippine military expenditures since 1990 show a clear trend toward less military spending, not more. What defense spending there is tends to be focused more on internal than external threats. This trend has not changed under any of the presidents, and Duterte appears set to only continue this trend.

The U.S.–RP Mutual Defense Treaty – No Free Ride

A common explanation for Philippine low military expenditures is that the country free-rides on a U.S. military alliance. Called "external balancing" in the scholarly literature, it is actually not clear what external balancing looks like. All the standard theories of alliances in the international relations literature assume that the smaller protégé seeks greater commitment from the more powerful patron and seeks to ensure the patron's involvement in a war the protégé may start. In this case, we would expect the smaller protégé to do everything possible to ensure the patron would have to be involved in any war that occurred, and the protégé would be prodding or urging the patron to engage in more confrontational behavior toward its adversary. That is, we would expect the Philippines to be actively seeking greater U.S. military commitments to it, to be actively taking more provocative or aggressive stances toward China, and to be actively seeking to encourage more aggressive American actions toward China.

However, by those expectations, the Philippines is not engaging in chain-ganging, free-riding, or external balancing. Most significantly, the Philippines has refused permanent U.S. military bases in the country. The Philippines has also not increased its naval maneuvers or

---

[6] Malcolm Cook, "Turning Back? Philippine Security Policy Under Duterte" (Sydney: Lowly Institute for International Policy, 2016), www.lowyinstitute.org/publications/turning-back-philippine-security-policy-under-duterte.

procurements in the South China Sea, and it is the Philippines that clearly prioritizes internal, not external, threats to its survival. In a number of ways, the Philippines appears to be taking a number of steps to reduce, not increase, U.S. involvement in its security.

As soon as the Philippines declined to renew the permanent bases lease with the United States in 1992, observers – particularly American observers – called the decision a mistake, predicting that the Philippines would regret the decision. As former Congressman Stephen J. Solarz said, "There is no doubt in my mind that in this instance the [Filipino] Senate was not speaking for the majority of the Filipino people … History will determine who is right and who is wrong."[7] In 1996, Dick Cheney predicted that closing the bases would be a "real tragedy for the Philippines."[8] Critics predicted dire economic consequences for the Philippines, a power vacuum in East Asia, and that it would "send a strong but wrong signal to the U.S."[9]

However, there is almost no evidence that anyone in the Philippines views the decision as a blunder. In the twenty-five years since the lease expired, no Philippine president has pushed for a renewed permanent American military base in the Philippines. So sensitive is the issue of U.S. bases that most politicians avoid the issue entirely, preferring to focus on temporary U.S. deployments. There is, in fact, a sizable coalition in the Philippines that opposes American bases on the grounds of protecting Philippine sovereignty.[10] As Philippines Foreign Secretary Perfecto Yasay said in 2016, the Philippines "cannot forever be the little brown brothers of America," a reference to a common pejorative Pinoy phase about wishing too closely to be American.[11] Attitudes toward the United States and its bases are conflicted: Filipinos

[7] U.S. Congress, House of Representatives, Committee on Foreign Affairs, *The Philippine Bases Treaty*, 102nd Cong., 1st sess., 1991, 7–8, babel.hathitrust. org/cgi/pt?id=pst.000020392741.

[8] Seth Mydans, "Subic Bay, Minus the U.S., Becomes Surprise Success," *New York Times*, November 23, 1996, ww.nytimes.com/1996/11/23/world/ subic-bay-minus-us-becomes-surprise-success.html.

[9] Rowena Carranza, "The Day the Impossible Happened," *Bulatlat*, September 16, 1991, www.bulatlat.com/news/2–32/2-32-bases.html; James E. Auer and Robyn Lim, "The Maritime Basis of American Security in East Asia," *Naval War College Review* 54, no. 1 (2001): 48.

[10] Andrew Yeo, *Activists, Alliances, and Anti-U.S. Base Protests* (New York: Cambridge University Press, 2011).

[11] Estrella Torres, "Yasay: PH 'Can't Forever Be Little Brown Brothers of America'," *Inquirer*, September 16, 2016, globalnation.inquirer.net/144982/ ph-cannot-forever-be-the-little-brown-brothers-of-america-yasay.

overwhelmingly trust and admire America, but there is also a sizable contingent who do not wish American bases on Philippine soil.

One of the key elements of the U.S.–Philippines Enhanced Defense Cooperation Agreement (EDCA) signed in April 2014 was a clear acknowledgment on all sides that EDCA did not involve permanent U.S. bases. The 2014 EDCA agreement "… explicitly prohibits the U.S. from establishing a permanent military presence or bases in the Philippines."[12] U.S. Ambassador Goldberg explicitly admitted that permanent U.S. bases were not a possibility, saying "This isn't a return to that era. These are different reasons and for 21st century issues, including maritime security," noting that the ninety-four years that the U.S. had permanent bases in the Philippines since 1898 was over.[13] The requirement that a permanent base be approved by the Senate, and perhaps a national referendum, made such a path virtually impossible, given Philippine domestic political opposition that almost surely would have defeated such a measure.

Philippine moves during the Aquino administration toward increased confrontation with China and a reinvigorated U.S. alliance were greeted with a sigh of relief by many in the American foreign policy-making establishment. As the U.S. ambassador to the Philippines said in 2014 about the signing of the EDCA between the United States and the Philippines, "This is really a pretty big deal." The United States has been clearly courting the Philippines – President Obama was the first foreign leader to call Duterte and congratulate him on his victory in the presidential election of 2016, the United States sent its two top diplomats to the Philippines in 2016, and the United States has strongly supported EDCA as a key of its Asian pivot. The conventional view in Washington, DC, was that finally, after more than two decades, the Philippines was realizing that they needed U.S. military presence.[14]

[12] CNN Philippines Staff, "What You Need To Know About EDCA," *CNN Philippines*, April 14, 2016, cnnphilippines.com/news/2016/01/13/what-you-need-to-know-about-edca.html.

[13] Jose Katigbak, "US, Philippines Agree on 5 Base Locations Under EDCA," *Philstar Global*, March 20, 2016, www.philstar.com:8080/headlines/2016/03/20/1564662/us-philippines-agree-5-base-locations-under-edca.

[14] Siddhartha Mahanta, "The Philippines to the United States: We Want You Back," *Foreign Policy*, June 1, 2015, foreignpolicy.com/2015/06/01/philippines-china-military-carter/; Dan De Luce, "China Fears Bring the U.S. Military Back to the Philippines," *Foreign Policy*, January 12, 2016, foreignpolicy.com/2016/01/12/china-fears-bring-the-u-s-military-back-to-the-philippines/.

However, the Aquino administration's moves were more a temporary swing rather than the beginning of an enduring shift in Philippine foreign policy orientation. In 2016, President Duterte began to reorient Philippine defense policy, making clear statements of a reluctance to have close relations with the United States. Regarding American forces in the Philippines, on September 13, 2016, Duterte said, "For as long as we stay with America, we will never have peace in that land ... The special forces, they have to go. They have to go in Mindanao, there are many whites there, they have to go. I do not want a rift with America, but they have to go."[15] Duterte has repeatedly mentioned American atrocities against Filipinos from the early 1900s when the United States colonized the islands. During the ASEAN annual meeting in Laos in September 2016, Duterte deliberately skipped a meeting between U.S. President Obama and the ASEAN leaders, and also referred to President Obama as a "son of a bitch" while mentioning the American atrocities in the Philippines from the early-twentieth century.[16]

To show how far Philippine defense policy has evolved, it is instructive to note that for decades, the question was whether or not the U.S.–Republic of the Philippines (RP) Mutual Defense Treaty covered the West Philippine Sea and obligated the United States to defend the Philippines.[17] Under Trump and Duterte, the question is the opposite: whether the Philippines will go along with U.S. confrontational policies. Indeed, President Duterte has made clear he does not want to be involved in military confrontations. When U.S. Secretary of State Tillerson said during his confirmation hearings in early 2017 that the United States might enact a naval blockade to deny China access

---

[15] "Duterte Wants US Forces out of Southern Philippines," *Fox News*, September 13, 2016, www.foxnews.com/world/2016/09/13/duterte-wants-us-forces-out-southern-philippines.html.

[16] Marina Koren, "The Philippine President's Vulgar Warning to Obama," *The Atlantic*, September 5, 2016, www.theatlantic.com/news/archive/2016/09/duterte-obama-extrajudicial-killings/498710/.

[17] "Ramos, Romulo View Status of Spratlys Dispute," *The Standard*, Foreign Broadcast Information Service Daily Reports (FBIS) East Asia, FBIS-EAS-95-036, February 23, 1995; Jay L. Batongbacal, "EDCA and the West Philippine Sea," *Rappler*, December 12, 2014, www.rappler.com/thought-leaders/77823-edca-west-philippine-sea-america; Prashanth Parameswaran, "What's Next for US–Philippine Military Ties?" *The Diplomat*, April 29, 2015, thediplomat.com/2015/04/whats-next-for-us-philippine-military-ties/.

to disputed islands in the South China Seas, the Philippine response was immediate and clearly distanced itself from the U.S. statements. Regarding a potential U.S. naval blockade of China, Philippine Foreign Affairs Secretary Perfecto Yasay said, "When America will be doing that they will be doing so to promote their national interest ... They have problems or issues with China they will deal with that but for all purposes we have also made it clear that we have our exclusive economic zone, our arbitral tribunal decision."[18]

What is actually often overlooked is that the Philippines has consistently been reluctant to have too close a U.S. embrace, and indeed may see the United States as the prime instigator of a conflict that would engulf the Philippines, a war it does not wish to be involved in. President Duterte made clear the Philippines would reduce joint Philippine–U.S. military patrols and exercises, and by late 2016 reductions had already begun.[19] Indeed, Duterte even discussed the idea of abrogating the entire Visiting Forces Agreement with the United States, saying, "America, you might also be put on notice. Prepare to leave the Philippines. Prepare for the eventual repeal or abrogation of the Visiting Forces Agreement."[20] Although this is unlikely to occur, that a sitting Philippine president would even broach the subject shows the distance that has emerged between the United States and the Philippines over the role and usefulness of the American forward presence.

And the resistance is not simply only under Duterte. When Secretary of State Hillary Clinton in 2010 hinted at greater U.S. involvement in the South China Sea dispute at the ASEAN Regional Forum in Hanoi, Philippine Foreign Secretary Alberto Romulo told Washington to keep out of the regional issue by saying bluntly, "it's ASEAN and China. Can I make myself clear? It's ASEAN and China. Is that clear enough?"[21] Adding to the United States' concern that the Philippines

[18] Arriane Merez, "US Only After Own Interest in Denying China Access to Disputed Seas," *ABS-CBN News*, January 13, 2017.

[19] Cris Larano, "Philippines Leader to End Joint Military Exercises, Naval Patrols with U.S.," *Wall Street Journal*, September 29, 2016, www.wsj.com/articles/philippines-leader-to-end-joint-military-exercises-joint-naval-patrols-with-u-s-1475086567.

[20] Pia Ranada, "Duterte Wants VFA Scrapped, but Will 'Wait' for Trump," *The Rappler*, December 17, 2016, www.rappler.com/nation/155785-duterte-visiting-forces-agreement-trump.

[21] Xiaokun Li, "US Puts on Display of Military Ties with Vietnam," *China Daily*, August 11, 2010, www.chinadaily.com.cn/cndy/2010-08/11/content_11133869.htm.

had "sided with China" was that President Aquino refused to send any representative to the Nobel ceremony in December 2010, in which Chinese dissident and human rights activist Liu Xiaobao would be awarded with the Nobel Peace Price.[22]

Domestic Politics Restrains Philippine Foreign Policy

Domestic politics in the Philippines has also continually limited the extent of military buildup, and is also likely to limit the extent of hostility in Philippine policy toward China. If one of the leading indicators of a country's foreign policy is public opinion, the Philippines shows little evidence of moving toward a more confrontational stance toward China. Enduring Filipino attitudes toward China are, perhaps somewhat surprisingly, enduringly positive. The Philippines has never experienced the type of violence against ethnic Chinese that occurred in Malaysia or Indonesia, for example. Public opinion polls consistently reveal that a majority of Filipinos have a positive view of China. As recently as June 2015, the Pew Global Attitudes opinion poll revealed that 54 percent of Filipinos had a favorable view of China, similar to Korea (61 percent favorable) and Australia (57 percent favorable).[23] Earlier, the "Asian Barometer" fourth-wave poll ending December 2015 revealed that 44 percent of Filipinos saw China having a positive influence in the region, and 63 percent seeing China as having a positive influence on the Philippines itself.[24]

The Philippine economy is also deeply tied into the Asian regional economy, and in particular China. China ($18 billion in total trade) is the Philippines' second largest trading partner after Japan ($19 billion in total trade). The Philippines was also a founding member of the Asian Infrastructure Investment Bank. In short, the Philippines has done nothing to limit its economic interactions with China, and instead has deepened them. In this way, the Philippines is simply a representative case of all ASEAN. As was noted earlier, all countries in the region have rapidly increased their economic and social relations with

---

[22] Willard Cheng, "PNoy Stands by Decision to Boycott Nobel Rite," *ABS-CBN News*, December, 13, 2010, news.abs-cbn.com/nation/12/13/10/pnoy-stands-decision-boycott-nobel-rite.

[23] Pew Research Center, *Global Attitudes and Trends*, June 23, 2015.

[24] "Survey Results," *Asian Barometer* (Taipei: Center for East Asia Democratic Studies, National Taiwan University, 2014), www.asianbarometer.org/survey/survey-results.

China. None have attempted to limit those relations in any meaningful manner, nor has any one attempted to limit its vulnerability to Chinese economic influence.

This relatively favorable view of China in public opinion and close economic relations are reflected by Philippine politicians. President Duterte, elected in 2016 to a six-year term, explicitly ruled out a military strategy toward China, saying in July 2016 that "We are not prepared to go to war. War is a dirty word."[25] Duterte has welcomed massive Chinese investment in the Philippines, saying, "Build us a railway just like the one you built in Africa and let's set aside disagreements for a while."[26] Duterte's first visit to China concluded with over $24 billion in economic pledges from China.[27]

President Duterte himself represents a dramatic change in Filipino domestic politics. For the past half-century, domestic politics has been dominated by the Marcos–Aquino axis, with presidents coming from either one side or the other. For example, his main opponent in the presidential election, Manuel Roxas, was thoroughly an establishment candidate. Roxas's grandfather founded the Liberal Party in 1946, and Roxas was the hand-picked protégé of outgoing president Benigno Aquino III, who was the son of Benigno Aquino II and former president Corazon Aquino (1986–1992). Duterte's victory was a rebuke to entrenched oligarchs in the Philippines; he is clearly an anti-establishment leader, and his power base is far different from those who have normally ruled. Indeed, Duterte represents a stark break from the past.

Metro Manila has always been the central locus of power. Duterte, coming from the southern island of Mindanao, represents a break in that tradition. Mindanao is not only heavily Muslim, it also is one of the poorest islands, and has a history of insurgency and violence. While mayor of Davao, the largest city in Mindanao, Duterte was

---

[25] Paterno Esmaquel II, "Duterte on PH–China Row: 'War Is a Dirty Word'," *Rappler*, July 7, 2016, www.rappler.com/nation/ 138712-duterte-philippines-china-war-dirty-word.

[26] Germalina Lacorte, "Duterte Tells China: Build Us a Railway and Let's Set Aside Differences for a While," *Inquirer*, February 29, 2016, globalnation.inquirer.net/137093/ duterte-tells-china-build-us-a-railway-and-lets-set-aside-differences-for-a-while.

[27] Andreo Calonzo and Cecilia Yap, "China Visit Helps Duterte Reap Funding Deals Worth $24 Billion," *Bloomberg*, October 21, 2016.

deeply involved in dealing with issues such as the various insurrections in Mindanao. Duterte is the first Philippine president to come from Mindanao, and his foreign policy, at least initially, reflects that experience and orientation. Duterte prioritizes domestic sovereignty and dealing with insurgency as a more important threat for the Philippines than disputed maritime claims. As Malcolm Cook notes:

Duterte's statements on the Muslim Mindanao peace process, military modernisation, and maritime rights disputes with China, including those prior to the presidential campaign, reflect a coherent view of the security challenges facing the Philippines. It is a view that is founded in Duterte's roots in Mindanao and his experience as mayor of Davao City. It is a different view of Philippine security to one that comes from a life in Metro Manila and study in the United States.[28]

Taken together, this view of the Philippine domestic politics leads to the conclusion that while there are unresolved maritime disputes, it is not at all clear whether this will fundamentally change or transform Philippine national defense policy or its priorities. The Philippine populace has surprisingly positive views of China. Domestic politics deemphasize the military, and when sovereignty issues are concerned, they are more likely to be related to internal insurgencies and border control, as the next section will discuss.

Internal Insurgency and Border Issues Continue to Dominate

Although maritime disputes with China have not been resolved, Philippine foreign policy is likely to be continually pulled back to the chronic domestic issues of insurgency and piracy. Indeed, key challenges to Philippine sovereignty that have a direct effect in terms of actual casualties arise from endemic insurgencies and separatist movements in Mindanao, and from piracy and smuggling in the Indonesia–Malaysia–Philippines waters. Most significant of these were Communist insurgency such as the New People's Army, secessionist groups on the island of Mindanao such as the Moro Islamic Liberation Front, and terrorist groups such as Abu Sayyaf.

---

[28] Cook, "Turning Back?"

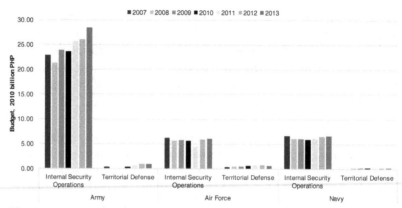

Figure 6.4 Internal and territorial defense budgets, 2007–2013.
Source: General Appropriations Acts of the Philippines (2007–2013).

Delfin Lorenzana, the defense minister under Duterte, said in June 2016 that "crushing Islamist militants in the Philippines will take precedence over territorial disputes in the South China Sea."[29] The military would continue to invest in more speed boats and helicopters to help eradicate insurgents on Jolo Island, rather than divert funds into maritime security. According to Lorenzana, "the defense budget should be spent on winning security at home rather than buying fighter jets to protect its waters, as the Philippines will not be going to war with any country."[30] It is thus no surprise that the portion of the military budget devoted to "internal security" has always dwarfed that devoted to "territorial defense." As noted previously, there has been an enduring focus on internal security. In 2013, the last year for which figures are available, the AFP devoted far more of its budget to internal security than it did to territorial defense (Figure 6.4). All branches of the military – the navy, air force, and army – are overwhelmingly focused on internal security.

Internal challenges have been endemic in the Philippines for decades, and the Philippines has been chiefly concerned with internal

[29] Manuel Mogato, "New Philippine Defense Chief Says Militant Threat More Pressing than South China Sea," *Reuters*, June 29, 2016, www.reuters.com/article/us-philippines-security-idUSKCN0ZF0WX.

[30] Mogato, "New Philippine Defense Chief Says Militant Threat More Pressing than South China Sea."

challenges to its security since its independence from the United States in 1946. For example, by 1975, seventy five percent of AFP troops were deployed in Mindanao.[31] In 1986, the AFP adopted the strategy of OPLAN Mamamayan, which established Special Operations Teams (SOTs) that not only sought to fight against guerillas and rebels, but also protected the people. Later, in September 1988, the AFP replaced OPLAN Mamamayan with OPLAN Lambat Bitag, with the immediate goal to slash the growth of insurgencies through military means by "unsheathing of the sword of war."[32] Due to this decades-long focus on internal insurgencies, the AFP has been geared primarily for counterinsurgency operations, with equipment consisting of mainly light tanks; armored fighting vehicles; light, assorted, and medium towed artillery; coastal and in-shore patrol vessels; and numerous transport and attack helicopters.[33]

In terms of direct threats, insurgency and piracy continue to be endemic issues, with consistently high numbers of casualties. For example, on April 9, 2016, twenty-three soldiers of the 44th Infantry Battalion were wounded in fighting against Abu Sayyaf in Basilan; on April 23, seven soldiers from Special Operations Command 10 and the 62nd Marine Company were wounded in Sulu. In summer 2016, militants kidnapped and threatened to execute two Canadians, a Norwegian, and a Filipino if the militants' ransom demands were not met. That summer, eighteen Indonesians and Malaysians sailors were kidnapped in three separate attacks in Philippine waters by "groups suspected of ties to the al-Qaeda linked Abu Sayyaf militant network in the Philippines."[34] Malaysia, Indonesian, and the Philippines have formed joint patrols to address the issue of piracy and kidnapping.[35] Following another kidnapping of seven Indonesian sailors in June

[31] Carolina Hernandez, *The AFP's Institutional Responses to Armed Conflict: A Continuing Quest for the Right Approach* (Philippine Institute for Development Studies [PIDS], 2006), 3.

[32] R. S. de Villa, *The Aquino Administration: Record and Legacy (1986–1992)* (Diliman, Quezon City: University of the Philippines Press, 1992), 93.

[33] R. C. de Castro, "The Twenty-First Century Armed Forces of the Philippines: Orphan of Counter-insurgency or Military Geared for the Long War of the Century?" *Contemporary Politics* 16, no. 2 (2010): 153–71.

[34] "Piracy Surge Turning Regional Waters into New Somalia'," *Borneo Post*, April 22, 2016, www.theborneopost.com/2016/04/22/piracy-surge-turning-regional-waters-into-new-somalia/.

[35] "Piracy Surge Turning Regional Waters into New Somalia."

2016, Malaysian, Indonesia, and Philippine naval and coast guards worked out a process to hold trilateral patrols.[36]

Internal insurgency issues continue to dominate Philippine security thinking. The casualties, kidnappings, and killings are endemic and have only ebbed and flowed but never been resolved. Piracy and coordination with Indonesia and Malaysia have been top priorities for successive Philippine presidents.

Maritime Disputes with China

In contrast to the military-first policies the Philippines has emphasized in dealing with the violence that plagues southern Philippines, the Philippines has pursued primarily institutional and diplomatic means of dealing with its maritime disputes. In 2013, the Philippines filed a case against China at the Permanent Court of Arbitration in the Hague, seeking to clarify the rights of the Philippines' exclusive economic zone (EEZ) and to adjudicate whether or not China had the right to develop various features. China refused to participate in the case, despite being a signatory of the UN Convention on the Law of the Seas. The ruling, released in July 2016, was favorable to the Philippine arguments. The Tribunal in the Hague ruled that China's "nine-dash line" had no basis in international law, and that Beijing's activities within the Philippines' two-hundred-nautical-mile EEZ, such as fishing and island construction, infringed on Manila's sovereign rights.

After the Hague ruling, which heavily favored the Philippines, all sides reacted cautiously. China denounced the ruling, but in the immediate aftermath did not undertake any particular actions. Duterte said "Let us create an environment where we can sit down and talk directly ... Can we declare war? It is not an option. I would not be stupid to do that. It will only be a massacre for all ... war is not an

---

[36] Ruben Sario, "Malaysia, Indonesia Want Philippines to Do More to Tackle Abu Sayyaf," *The Star*, June 26, 2016, www.newsjs.com/url.php?p=http://www.thestar.com.my/news/nation/2016/06/26/anifah-malaysia-indonesia-concerned-over-kidnappings-by-abu-sayyaf/; Marguerite Afra Sapiie, "Indonesia to Start Joint Sea Patrols with Malaysia, Philippines," *Jakarta Post*, August 2, 2016, www.thejakartapost.com/news/2016/08/02/indonesia-to-start-joint-sea-patrols-with-malaysia-philippines.html.

option nowadays."[37] Duterte followed up his rhetoric with a number of initiatives aimed at reducing tensions and finding mutual ways to accommodate both countries in the South China Seas. There were initial meetings between the Chinese and Philippine coast guards about a joint committee that would include "maritime cooperation, including combating drug trafficking and other maritime crimes, marine environmental protection, maritime search and rescue, and capacity-building in related areas."[38] In November 2016, President Duterte announced that he would sign an executive order declaring part of the disputed Scarborough Shoal as a sanctuary off-limits to all fishermen.[39] This would have the function of allowing fish stocks to be replenished and would also be a face-saving way to begin resolving the dispute between China and the Philippines. The Philippines and China have also begun discussing ways of jointly exploring for natural resources, particularly oil, in the West Philippine Sea.[40] In June 2017, for example, Jose de Venecia Jr., a former Speaker of the House of Representatives and Duterte's special envoy for inter-cultural dialogue, said "Why are we willing to go to war, why is China willing to go to war…when we can have a commonsensical, practical, imaginative, pragmatic oil negotiation in the South China Sea where everyone participates."[41]

Perhaps most significantly, in September 2016, Duterte announced that he wished to stop all joint naval patrols between the United States and the Philippines. Duterte also called for the removal of all American military forces in Mindanao. The Philippines also decided to move joint U.S.–Philippine naval maneuvers out of the South China Seas

[37] Christina Mendez, "Duterte Ready to Face China on Territorial Issue," *philstar*, August 18, 2016, www.philstar.com/headlines/2016/08/18/1614692/ duterte-ready-face-china-territorial-issue.

[38] "PH, China Coast Guards Get Friendly," *ABS-CBN News*, December 16, 2016.

[39] Manuel Mogato, "With Support of China's Xi, Philippine Leader to Ban Fishing in Disputed Lagoon," *Reuters*, November 21, 2016, www.reuters.com/ article/us-southchinasea-philippines-china-idUSKBN13G0QA.

[40] Xianne Arcangel, "Envoy Says PHL Studying Joint Exploration with China in Disputed Waters," *GMA News Online*, January 2, 2017, www.gmanetwork .com/news/story/594371/news/nation/envoy-says-phl-studying-joint-exploration-with-china-in-disputed-waters#sthash.km1QZlM4.dpuf.

[41] N.a., "Duterte's envoy agrees to joint drilling program in the West Philippine Seas," *Update.PH* June 12, 2017, https://www.update.ph/2017/06/dutertes-envoy-agrees-for-joint-drilling-program-in-west-philippine-sea/18103?utm_content=bufferda48a&utm_medium=social&utm_source=twitter.com&utm_campaign=buffer.

in early 2017.[42] On September 28, Duterte said that the joint military exercises between the United States and the Philippines scheduled for October 2016 would be the last: "I will serve notice to you now that this will be the last military exercise."[43] In late 2016, the Philippines canceled an arms order for twenty-six thousand rifles from the United States and purchased them from China instead.[44] Although it is not yet clear that Duterte would follow through with plans to terminate joint patrols and exercises, even the discussion of it was a major change in Philippine foreign policy. In May 2017, the Philippine Coast Guard sent 20 officers to China for joint training with the Chinese Coast Guard about law enforcement, search and rescue, and communication.[45] As Philippine ambassador to China, Jose "Chito" Sta. Romana, described it in early 2017, the Philippines had been "... one-sidedly imbalanced in favor of the [United States]. We are not abandoning our alliance with the [United States] ... We are basically trying to normalize our relations with China."[46]

Conclusion: No External Balancing in the Philippines

The Philippines is not obviously engaging in costly signaling and external balancing. There is little evidence that it is free-riding on the U.S.–RP Mutual Defense Treaty. The Philippines has no military to speak of, and has spent a generation reducing that funding further. The Philippine navy's share of the overall military budget has contracted 25 percent in the past two decades. The main issues are domestic insurgency, terrorism, and piracy.

[42] Christina Mendez, "No More Phl-US Military Exercises in SCS," *Philippine Star*, December 30, 2016, www.philstar.com:8080/headlines/2016/12/31/1658267/no-more-phl-us-military-exercises-scs.

[43] Larano, "Philippines Leader to End Joint Military Exercises, Naval Patrols with U.S."

[44] "Philippines' Duterte Agrees to Buy Chinese Firearms," *RT News*, December 13, 2016, www.rt.com/news/369956-duterte-china-philippines-arms/.

[45] Zander Cayabyab, "PH Coast Guard officers sent to China for seminar, training," *ABS-CBN News*, May 14, 2017, http://news.abs-cbn.com/news/05/14/17/ph-coast-guard-officers-sent-to-china-for-seminar-training?utm_content=buffer4a7f0&utm_medium=social&utm_source=twitter.com&utm_campaign=buffer.

[46] "Duterte Drifting from US to China, Says New PH Envoy," *Inquirer*, January 4, 2017, globalnation.inquirer.net/151173/duterte-drifting-us-china-says-new-ph-envoy.

There is virtually no evidence that the Philippines plans to fight a war against China, nor that it is attempting to "chain-gang" the United States into supporting it. Duterte has clearly said he does not wish to incite competition with China. Duterte has even initially begun to reduce or limit the American military presence in the Philippines. Indeed, with over 50 percent of Filipinos holding a positive view of China in 2015, and with Philippines–China trade increasing at double digits annually, that is not surprising. Maritime disputes remain undecided, but it is also clear that the Philippines plans to use institutional, diplomatic, and rhetorical tools to try to solve the problem, but does not plan to use military tools to that end.

Rather than free-riding on the United States, Philippine strategy toward the United States in 2016 appeared to be moving back to the general strategy of the past quarter-century, which has been to limit American access and influence in the Philippines.

As Foreign Affairs Secretary Perfecto Yasay said in 2016:

Washington has failed us – Washington has for too long employed a "carrot and stick" approach "to force Filipinos into submission to American demands and interests ... Breaking away from the shackling dependency of the Philippines to effectively address both internal and external security threats has become imperative in putting an end to our nation's subservience to United States' interests.[47]

---

[47] Joel Guinto, "America has 'failed' Philippines, Yasay says," *ABS-CBN News*, October 3, 2016, http://news.abs-cbn.com/news/10/06/16/america-has-failed-philippines-yasay-says.

7 | Vietnam: Who's Chasing Whom in Vietnam–U.S. Relations

> Every Vietnamese leader must be able to stand up to China and get along with China and if anyone thinks this cannot be done at the same time, he does not deserve to be a leader.
>
> – Senior Vietnamese official, 2016[1]

Vietnam continues the case studies of countries that are not sending costly signals about a willingness to use force against China. Similar to South Korea and the Philippines, Vietnam shows few signs of planning to emphasize military force in its overall strategy for dealing with China. Indeed, Vietnam and the Philippines are an interesting pair-wise comparison: both are smaller countries that are potentially in adversarial relations with China. In both cases, the United States looms as a potential patron that could provide a powerful balance to Chinese power. Both countries are in Southeast Asia, and both have a long history of relations with China and some unresolved disputes. Both also have deep economic ties with both China and the United States. Finally, in both cases, there has been increasing speculation from mostly American and Western observers that both Vietnam and the Philippines are beginning to balance against China and seek American support. For example, Yahri-Milo and her co-authors argued in 2016 that, "China's rapid military modernization and increasingly assertive behavior will likely fuel the perception that the United States and many regional states have common security interests…Vietnam could become a major security partner of the United States," while Liff and Ikenberry argued back in 2014 that "U.S.-Vietnam military ties are deepening rapidly…and Vietnam is also reaching out to U.S. allies."[2]

---

[1] Quoted in Bilihari Kausikan, "Dodging and Hedging in Southeast Asia," *The American Interest* 12, no. 5 (January 2017), https://www.the-american-interest .com/2017/01/12/dodging-and-hedging-in-southeast-asia/.

[2] Keren Yarhi-Milo, Alexander Lanoszka, and Zack Cooper, "To Arm or to Ally? The Patron's Dilemma and the Strategic Logic of Arms Transfers and

These perspectives assume an external threat from China, and also assume Vietnam's first or most obvious reaction is to actively seek protection from the United States.

Yet in each of these cases, there is scant evidence that the smaller country is pursuing the United States, nor is there evidence of a nascent balancing strategy towards China. Is Vietnam chasing the United States because it fears a rising China? Or is the U.S. pursuing Vietnam in order to extend or retain its own hegemonic ambitions and influence?

Who's chasing whom?

A close examination of Vietnamese foreign policy behavior leads to the conclusion that the United States is the ardent suitor, and Vietnam is the reluctant date. The literature on balancing, external balancing, and alliances overwhelmingly begins with the assumption that two states already have a military alliance, and that the smaller protégé seeks greater support from the powerful patron. This chapter will show that Vietnam is not particularly worried about its relationship with China, and indeed faces no existential threat from China, and therefore Vietnam is cautious in its relationship with the United States. For its part, the U.S. is eager to retain its hegemonic position in East Asia, and is perhaps even attempting to create an incipient containment coalition against China. Vietnam and the United States are nowhere near forging a military alliance. The relationship has only begun to move past initial diplomatic recognition. Thus, before characterizing Vietnam's security strategy as "external balancing" with the United States, and before characterizing it even as "hedging," it is important to describe accurately the relationship, and in particular to note how distant the relationship actually is at the present time.

Vietnam appears to be attempting to build stable and close relations with both the United States and China. In both cases, Vietnam has substantially upgraded ties in the past twenty-five years. Vietnam normalized relations with China in 1991 and the United States in 1995. Vietnam formally demarcated its land border with China in 1999, and the border remained essentially the same as when it was first formally

Alliances," *International Security* 41, no. 2 (2016): 138; Adam Liff and G. John Ikenberry, "Racing toward Tragedy?: China's Rise, Military Competition in the Asia Pacific, and the Security Dilemma," *International Security* 39, no. 2 (2014): 81.

demarcated in 1079, over nine centuries earlier.[3] Since that time, trade and economic relations between Vietnam and both countries have surged. China is now Vietnam's largest trading partner, with total trade over $62 billion annually. For its part, the United States is Vietnam's largest export market, taking $30 billion of Vietnam's exports, but imports from the United States are only 3 percent of Vietnam's total imports.

The conclusion that Vietnam is not trying particularly hard to improve relations with the United States is buttressed by examining in-depth interactions between Vietnam and the United States. In addition to exploring military expenditures and Vietnam's security strategy, we explore who initiates invitations to Vietnamese leaders and where Vietnamese leaders choose to travel, in order to provide insight into the direction of pursuit in relationship building. The study of high-level visits is a common method by which to assess a country's relations with another country.[4] By constructing an original dataset on Vietnamese high-level exchange, we present a series of expectations concerning how the high-level exchange patterns are different when small powers are the suitors versus when they are being pursued. The data and a key case study reveal that it is the United States that often initiates and reiterates invitations to Vietnamese leaders to visit the United States, while Vietnamese responses are often cautious and restricted. We also find that the interaction between Vietnam and its neighboring countries in the region such as Laos, Cambodia, and Thailand is much more vibrant than examined in the existing literature.

As with the case of the Philippines, smaller powers have a surprising amount of autonomy and agency in crafting their foreign policies. There are in fact sound theoretical reasons to expect that smaller powers might not desire close relations with a larger power. The first question that must be answered is whether or not the smaller power actually has a threat perception from an adversary. External threat needs to be shown, not assumed. Especially if the threat is not existential, it is not clear that a smaller power will seek an alliance to mitigate

---

[3] James A. Anderson, "Distinguishing Between China and Vietnam: Three Relational Equilibriums in Sino–Vietnamese Relations," *Journal of East Asian Studies* 13 (2013): 259–80.

[4] See, for example, the Center for Strategic and International Studies "Beyond Parallel" database of high-level Chinese and North Korean visits at beyondparallel.csis.org/database/.

it. Second, if a smaller power fears abandonment, it may be very cautious about making any firm *ex ante* commitment to a larger power. If the larger power can abrogate its responsibilities at any time, the smaller power can very likely be left *ex post* having annoyed a third party, but with no alliance support from its larger ally. For example, if the Trump administration does take a more confrontational approach to China, it is not clear that it would be sustained. As a result, Asian countries are likely to be highly cautious about too eagerly joining an American-led coalition. Furthermore, to actively seek relations with one large power against another large power is to clarify and reinforce the perception and designation of that third power as an adversary.

The explanation for continued absence of Vietnamese external balancing in the form of alliance seeking with the United States, and of concomitant low military expenditures, is actually quite simple: Vietnam does not fear for its survival, and hence it is not behaving as if it does. Competing maritime claims in the South China Seas do not deny the right of Vietnam to exist.[5] The United States and China may be facing off over regional hegemony, but few other states feel the necessity to choose sides. Given that the stakes are actually fairly low, it is not surprising that Vietnam does not yet appear willing to make the costly domestic and economic trade-offs that would be required for major and sustained alliance pursuit of the United States.

Vietnamese Military Priorities: No Costly Signals

We begin with an examination of Vietnam's military priorities. While there is increasing talk of Vietnamese military modernization, and much speculation about Vietnamese militarization, a careful examination of Vietnamese military spending leads to the conclusion that Vietnam's defense policy is following normal modernization, not enhanced or even arms-racing with another country. Vietnam is not attempting to keep up with China, and costly signals about a willingness to use force are absent. Most clearly, military expenditures as a proportion of GDP have fallen steadily since the 1980s and have remained low for well over a decade. In 2015, Vietnam devoted 2.3 percent of GDP to the military, a proportion that has remained roughly the same for over a

---

[5] Michael Swaine and Taylor Fravel, "China's Assertive Behavior, Part Two: the Maritime Periphery," *China Leadership Monitor* 35 (2011): 1–29.

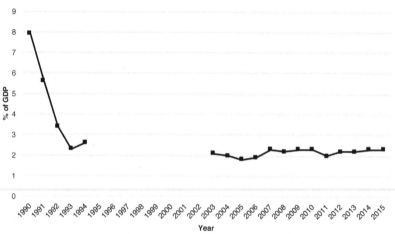

Figure 7.1 Vietnamese military expenditures, 1990–2015 (% of GDP).
Source: SIPRI 2016.

decade (Figure 7.1). Put differently, since 2003, the Vietnamese government has not seen it necessary to increase the proportion of its economy that it devotes to the military. Absolute spending on the military is also low – $4.5 billion in 2015. This compares to over $200 billion in defense spending by China and $601 billion in spending by the United States.

When Vietnam was actively involved in border skirmishing with China, and deeply involved in fighting in Cambodia during the 1980s, the country devoted between 7 and 9 percent of its GDP to defense. A reduction of military expenditures to two percent is a dramatic, bringing Vietnamese spending into line with most countries in the region. In terms of procurement, the Vietnamese navy had only two surface combatants in 2015, although it has ordered four more from Russia, which will bring the total number of its surface combatants to six (Table 7.1). Yet in 2000, Vietnam already had six frigates, which were subsequently decommissioned. Thus, Vietnam's order of six modern frigates will only bring them back to the level they had previously. Vietnam has also ordered six submarines, which while symbolically important, will provide the Vietnamese with a modest fighting force at best. Vietnam's troop levels have also contracted (Table 7.2). In 1990, Vietnam had 900,000 soldiers in uniform. In 2015, that was 412,000, a reduction of more than 50 percent.

Table 7.1. *Principal surface combatants, 2000–2015 (China and Vietnam)*

	1987	2000	2015	Change, 1987–2015	2020 (est.)
China	53	60	71	+18	71
Vietnam	7	6	2	−5	6

Source: IISS, *The Military Balance*, various years.

Table 7.2. *Vietnam's military deployments, 1980–2016*

	Army personnel	Naval personnel	Air force personnel
2016	412,000	13,000	30,000
2006	412,000	13,000	30,000
1990	900,000	13,000	12,000
1985	1,000,000	13,000	15,000
1980	1,000,000	4,000	25,000

Source: IISS, *The Military Balance*, various years.

This close examination of Vietnamese military expenditures and priorities reveals that there is almost no evidence that Vietnam is preparing to use its military in a conflict with China. Vietnam is not sending any costly signals about its military by making costly investments beyond routine modernization. Defense spending as a proportion of the economy is one-third of what it was during the 1980s, and has not significantly increased since the early 2000s. In combination with dramatically increased economic interactions and surging interactions in many areas, the evidence appears to lead to the conclusion that Vietnam is rapidly improving relations with both China and the United States.

Vietnam's Surprising Relations with China in Premodern Times

Part of the reason some observers believe Vietnam wants to hedge against China is because there is a myth that Vietnam's history was one of constant warfare, particularly against an aggressive China. Yet this view is an invention of the twentieth century, a nationalist Vietnamese response to French colonialism and foreign intervention.

The actual historical record shows clearly that Vietnam–China relations were unusually peaceful and stable. Liam Kelley observes that:

So thoroughly did the Western academy adopt the modern Vietnamese nationalist view of the past in the 1960s, 1970s and even 1980s that we have yet to fully disengage from this conceptual framework ... [with] emphasis on the historical importance of foreign intrusions, especially those of a supposedly expansionist China, as a major element ...[6]

Historically, the Dai-Viet were much more concerned with internal stability than with China, and indeed reveal almost no military attention to their relations with China, which were conducted extensively through the tribute system of institutions and principles. Rather, Vietnamese leaders were clearly more concerned with quelling chronic domestic instability and in relations with the Champa to their south and west. Despite China being by far the most powerful actor in the system, war with China, and even preparations for war against China, was vanishingly rare. James Anderson notes that:

By 1086 a clear border had been mapped out between the two states, the first such court-negotiated border in China's history. After the establishment of this court-negotiated border, there would still be challenges to the Đại Việt's insistence on self-rule. However, the existence of a formal border between the two polities was successfully challenged only once in the next eight hundred years.[7]

Indeed, the unusual stability of the Vietnam–China relationship is reflected in not only the longevity of the two sides, but in actual fighting. Kang, Nguyen, Fu, and Shaw measured Vietnamese wars and other violence from 1389 to 1789, using a key nineteenth-century Vietnamese language primary source, 钦定越史通鉴纲目 ("The Imperially Ordered Annotated Text Completely Reflecting the History of Viet," originally commissioned in 1856 and last published in 1884).[8] The annals were written before the arrival of the West in Vietnam, and

[6] Liam Kelley, "Vietnam as a Domain of Manifest Civility (Văn Hiến chi Bang)," *Journal of Southeast Asian Studies* 34, no. 1 (February 2003): 63–76.

[7] Anderson, "Distinguishing Between China and Vietnam," 282.

[8] David Kang, Dat Nguyen, Ronan Tse-min Fu, and Meredith Shaw, "Vietnamese Wars in Early Modern East Asia, 1389–1789: Introducing New Data," paper

thus provide a fascinating perspective on how Vietnamese at the time viewed themselves and their foreign relations. They find that of 264 total incidents of violence reported from 1389 to 1789, only 29.1 percent of total entries are external, while 70.9 percent deal with internal violence of some type. In other words, by far the Vietnamese court was more concerned with internal than external threats to its survival. In terms of who is listed in the annals, China features in 8.8 percent of entries, Champa in 3.2 percent of entries, and Laos in 1.1 percent of entries. Put differently, the only China–Vietnam war during those four hundred years occurred during the 1408–1420 Ming occupation of Vietnam. For centuries, China and Vietnam had stable relations, not war.

This historical perspective is important not only to set the proper context for understanding contemporary relations. Vietnamese leaders spent centuries learning to deal with a powerful China. But more important than that is to show how long the two countries have lived next to each other. While the past is not predictor of the future, the existence of a centuries-long relationship is at least suggestive evidence that the two sides have managed to craft stable relations for quite some time.

High-Level Exchanges by Both Vietnam and America

In the late-twentieth century, Vietnam once again reemerged as an independent nation after almost a century of colonization and conflict. Given that Vietnam appears to be improving relations with both the United States and China, it is perhaps difficult to assess whether Vietnam pursues closer relations with the United States as a hedge against China, or whether the United States pursues closer relations with Vietnam as it attempts to retain a predominant position in the region. A key first step is to investigate whether, in fact, the small power feels or perceives a direct external security threat. More directly to the question of whether the small power is pursuing an alliance with the U.S., or is "hedging" with the United States, we need to assess who is chasing whom.

To that end, the allocation of high-level diplomatic visits – a scarce resource – can offer insights into the direction of pursuit in relationship

prepared for the annual meetings of the International Studies Association, February 21, 2017.

building. Specifically, who initiate invitations to the leaders of the small power, and where the leaders of the small power choose to visit can be important messages, as high-level visits often require trade-offs of prioritizing certain destinations over others, the high opportunity cost of leaders' absence from their normal duties, and the mobilization and commitment of a significant level of scarce diplomatic resources. After all, high-profile exchange often involves extensive preparation such as lower-level officials' preparatory visits, especially for negotiating economic and other agreements that will be signed during the top leader's visit.[9] Finding that big powers such as the United States frequently send out and iterate invitations to Vietnamese leaders with only restricted responses from Vietnam would indicate that the great power is the suitor, and that small powers are typically hesitant to embrace the great power.

The direction of visits by high-level political officials can also help assess the existing literature reviewed in the preceding: if the more common assumption holds, and the smaller power is pursuing support of a larger power, then we would expect to find that Vietnamese leaders are more likely, *ceteris paribus*, to visit the United States than other countries, especially if they do believe that China is becoming more assertive. Furthermore, we should find that the larger power is wary of being entrapped into a war with another major power over which it has marginal interests, or which is of marginal strategic importance. By contrast, if the small power is being pursued, we expect to find that the smaller power is cautious about too obviously or closely aligning itself with the larger power, while the larger power will be attempting to convince or cajole the smaller power into more obviously aligning with it.

There are other ways to explore the direction of pursuit, as well. A corollary of this is that if the smaller power is pursuing the large power, the leaders of the smaller power should be more likely to court the regional allies of the large power and interact more with them. While we would expect that Vietnam might interact more with its neighboring countries regardless of its intentions, finding that Vietnam

---

[9] Scott L. Kastner and Phillip C. Saunders, "Is China a Status Quo or Revisionist State? Leadership Travel as an Empirical Indicator of Foreign Policy Priorities," *International Studies Quarterly* 56, no. 1 (2012): 165.

has made particular efforts to engage the regional allies of the United States would indicate well small powers' pursuit of a large power. By contrast, if the small power were being pursued, we would expect that leaders of U.S. regional allies are more likely, *ceteris paribus*, to visit Vietnam.

A clear picture of the direction of pursuit can also help us test the dynamics between the large power and other countries in the region. Specifically, if the large power is pursuing the small power, would this make it view the small power as more important than other regional countries, even more than its regional allies? For example, leaders of the United States may show a higher incidence of visits to Vietnam than other regional countries, including its allies. Such allocation of scarce diplomatic resources would indicate the special importance bestowed by the United States on Vietnam. Similarly, if we find the small power pays more visits to the large power and its allies than to other small powers in the region, then we might conclude that the small power is the ardent suitor.

To test these hypotheses, we first constructed an original dataset on Vietnamese high-level exchanges from January 2005 to the end of June 2016, in order to identify the patterns and trend of the high-level exchange patterns of Vietnam. In total, we examined in-depth 683 high-level exchanges between Vietnam and other countries from January 2005 to June 30, 2016. For each visit, we coded the date, the locale, host country, visiting country, a variable indicating whether it is an incoming visit to or outgoing visit from Vietnam, the positions and names of the foreign leaders, the positions and names of the Vietnamese leaders, and brief remarks that outline the nature or the major theme of each exchange.

In addition, we extend and expand the scope of the dataset on U.S. high-level visits found in Lebovic and Saunders, which analyzed all foreign visits by U.S. president and secretary of state based on the U.S. State Department's Office of the Historian until 2010.[10] We updated their data on outgoing visits by the U.S. president and secretary of state to June 2016 and added all visits made by U.S. defense

---

[10] James H. Lebovic and Elizabeth N. Saunders, "The Diplomatic Core: The Determinants of High-Level US Diplomatic Visits, 1946–2010," *International Studies Quarterly* 60, no. 1 (2016): 107–23.

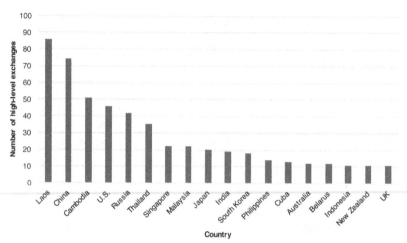

Figure 7.2 Vietnamese high-level exchanges, January 2005–June 2016.

secretary since 2005, based on information published by the U.S. Department of Defense. This gives us a total of 1,226 high-level visits done by U.S. president, secretary of state, and secretary of defense from January 2005 to June 2016.

Figure 7.2 shows all the eighteen countries that had more than ten high-level exchanges with Vietnam (incoming and outgoing combined) over the years 2005 through 2016.

Two observations that are against the conventional wisdom immediately stand out. First, the country that interacts most frequently with Vietnam is not a large power such as China or the United States, but a small power that sits next to it on the Southeast Asian mainland – Laos. Specifically, Vietnam and Laos have had more than ten exchanges more than occurred between Vietnam and China, forty more exchanges than took place between Vietnam and the United States, and forty-four more exchanges than occurred between Vietnam and Russia. The exchange between Vietnam and another neighboring small power – Cambodia – was also very frequent.

A closer examination of the exchanges among Vietnam, Laos, and Cambodia reveals that these exchanges are not only frequent, but also very high profile. For instance, after coming in office in April 2016, the first-ever foreign activity made by Vietnamese President Tran Dai Quang as the state president was his visit to Laos and Cambodia in June 2016, during which he met with Laos' party general secretary, president, and the king of Cambodia.[11] Three months later, the Vietnamese prime minister met again with the Lao party general secretary and president on the sidelines of the ASEAN Summit, and committed that "Vietnam always gives the top priority to the special solidarity with Laos," and pledged that he will instruct the ministries, agencies, and localities to continue realizing high-level agreements between the two countries.[12]

In addition, among the 86 total exchanges between Laos and Vietnam, ten were at the presidential level, four were at the level of party general secretary, twenty-six were made at the ministerial and vice-ministerial level (minister and deputy minister of defense, prime minister, and deputy prime minister), and four were conducted by chief commanders of certain military regions or high-ranking military officials such as the chief of the general staff of the armed forces. Only five out of eighty-five are at the agency level, including the governmental special sections of bilateral relationship or Communist Party of Vietnam (CPV) Politburo member. By contrast, among the forty-six total exchanges between Vietnam and the United States, only five were at the presidential level, one by the party general Secretary of Vietnam, twenty-five were at the ministerial and vice-ministerial level (secretary of state, secretary of defense, foreign minister, and prime minister), while the rest were mostly initiated by the United States by regional military commanders, such as the commander of the Pacific Command, commander of the Pacific Fleet, and commander for the Pacific Air.

The breakdown of the high-level exchanges (Figure 7.3) further demonstrates the nature of the direction of pursuit. What should be noted is that the data indeed do not draw a clear-cut division among the United States, its allies, and non-U.S. allies. However, important patterns can still be discerned and are particularly notable. Specifically, echoing the observation above, Vietnam has to date initiated far more outgoing visits to China (twelve more outgoing visits to China than

---

[11] "President's Visits to Laos, Cambodia – a Success: Deputy FM," *VietnamPlus*, June 17, 2016, en.vietnamplus.vn/presidents-visits-to-laos-cambodia-a-success-deputy-fm/94863.vnp.

[12] "Vietnam Gives Top Priority to Relationship with Laos: PM," *People's Army Newspaper: Organ of the Military Central Commission and Vietnamese Ministry of National Defense*, September 7, 2016, en.qdnd.vn/vietnam-and-asean/vietnam-gives-top-priority-to-relationship-with-laos-pm/421200.html.

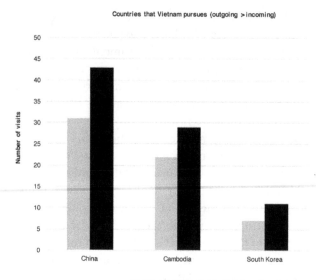

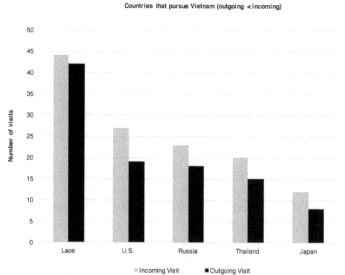

Figure 7.3 Who is chasing whom? Breakdown of Vietnamese high-level exchanges, January 2005–June 2016.
Sources: Asia News Monitor, other news sources.

incoming ones) and Cambodia (seven more outgoing than incoming visits). It has almost an equal number of outgoing visits to and incoming visits from Laos. By contrast, the U.S. and most of its regional allies have paid more visits to Vietnam than the way around. For instance, in 2010 alone, U.S. Secretary of State Hillary Clinton visited Hanoi twice in July and October, respectively, reiterating the Obama administration's commitment "to broad, deep, and sustained engagement in Asia."[13] In addition to her visits, U.S. Secretary of Defense Robert Gates also visited Hanoi in October, with the aim to "advance the defense ties … and to establish a broader set of more practical cooperation activities with the Vietnamese military and defense establishment."[14] The allocation of three high-level visits to Vietnam within such a short period of time clearly shows the desire of the United States to have a closer and more comprehensive relationship with Vietnam, a country that is, according to Pentagon Press Secretary Geoff Morrell, "a close and leading U.S. partner in Southeast Asia."[15]

The comparison of incoming and outgoing visits in Figure 7.3 also leads to our second observation against the conventional wisdom. Specifically, we find no evidence that Vietnam is pursuing the United States or its regional allies to balance or hedge against an increasingly assertive China. On the contrary, the high frequency of high-level exchanges between Vietnam and China and the fact that Vietnam has paid more visits to China both indicate that instead of allying with the United States, Vietnam is more inclined to rely on bilateral exchanges and dialogues with China to exchange views between the two parties and the two countries. For instance, in the year of 2015, the Vietnamese party general secretary, president, prime minister, and deputy prime minister made six outgoing visits to meet with their Chinese counterparts, with a common focus on trust building and fostering future high-level exchanges. Reciprocally, China also paid six visits to Vietnam, all of which were above the ministerial level. By contrast, there were only five exchanges with the United States in total, with a focus more on finding U.S. personnel missing in action (MIAs) and cleaning toxic dioxin left from the wars.

---

[13] U.S. Department of State, "Comments by Secretary Clinton in Hanoi, Vietnam: Discusses U.S.–Vietnam Relations, ASEAN Forum, North Korea," July 23, 2010, iipdigital.usembassy.gov/st/english/texttrans/2010/07/20100723164658su0.4912989.html#ixzz3xFZknY1m.

[14] John D. Banusiewicz, "Gates Arrives in Vietnam for Bilateral Meetings, Conference," *DoD News*, October 10, 2010, archive.defense.gov/news/newsarticle.aspx?id=61215.

[15] Al Pessin, "Gates to Visit 'Close Partner' Vietnam," *Voice of America*, October 6, 2010, www.voanews.com/a/gates-to-visit-close-partner-vietnam-104516579/166465.html.

Also, in the first six months of 2016, the Vietnamese prime minister, foreign minister, and deputy prime minister have already paid three visits to China to meet with their counterparts. Meanwhile, Chinese Defense Minister and State Councilor Yang Jiechi, who outranks China's foreign minister, also visited Vietnam in March and June and were received by the Vietnamese defense minister and president, and the Vietnamese Communist Party general secretary. Just as emphasized in multiple joint statements issued during these exchanges, Vietnam and China both view the maintaining of regular high-level contacts between the two parties and states as key to strengthening political trust and will continue to make visits on a regular basis, send special envoys, talk on the hotline, organize annual meetings, and hold meetings on the sidelines of multilateral forums to promptly exchange views on regional and international issues of shared concern.[16]

A concrete example illustrates the nature of exchanges between China and Vietnam. In 2014, a thirteen-member high-level Vietnamese military delegation, led by its minister of national defense, General Phung Quang Thanh, visited his counterparts in Beijing. Apart from usual pleasantries, General Thanh proposed five ways to rebuild confidence and trust with reassurance that "force would not be used."[17] Reciprocally, General Fan Changlong, who is also the vice-chair of the central military commission and member of the Chinese Communist Party Politburo, urged the two militaries to contribute "positive energy." Fan emphasized, "A neighboring country cannot be moved away ... We should make our troops well-behaved."[18] As Carl Thayer, a Southeast Asia regional specialist who is close with Vietnamese party and defense sectors, pointed out, during these meetings, military commanders on both sides of the border and at sea have met their respective counterparts. "These commanders have all witnessed the

---

[16] "Viet Nam, China Issue Joint Statement," *Viet Nam News*, November 6, 2015, vietnamnews.vn/politics-laws/278187/viet-nam-china-issue-joint-statement.html#GvmrMZEH1E9WILi4.97.

[17] Carlyle Thayer, "China–Vietnam Defense Hotline Agreed: What Next?" *The Diplomat*, October 24, 2014, thediplomat.com/2014/10/china-vietnam-defense-hotline-agreed-what-next/.

[18] "China, Vietnam Agree to Properly Address Disputes," *Xinhua News Agency*, October 18, 2014, news.xinhua.net.com/english/china/2014-10/18/c_133726371.htm.

verbal understandings reached by their respective ministers. Military commanders on both sides can be expected to carry out their duties accordingly."[19]

In short, the examination of Vietnamese incoming and outgoing visits reveal three features: first, the interaction between Vietnam and its neighboring small powers are far more frequent and high-profile than examined in existing literature. Second, Vietnam has been actively seeking direct dialogue with China through regular high-level exchanges on key issues. Third, while the exchanges between Vietnam and its neighboring powers are equally or even more actively initiated by Vietnam, exchanges between Vietnam and the United States are more actively initiated by the United States, especially when it comes to those high-level exchanges on security and defense led by military and security officials.

A closer examination of the U.S. visits to the region further confirms that the United States is the ardent suitor. Specifically, we compare the top ten countries visited by the U.S. president, the secretary of state, and the secretary of defense from 2005 to June 2016 (Figure 7.4) versus key countries in Asia. Three observations stand out.

First, on a global scale, countries that are most frequently visited by the United States are its North Atlantic Treaty Organization (NATO) allies and key countries in Middle East, such as France, the United Kingdom, Germany, Belgium, Israel, Afghanistan, and Iraq. Leaders of the United States and these countries frequently meet at bilateral and multilateral forums, with an emphasis on deterring against two major threats: the continuing threat of terrorism, and the rising threat of Russian aggression.[20] This demonstrates that despite the intensified speculation about the instability in the South China Sea, counterterrorism and coalition with NATO have continued to be the top priority of national and defense leaders of the United States.

Second, within the region of East Asia, countries visited mostly by the United States are South Korea, China, and Japan, the most important stakeholders for the geopolitical balance on the Korean peninsula.

---

[19] Thayer, "China–Vietnam Defense Hotline Agreed."

[20] "Remarks Previewing the FY 2017 Defense Budget: As Delivered by Secretary of Defense Ash Carter," *U.S. Department of Defense*, February 2, 2016, www.defense.gov/News/Speeches/Speech-View/Article/648466/ remarks-previewing-the-fy-2017-defense-budget.

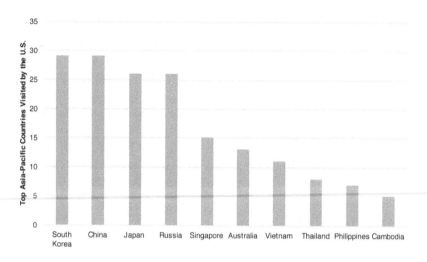

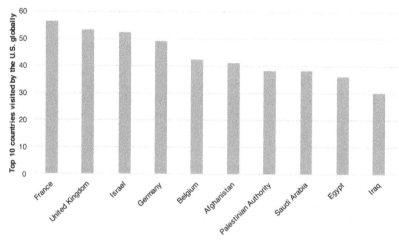

Figure 7.4 U.S. high-level visits to Asia-Pacific region versus global top ten, January 2005–June 2016.

In the following section, we will further examine the themes of these visits. However, initial examination of the news coverage on these visits demonstrates that even within Asia, North Korea has continued to be the most important factor shaping the interests of the United States in the region.

Third, within the region of Southeast Asia, the United States has paid more visits to Vietnam than to its regional allies, including

Thailand and the Philippines. This observation is particularly important for clarifying the direction of pursuit between small and large powers. Our third pair of hypotheses indicates that if the large power were pursuing the small power, we would expect that leaders of the large power visit the small power more frequently than other regional countries. The fact that the leaders of the United States show a higher incidence of visits to Vietnam even more than to its regional allies provides strong support for this hypothesis.

However, aggregating visits cannot reflect changes in the trend of U.S. visits to the region. Thus, since the South China Sea did not become an issue until 2009, data before 2010 might skew the picture of the U.S. visits to the region. To account for this, we also looked at U.S. visits to the region from 2010 to 2016.[21]

Figure 7.5 demonstrates even more clearly the strategic importance of Vietnam to the United States. While data from 2005 to 2016 show that the United States visited Vietnam more frequently than Thailand, the Philippines, and Cambodia, data from 2010 show that the United States has paid more visits to Vietnam than most countries in Asia-Pacific region, ranging from big powers such as Russia, to key players in ASEAN such as Singapore, and especially to the regional allies of the United States, including Australia, the Philippines, and Thailand.

We now summarize the findings from the dataset on high-level exchanges. First, the interaction (or lack thereof) between Vietnam and its neighboring small powers are far more frequent and prominent than examined in existing literature. This indicates that when allocating its limited diplomatic resources, small powers do not necessarily always prioritize large powers.

Second, we find no evidence that Vietnam has joined a containment coalition against China. On the contrary, the high-level exchanges between China and Vietnam are more regular and frequent than that between Vietnam and any other major powers, thus opening more channels for direct exchange of views on issues of concern between these two parties and countries. In addition, instead of balancing or hedging against China, the fact that Vietnam has paid more outgoing

---

[21] In an additional test, we also plotted the U.S. visits to the region by country over years, which shows similar trend as the aggregated number.

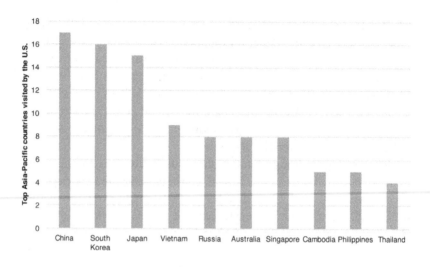

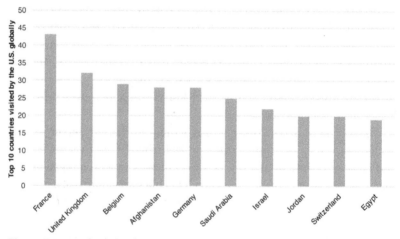

Figure 7.5 U.S. high-level visits to Asia-Pacific region versus global top ten, January 2010–June 2016.

visits to China indicates that Vietnam at least is consciously preserving, if not actively seeking, direct dialogue with China.

Lastly, if standard theories are correct, the weaker and more vulnerable country (Vietnam) should be the one initiating and pursuing greater relations with the powerful ally (the United States) that can provide support. However, while the exchanges between Vietnam and its neighboring powers are equally or even more actively initiated by Vietnam, the exchanges between Vietnam and the United States are more actively initiated by the United States. Especially since 2010, the United States has paid more outgoing visits to Vietnam, even more than big powers such as Russia or its own allies such as Thailand and the Philippines.

Case Study: Vietnamese Party General Secretary Nguyen Phu Trong's Visit to the United States

We now turn to several cases to further illustrate these dynamics: the historic visit of Vietnamese party general secretary to the United States in July 2015, the opening of Cam Ranh International Port in March 2015, and the recent lift of embargo on arms sale during President Obama's visit. From July 5 to July 10, 2015,[22] the United States hosted the first-ever visit by General Secretary of the Vietnamese Communist Party Nguyen Phu Trong. This "groundbreaking" visit has been lauded in Western analysis as a tipping point in the U.S.–China–Vietnam triangle, a major step forward in the quiet yet profound shift in Vietnam's domestic politics.[23]

However, what is often overlooked in Western analysis is where the party general secretary visited before his visit to the United States, and the substantive rather than symbolic achievements coming out of this U.S. visit. There was clear hesitance on the part of Vietnam in embracing the U.S. invitation, careful management of Chinese perceptions before embarking for the United States, and the lack of substantive agreements out of this U.S. visit.

The Obama administration's invitation to the party general secretary to visit the United States was first made public by U.S. Secretary of State John Kerry on February 14, 2015, during a telephone conversation with Vietnamese Deputy Prime Minister and Foreign Minister

---

[22] Media have conflicting coverage on the exact starting and ending date of this visit. Here, we use the dates in the news released by the Vietnamese Embassy in the United States. Retrieved from vietnamembassy-usa.org/news/2015/07/general-secretary-nguyen-phu-trong-concludes-us-visit.

[23] Alexander L. Vuving, "A Tipping Point in the US–China–Vietnam Triangle," *The Diplomat*, July 6, 2015, thediplomat.com/2015/07/a-tipping-point-in-the-u-s-china-vietnam-triangle/.

Pham Binh Minh[24] for Lunar New Year's greetings.[25] Later that month on February 23, this invitation was again discussed when Vietnamese Ambassador to the U.S. Pham Quang Vinh presented his credentials to President Barack Obama at the White House.[26] The party general secretary's visit to the United States was confirmed only few days later by the Vietnamese Ministry of Foreign Affairs on February 25, 2015, with no confirmed date for the visit yet at that point.[27]

However, after confirming his U.S. visit, the general secretary first went to Beijing in April, three months before going to Washington. During his four-day visit, the party leader met with his Chinese counterpart Xi Jinping, Premier Li Keqiang, Chair of the National People's Congress Zhang Dejiang, and Chair of the Chinese People's Consultative Conference Yu Zhengsheng, with a particular theme of "enhancing the political trust in each other."[28] Commentary published by Xinhua News Agency, China's state-run news agency, on Nguyen

---

[24] A side note is that during the lunar new year of 2015, Vietnam in total had three phone conversations with foreign countries: China, Japan, and the United States. The phone talk with China was between Party General Secretary Nguyen Phu Trong and his Chinese counterpart Xi Jinping on February 11, during which they agreed to visit their respective countries in 2015. Conversation with Japan was between Japanese Prime Minister Shinzo Abe and Vietnamese Prime Minister Nguyen Tan Dung, during which Japan committed to continuing to provide official development assistance (ODA) for Vietnamese socioeconomic development and the Trans-Pacific Partnership (TPP). Conversation with the United States was conducted by Vietnamese deputy prime minister, who has lowest ranking in terms of official profiles.

[25] "Deputy PM, US Secretary of State Talk Bilateral Ties over Phone," Asia News Monitor, February 16, 2015, vietnamembassy-usa.org/news/2015/06/secretary-defense-ashton-carter-visited-vietnam.

[26] "Ambassador Pham Quang Vinh Presented Credentials to President Barack Obama," Embassy of the Socialist Republic of Vietnam in the United States of America, February 25, 2015, vietnamembassy-usa.org/news/2015/02/ambassador-pham-quang-vinh-presented-credentials-president-barack-obama.

[27] "Vietnam Party Chief to Visit US in 2015, Ministry Confirms," *Tuoi Tre News*, February 26, 2015, tuoitrenews.vn/politics/26288/vietnam-party-chief-to-visit-us-in-2015-ministry-confirms.

[28] "China's Party General Secretary Meet with Vietnamese Counterpart (习近平同越共中央总书记阮富仲举行会谈)," Xinhua News, April 7, 2015. The article reads, "Party General Secretary Nguyen Phu Trong expressed Vietnamese wish to strengthen high-level exchanges between Vietnam and China, and to enhance mutual political trust (阮富仲表示, 越方希望双方加强两国领导人互访和接触, 增强政治互信)."

Phu Trong's visit is instructive. Title "No Room for Wedge in China–Vietnam Relations," the commentary reads,

The timing of the trip is riveting … it takes place ahead of a Washington-announced visit by Trong to the United States … top-level diplomacy between Beijing and Hanoi sends out a clear albeit delicate message … Beijing and Hanoi are mature enough to handle their relations beyond the bilateral scope. They will not chase after other interests at the cost of China–Vietnam relations, nor will they allow anybody to drive a wedge between them. Interpretations of Trong's expected U.S. trip as a move to counterbalance China smell of Cold War–era machination and confrontationalism, which should have long been dumped to the dustbin of history … China unequivocally encourages its neighbors to follow development paths and cultivate foreign relations in line with their respective realities. And it is widely accepted common sense that such pursuits should be conducive both to national development and to regional peace.[29]

The Vietnamese state-run news agency VNA, as well as the newspaper of the CPV, *Nhan Dan* (The People), also sent out similar messages. For example, the Vietnamese official perspective was that the trip

… aims to continue solidifying and maintaining the friendly and stable situation, creating more momentum for healthy China–Vietnam relations and creating favorable conditions to continue resolving disputes between the two countries, contributing to the maintenance and consolidation of a peaceful and stable environment for national development and construction.[30]

Following Trong's visit to Beijing, and before his visit to the United States, there were two additional high-level exchanges between Vietnam and China. During these two visits, China's State Councilor Yang Jiechi, who outranks China's foreign minister, Premier Li Keqiang, and Foreign Minister Wang Yi met with the Vietnamese deputy prime minister and Foreign Minister Pham Binh Minh in Beijing and Hanoi,

[29] Yushan Deng, "Commentary: No Room for Wedge in China–Vietnam Relations," *Xinhua News Agency*, April 7, 2015, news.xinhuanet.com/english/2015-04/07/c/134129188.htm.

[30] "Promoting Healthy and Stable Development of Vietnam–China Friendly and Cooperative Relations," *Vietnam Breaking News*, April 7, 2015, www.vietnambreakingnews.com/2015/04/promoting-healthy-and-stable-development-of-vietnam-china-friendly-and-cooperative-relations/.

respectively. The importance of regular meetings between the two countries' high-level leaders to enhance political trust was emphasized in each exchange, with multiple initiatives being set up to strengthen cooperation among ministries, sectors, and localities. In addition, both sides have committed to effectively using government-level negotiation mechanisms for the Vietnam–China territorial border, and to avoiding any actions that complicate disputes in the South China Sea.

In fact, we often observe meetings between Vietnamese and Chinese leaders to precede those between leaders of Vietnam and the United States. For instance, Vietnamese State President Truong Tan Sang visited the United States for the first time in July 2013. During that visit, President Truong Tan Sang and President Obama announced their decision to "form a U.S.–Vietnam Comprehensive Partnership to provide an overarching framework for advancing the relationship."[31] However, President Truong Tan Sang had visited China one month earlier in June, in his first-ever visit as the head of state.[32]

Another example is the postponed visit by President Obama to Vietnam. Back in 2015, when receiving Vietnam's Communist Party leader at the White House, President Obama pledged that he was looking forward to making his first visit to the nation "sometime in the future."[33] Given that President Obama was scheduled to attend an Asia-Pacific Economic Cooperation (APEC) meeting in the Philippines and the East Asia Summit 2015 in Malaysia in November, it was widely expected that President Obama would visit also Vietnam. The United States, to mark the twentieth anniversary of U.S.–Vietnam ties.[34]

---

[31] Megan Slack, "President Obama Meets with President Truong Tan Sang of Vietnam," White House, July 25, 2013, www.whitehouse.gov/blog/2013/07/25/president-obama-meets-president-truong-tan-sang-vietnam.

[32] "President Sang's Visit to Lift Vietnam–China Ties," *Viet Nam News*, June 18, 2013, vietnamnews.vn/politics-laws/240925/president-sangs-visit-to-lift-vietnam-china-ties.html#2BiQZEYTQFpPs7B5.97.

[33] David Nakamura, "Obama Pledges to Visit Vietnam During Meeting with Communist Party Chief," *Washington Post*, July 7, 2015, www.washingtonpost.com/news/post-politics/wp/2015/07/07/obama-meets-with-vietnamese-communist-party-leader-at-white-house/.

[34] Dave Boyer, "Obama Says He'll Visit Vietnam Soon, Meets with Leader Nguyen Phu Trong," *Washington Times*, July 7, 2015, www.washingtontimes.com/news/2015/jul/7/obama-says-hell-visit-vietnam-soon-meets-with-lead/. Also see M. K. Bhadrakumar, "Vietnam and the Zen of juggling," *Asia Times*, April 6, 2015, www.atimes.com/vietnam-and-the-zen-of-juggling/.

However, Obama's trip was postponed,[35] while Vietnam welcomed Chinese President Xi with a red-carpet ceremony, despite the extremely short notice of Xi's intention to visit in November. To welcome Xi, Vietnam had to juggle the long-scheduled visits of the presidents of Italy and Iceland.[36] In addition, Xi was the first world leader to send a special envoy to congratulate Nguyen in person after the Twelfth Party Congress in January 2016, and the special envoy of Nguyen was the first foreign guest Xi met after the Lunar New Year in 2016.[37]

A close examination and comparison of the joint statements issued during the Vietnamese leaders' visits to China and to the United States further illustrates the lack of actual momentum in these visits. Back in July 2013, Vietnam's president and his U.S. counterpart agreed on nine areas of cooperation, including political and economic relations, security ties, human rights, and cooperation on tackling environmental issues. However, the majority of U.S.–Vietnam military cooperation since then involved only joint efforts to address war legacies, including Agent Orange/dioxin, unexploded ordnance, the search for remains of U.S. MIAs, and the provision of information about Vietnamese soldiers missing in action.[38] Even the annual Naval Exchange Activity (NEA), established in 2010, has been confined to noncombat training and skills exchanges in military medicine, search and rescue, maritime law, shipboard damage control, legal symposia, band concerts, community service events, and team sports.[39] With that in mind, the joint statement issued during the 2016 visit again gave priority to "humanitarian

---

[35] Xinxin Tong, "No Surprise, Obama Skips Vietnam Visit," *CCTV News*, November 11, 2015, english.cntv.cn/2015/11/11/ARTI1447228837199370.shtml.

[36] Carlyle Thayer, "Obama's Visit to Vietnam: A Turning Point?" *The Diplomat*, May 31, 2016, thediplomat.com/2016/05/obamas-visit-to-vietnam-a-turning-point/.

[37] Yun Sun, "China's Perspective on the US–Vietnam Rapprochement," *PacNet* No 48A (Honolulu, Hawaii: Pacific Forum, CSIS, June 6, 2016), csis-prod.s3.amazonaws.com/s3fs-public/publication/160606_PacNet_1648A.pdf, 5.

[38] "Deputy Defence Minister Receives US Ambassador," *Talk Vietnam*, March 8, 2016.

[39] Patrick Barta, "U.S., Vietnam in Exercises Amid Tensions with China," *Wall Street Journal*, July 16, 2011, www.wsj.com/articles/SB10001424052702304223804576447412748465574. Also see Commander Task Force 73 Public Affairs, "US Navy Kicks Off Naval Engagement Activities with Vietnam," *America's Navy*, April 6, 2015, www.navy.mil/submit/display.asp?story_id=86422.

cooperation, war legacy, maritime security, peacekeeping, and humanitarian assistance and disaster relief," as well as to work toward concluding the Trans-Pacific Partnership preferential trade pact.[40]

Nor did this "ground-breaking" meeting advance the U.S.'s call for preferential access to Vietnam's deep-sea port at Cam Ranh Bay. Right before Trong's visit to the United States, the United States had "urged Vietnamese officials to ensure that Russia is not able to use its access to Cam Ranh Bay to conduct activities that could raise tensions in the region," including "provocative" flights near the U.S. Pacific Ocean territory of Guam.[41] However, consistent with its "three no's" policy against foreign alliances, bases, or reliance, Vietnam had no response to the U.S. requests,[42] nor the alleged requests from the United States on exclusive foreign rights to the facilities. Thus, as Shawn Crispin points out, instead of being monumental as some are making it out to be, the 2016 visit at best advanced the budding "comprehensive partnership" launched in 2013 and still remains largely symbolic and limited.[43]

On the other hand, the joint statements issued between China and Vietnam included many more substantive cooperative projects. In the realm of military and security cooperation alone, the 2013 joint statement highlights the importance of maintaining high-level contacts between the two armies, especially the usage of the direct telephone line between the two defense ministries to enhance mutual trust. The statement also inked more joint land, sea, and naval patrols, based on the principles of easy things first and step-by-step, especially in the Tonkin Gulf. The two sides also agreed to stay calm and restrain themselves so as not to complicate and expand disputes. In the joint statement issued during Xi's visit in 2015, the two sides spoke highly

---

[40] "United States–Vietnam Joint Vision Statement," White House Office of the Press Secretary, July 7, 2015, www.whitehouse.gov/the-press-office/2015/07/07/united-states-%E2%80%93-vietnam-joint-vision-statement.

[41] David Brunnstrom, "U.S. Asks Vietnam to Stop Helping Russian Bomber Flights, *Reuters*, March 11, 2015, www.reuters.com/article/us-usa-vietnam-russia-exclusive-idUSKBN0M71NA20150311.

[42] "US Wants Vietnam to Stop Russian Aircraft Refueling at Navy Base – Report," *RT*, March 12, 2015, www.rt.com/news/239909-us-vietnam-base-russia/.

[43] S. Shawn and W. Crispin, "Limits of US–Vietnam Relations Revealed in Communist Party Leader Visit," *The Diplomat*, July 10, 2015, thediplomat.com/2015/07/limits-of-us-vietnam-relations-revealed-in-communist-party-leader-visit/.

of the continued high-level exchanges between two armies, and have emphasized again the usage of the direct hotline between two defense ministries to manage and control crises at sea. They also expanded cooperation between the two armies to realms including party and political affairs in the army, personnel training, joint patrols, visits by naval ships, as well as law enforcement at sea between the two countries' maritime police. Following these statements, the coast guards of Vietnam and China conducted a total of eleven joint patrols as of April 2016.[44]

In short, the unprecedented visit of the Vietnamese party general secretary has been lauded by the Western analysis as an indicator of Vietnam's pivoting toward the United States; however, we found little evidence to support this argument. To be clear, we do not claim that Vietnam, as an independent and self-reliant country, always seeks assurance from Beijing before moving closer to Washington. However, by pointing out that Vietnamese leaders often meet their Chinese counterparts prior to their meetings with the U.S. leaders, as well as the lack of substantive progress in defense cooperation after Vietnamese leaders' visits to the United States, we argue that small powers such as Vietnam can be, and have indeed been, very versatile and strategic in handling their relationships with the large powers. Instead of allying with one to balance or hedge against the other, they instead can have a surprising amount of autonomy and agency in maneuvering among large powers.

Conclusion

Most theory predicts that a small state will approach a powerful patron. Yet in Southeast Asia, it is the great powers as the suitor, while small powers are typically hesitant to embrace the great power. We show this by examining in depth the interaction between Vietnam and the United States, by constructing an original dataset on Vietnamese high-level exchange along with an in-depth case study. We find that the interaction between Vietnam and its neighboring countries in the

---

[44] "Vietnam–China Joint Fishery Patrol Concludes," *People's Army Newspaper: Organ of the Military Central Commission and Vietnamese Ministry of National Defense*, April 24, 2016, en.qdnd.vn/defence-cooperation/vietnam-china-joint-fishery-patrol-concludes/407940.html.

region such as Laos and Thailand is much more vibrant than examined in existing literature. Altogether, we demonstrate that not only the causality of relationship between big and small powers runs the opposite way than is usually theoretically expected, the dynamics within the region is also far more vibrant and stable than is usually expected.

There is good evidence that Vietnam desires good relations with both the United States and China. Clearly Vietnam is attempting to chart an independent course between the two countries. But just as clearly, it is hardly about to join a containment coalition against China. As Evelyn Goh notes, Vietnam's "leadership, especially the older generation, still fears the subversive intent of the United States" and is unwilling to trade Vietnam's autonomy for risky permanent alignment with an offshore power.[45]

The Vietnamese case is particularly interesting, because it is widely perceived that Vietnam fears China and is seeking to hedge with its relations with the United States. Yet the data presented in this chapter lead to the counterintuitive conclusion that – at least as of 2016 – it is the United States that is pursuing Vietnam, not the other way around. While Vietnam is willing to improve its relations with the United States, it fairly clearly does not expect to fight a war with China, nor does it have any great expectations for what closer relations with the United States might bring. And it is particularly important to note that relations are far from actually being a military alliance. The U.S.–Vietnam relationship is more symbolic than anything else of a widening Vietnamese foreign policy that is increasingly globalized.

---

[45] Evelyn Goh, "Southeast Asian Strategies Toward the Great Powers: Still Hedging After All These Years?" *Asan Special Forum* (Seoul: Asan Forum, February 22, 2016), www.theasanforum.org/southeast-asian-strategies-toward-the-great-powers-still-hedging-after-all-these-years/.

8 | Comprehensive Security in Japan, Indonesia, Singapore, and Australia

There is a school of thought that believes concern about China's increasingly assertive behavior will make ASEAN naturally gravitate towards the US and its allies. This is true, but only to a degree. You will misinterpret developments in Southeast Asia if you lose sight of this fact.

– Retired Singaporean diplomat Bilahari Kausikan, May 12, 2016[1]

South Korea, the Philippines, and Vietnam are particularly vivid case studies that show the nuanced and complex manner in which East Asian countries view their security environments. Each one of those case studies revealed substantial efforts at comprehensive security involving economic, social, and diplomatic relations and an effort to increase regional integration while avoiding military-first solutions to issues. None of these countries is sending clear costly signals about their willingness to fight over issues, in stark contrast to North Korea. But these countries are not alone, and indeed most countries in the region have similarly comprehensive approaches to their security.

This chapter examines four other important countries in the region. Japan and Australia are both close U.S. allies but not nearly as committed to containment strategies toward China as many American policy makers wish. Indonesia and Singapore are not U.S. allies but are significant and important actors in the region itself. No matter their similarities and differences, however, all four cases reveal a common approach to security: none is using costly signals, military means, or preparations for war in its dealing with China. All are emphasizing comprehensive security and a range of diplomatic, economic, and social priorities and instruments in dealing with each other. All four countries have been deeply involved in regional integration and show every indication of continuing and deepening the trend toward regional integration. All have reduced or maintained low military

[1] Kausikan, "Security Challenges in Asia."

expenditures. And, none, not even Japan, show any appetite for join-ing a coalition led by the United States that would aim at containing or isolating China. These countries have numerous reasons why they would like to maintain good relations with both China and the United States, and do not particularly want to choose sides.

Japan Is Not a Leader

Japan's regional role is diminishing, not increasing. From its height in the 1980s as the economic powerhouse of Asia, today Japan is a middle power that sporadically retains great power ambitions. This basic fact should be the starting point for any analysis of Japanese grand strat-egy in the twenty-first century. Japanese people and leaders do not hold warm views of China or, for that matter, of Korea. Japan also is a stalwart U.S. ally. But there is also little apparent evidence that Japan is capable of engaging in regional leadership, or even in an activist or "normal" foreign policy. Japan's current leadership, and Prime Minister Abe Shinzo in particular, has attempted to make Japan more active in foreign affairs and is attempting to change Japan's constitution to allow him to be more assertive. But this is a defensive action, a rear-guard attempt to slow down Japan's relative diplomatic decline. It is also not supported by the majority of Japanese, and it appears that Japan is mov-ing slowly toward middle power status. Japan is rich and important for sure, but is increasingly neither a leader nor a great power.

Prime Minister Abe Shinzo entered office for a second time in 2012 determined to end all doubts about Japan's role and position in Asia. Yet Abe is working from a position of weakness – Japan is no longer the Japan of the 1980s, where Japan's economy comprised 75 percent of the total regional GDP. Rather, today Japan is a middle power that retains a diminishing trajectory. As was shown in Chapter 1, the speed with which China eclipsed Japan as the economic center of gravity in East Asia has been astonishing. As Brad Glosserman writes, "the inability of Abenomics to gain traction means that Tokyo's interna-tional influence is likely to be at its apogee, and will level off and eventually decline. Tokyo won't be irrelevant, but we may well be wit-nessing 'Peak Japan'."[2] Furthermore, as T. J. Pempel wrote in 2015,

[2] Brad Glosserman, "The Regional Implications of 'Peak Japan'," *Strategist*, March 31, 2016, www.aspistrategist.org.au/the-regional-implications-of-peak-japan/.

"Japan is not back at all in regaining a commanding position within East Asia, in part due to its slow economic transformation, but due also to the atavistic positions taken by Abe's government on the historical interpretations of Japanese behavior in World War II."[3]

Indeed, there is little evidence, other than Abe's pronouncements, that Japan is in any position to return to a position of leadership in East Asia. Japan has long been a "reactive state," one that was consistently criticized for not assuming a "normal" posture.[4] A generation ago, that criticism was aimed at a Japan that was not willing to militarize under the U.S. alliance system and assume greater responsibility; today that criticism appears unlikely to prod a Japan into adopting a clear antagonistic position against China. In short, while Abe seeks to make Japan an active regional and global power, it is not clear whether the rest of his public will go along with him. The country as a whole appears to be more focused inward than outward. There is no indication that Japan as a nation is eager for an activist and leadership role. This is due partly to structural factors, but due also to the atavistic positions taken by Abe's government. It is unlikely that Abe can galvanize the national will to create and sustain a military that could project power or threaten its neighbors. As Robert Dujarric wrote about Japan, "Stasis, lethargy, and fatalism, along with a pleasant lifestyle, best describe the archipelago in 2016."[5]

The Abe government has adopted an aggressive domestic policy agenda that seeks first to reenergize the Japanese economy, which will then serve as the foundation of a higher-profile international role. Abe's confidence and focus have sparked criticism of and concern about Japan's "remilitarization," as well as increasing concerns that Japan and China are leading an East Asian arms race with potentially dangerous implications.[6] The prospect of a remilitarized Japan

---

[3] T. J. Pempel, "Back to the Future? Japan's Search for a Meaningful New Role in the Emerging Regional Order," *Asian Perspective* 39, no. 3 (July 2015): 361–80.

[4] Chalmers Johnson, "Japan in Search of a 'Normal' Role," *Daedalus* 121, no. 4 (Fall 1992): 1–33; Kent Calder, "Japanese Foreign Economic Policy Formation: Explaining the Reactive State," *World Politics* 40, no. 4 (July 1988): 517–41.

[5] Robert Dujarric, "Japan Without Ambition," *The Diplomat*, January 22, 2016, thediplomat.com/2016/01/japan-without-ambition/.

[6] Bruce Einhorn, "China, Japan, and India's Arms Race," *Bloomberg*, August 16, 2013, www.bloomberg.com/news/articles/2013-08-16/china-japan-and-indias-asian-arms-race.

is fantasy, as are fears about impending war in East Asia, even though the risk of miscalculation or an accidental clash is real.

A key goal of the Abe administration has been to change Japan's regional security role. His government has passed legislation – a secrecy law, established a National Security Council – that will allow it to function better in a crisis. It has produced a National Security Strategy. It has reinterpreted the pacifist constitution to allow the country to exercise the right of collective self-defense. It has revived discussions on the acquisition of offensive strike capabilities. Most significantly, it wants to revive pride and patriotism among the Japanese people.

Yet even this is limited. Reinterpretation of the constitution is subject to very limiting conditions. The public remains fundamentally hostile toward an activist foreign policy and profoundly suspicious of any role for the military. Japan only has "Self-Defense Forces"; that may be linguistic legerdemain, but it is a sign of the mental hurdles the country faces before it can "remilitarize." A majority of Japanese people oppose Abe's Yasukuni Shrine visits rather than support them; opinion polls consistently show that with the exception of environmental issues, few Japanese believe their country should play a regional role, and even fewer believe it should play a global role. For example, a 2014 *Asahi Shimbun* poll found that only 21 percent of Japanese thought the constitution should recognize the Self-Defense Forces as a military; only 29 percent wanted to change Article 9 (the "Peace" constitution), and only 29 percent wanted to lift the ban on exercising the right to collective self defense (Table 8.1). Such results are consistent over time. A Gallup poll from 2014 found that only 10 percent of Japanese "would be willing to fight" if their country were involved in a war, for example.[7] A May 3, 2016 poll found that 68 percent of voters felt no need to amend Article 9, against only 27 percent in favor. In short, Japanese voters have consistently, over years, and by large margins, supported Japan's current international profile. When asked why they supported keeping the constitution as is, 72 percent responded because "the constitution has brought about peace."[8] Abe has realized this is a goal he is unlikely to achieve, and in June 2016 even admitted

---

[7] WIN/Gallup International 2014 Survey, www.wingia.com/en/services/end_of_year_survey_2014/regional_country_results/8/46/.
[8] "ASAHI Poll: Majority of Voters Feel No Need to Revise Constitution," *Asahi Shimbun*, May 3, 2016, www.asahi.com/ajw/artIcles/AJ201605030043.html.

Table 8.1. *Japanese opinion poll, 2014*

	Should recognize	Should not recognize
Whether to recognize Self-Defense as a military in the constitution	25%	68%
	Should alter	Should not change
Whether to change Article 9	29%	64%
	Should lift ban	Should not lift ban
Whether to lift the ban on exercising the right to collective self-defense	29%	63%

Source: Asahi Shimbun (April 7, 2014).

that Article 9 was not going to change, saying "no agreement whatsoever has been reached, and I believe it is difficult under the current circumstances to revise article 9."[9]

There are other equally powerful limits on Japan's future defense capabilities. The first is the budget. As noted in Chapter 3, Japan's military expenditures are modest, even under Abe. The five-year plan put forth by Abe increased 2014 defense spending by 0.8 percent, and proposes annual 3 percent increases until 2018. The increases might total $9 billion if they are fully implemented – a 16 percent increase over today's military budget. That hardly qualifies as remilitarization. To put these proposed increases in context, between 1990 and 2015, Japanese defense expenditures rose just 8 *percent* when adjusted for inflation. Japan actually *decreased* its defense spending slightly in 2015 ($46.3 billion) compared to its height in 2011 ($47.1 billion), and since 2001 the military budget has *decreased* 0.2 percent in real terms (Figure 8.1). China, by comparison, spent $214 billion on defense in 2015, and has averaged 7 percent increases over the past decade. South Korea spends 50 percent more on defense (per capita) than does Japan. When put in perspective, Abe's proposed defense increases are actually restrained.

This restraint is even more pronounced when looking at the type of weapons the Japanese military is purchasing. The Japanese Maritime

[9] Kiyoshi Takenaka, "Japan PM: Hard for Now to Revise Arms-Renouncing Article of Constitution," *Reuters*, June 24, 2016, uk.reuters.com/article/ uk-japan-politics-idUKKCN0ZA399.

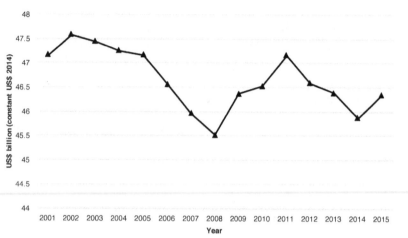

Figure 8.1 Japanese military expenditures, 2001–2015 (constant U.S.$ 2014).
Source: SIPRI 2016.

Self-Defense Force (JMSDF) is already a powerful defensive maritime force, and few analysts see the planned expansion as being a real attempt to create a blue-water navy that can project power. In October 2013, Admiral Katsutoshi Kawano, chief of staff at the JMSDF, emphasized capabilities such as minesweeping, antisubmarine warfare, antipiracy operations, and modernization of command and control as future key priorities. There are also substantial limitations on what Japan could purchase in the future.[10] As Philipe De Koning and Phillip Lipscy point out, Japan's personnel costs are so great that "Japan's focus has shifted from acquisition to preservation, and maintenance costs have skyrocketed: at the end of the Cold War, maintenance spending was roughly 45 percent the size of procurement expenditures; it is now 150 percent."[11] In short, while the Japanese military is powerful, and defense of its islands is a priority, this is a far cry from being able to project power beyond its own islands.

[10] James Hardy, "Japan's Navy: Sailing Towards the Future," *The Diplomat,* January 21, 2013, thediplomat.com/2013/01/japans-navy-steaming-towards-the-future/.

[11] Philipe De Koning and Phillip Y. Lipscy, "The Land of the Sinking Sun," *Foreign Policy,* July 30, 2013, foreignpolicy.com/2013/07/30/the-land-of-the-sinking-sun/.

Also, at this time the defense budgets are merely a *projected* increase: the difference between what Abe wants and what Abe gets may be large. Increasing the defense budget depends on the state of the overall Japanese economy. Inflation can dissipate any rise in defense spending. And if the overall economy performs poorly, it will be difficult to muster resources to spend more on the military. The record thus far is mixed. The Bank of Japan is doing its best to end the country's deflation, and prices are slowly rising (although the goal of 2 percent inflation remains beyond reach). The government continues to apply stimulus measures, but growth has been elusive. After the April 1 consumption tax hike, GDP fell 1.8 percent in the second quarter of 2014. Indeed, with the –1.4 percent growth for the first quarter of 2016, Japan had experienced the fifth contraction in the twelve quarters that Prime Minister Shinzo Abe has been in office.

Perhaps more significant for understanding Japan's future strategy choices is its economic relations with the region. Japan has always been more focused on the U.S. market than on East Asia. For example, Japan chose not to join the China-led Asian Infrastructure Investment Bank (AIIB) and did sign and pass the TPP. As Saori Katada writes about Japan's decision not to initially join the AIIB: "the government's decision to distance itself from the bank emerged from defensive concerns that it needed to maintain its position in the retreating global hierarchy."[12] Yet Japan's economic focus itself has still clearly shifted over the years. In the 1980s, the United States was by far Japan's most important trading partner. Today, Japanese investment and trade has shifted to focus on China as well as the region. By 2015, ASEAN took 15 percent of total Japanese trade; China, including Hong Kong, over 20 percent of Japanese trade; and the United States comprised 20 percent of Japanese exports and 10 percent of Japanese imports.

Economists can explain the quarterly gyrations in economic growth, but more troubling is the "third arrow" of Abenomics, structural reform, for which there is little evidence of success. Proponents say it is too soon to judge the reform efforts, but there need to be positive signs soon or Japan will face the worst of all possible worlds: rising inflation, stagnant

---

[12] Saori Katada, "At the Crossroads: The TPP, AIIB, and Japan's Foreign Economic Strategy," *AsiaPacific Issues* No. 125 (Honolulu: East-West Center, 2016), 7.

wages, and rising government debt. In that world, Abe's ambitions will be impossible to realize.

More troubling still are demographic trends. Nearly 26 percent of Japan's population is older than sixty-five, and the number will top 33 percent by 2035. From a peak population of 128 million in 2008, optimistic Japanese government estimates hope that the population will remain above 100 million by 2060. This is a "demographic crunch of a size that no other country has faced before."[13] Nearly 26 percent of Japan's population is older than sixty-five, and the number will top 33 percent by 2035.[14] That means increasing difficulty in financing pensions and shrinking tax revenues at the same time that government budgets – or at least public welfare spending, already more than 31 percent of GDP – will rise. Older populations will resist spending limited tax dollars on a military, especially if it means less money for health and long-term care. And old people vote, meaning those preferences will be heard. Older populations are more conservative and less inclined to take risks – including embarking on military adventures. And that proclivity will be further reduced when it means sending the country's most precious resource – its young people – into harm's way.

The persistent belief among some in Japan that the country needs to be "more normal" and shoulder more responsibilities in the provision of international or regional security public goods is countered by an equally powerful and compelling belief among a larger group of Japanese that one of the most important contributions that their country can make in this endeavor is serving as an example of a resolute "peace seeking country."[15] Some observers see pacifism as a way of cheap riding on the United States, but that is too cynical an explanation in all cases. Many Japanese honestly believe that their country's constitution is an important and unique instrument for peace. For them, the country's postwar history is a shining example of the constitution's power and Japan's "soft power." The nomination of Article

[13] Shiro Armstrong, "The Consequences of Japan's Shrinking," *East Asia Forum*, May 15, 2016, www.eastasiaforum.org/2016/05/15/the-consequences-of-japans-shrinking/.

[14] Dujarric, "Japan Without Ambition."

[15] Chalmers Johnson, "Japan in Search of a 'Normal' Role," *Daedalus* 121, no. 4 (Fall 1992): 1–33; Kent Calder, "Japanese Foreign Economic Policy Formation: Explaining the Reactive State," *World Politics* 40, no. 4 (July 1988): 517–41.

9 for the 2014 Nobel Peace Prize is one expression of this mindset. Even as the Abe government pursues constitutional reinterpretation – or perhaps because of it – this belief acts as a counterweight to any precipitous action.

In short, while Abe seeks to make Japan an active regional and global power, it is not clear whether the rest of his public will go along with him. It is also not clear whether Abe can muster the necessary economic and political capital he needs to move the country in his direction – the people and country as a whole appear to be more focused inward than outward. As Shiro Armstrong concludes, "Acknowledging that Japan's aggregate economy will inevitably start to shrink as the population decline accelerates is the starting point. Accepting the implications of that for Japan's place in the world and refashioning Japan's national agenda accordingly will clearly take much longer."[16]

Perhaps the most powerful limits on Japan's global role are external, however. There have been dire warnings that Europe's experience with 1914 might repeat itself a century later in Asia, with nationalism, modernization, and territorial disputes leading to war.[17] However, Japan's twentieth-century transformation – and the imperialism that it produced – occurred in a distinctive environment. In the late-nineteenth century, Japan faced Western imperial powers that had colonized virtually all of South, Southeast, and East Asia and had forcibly opened Japan to international trade. The Qing Dynasty – for more than two hundred years the unquestioned regional hegemon – was in disarray, facing internal rebellions and extraordinary Western pressure. The entire regional system of norms and institutions that had traditionally governed relations in East Asia was disintegrating as the Western, Westphalian system of modern international relations became paramount. Throughout East Asia, there was power vacuum, and perhaps more importantly a profound intellectual vacuum, as all East Asian nations attempted to understand, react, and adjust to the arrival of the West.

Japan in the late-nineteenth century faced a stark choice: wait to be colonized and possibly disappear as a nation, or undertake radical

---

[16] Armstrong, "The Consequences of Japan's Shrinking."
[17] See, among many, Gideon Rachman, "The Shadow of 1914 Falls over the Pacific," *Financial Times*, February 19, 2013, www.ft.com/content/e29e200a-6ebb-11e2-9ded-00144feab49a.

changes.[18] It chose the latter path, and did so exceptionally well. Within a generation, it was the leading nation within Asia and had defeated a Western imperial power in battle. Japan became a global industrial and military force to be reckoned with, adopting Western policies and practices and, in many respects, outperforming its "mentors" in the West, not always in good ways.

The international environment that Japan faces in 2017 is the mirror image of that of a century ago. No Western powers threaten the region, and China is once again a wealthy and powerful country. India too is emerging, and other middle powers, such as South Korea and Indonesia, are seeking international space. There is no military or intellectual vacuum to fill. These other countries in the region have various means to assert their interests and check the resurgence of a revanchist power, whether it be China or Japan. The gap between Japan and its neighbors is far smaller today than it was a century ago. South Korea today is a rich, powerful democracy seeking its own vision for the future; Indonesia, Malaysia, Thailand, and Vietnam are no longer colonies but instead have become politically stable and relatively wealthy countries in their own right. Moreover, the norms of the international system have changed. Unilateral changes in the status quo are no longer acceptable. Perhaps most obviously, the region's economies are deeply intertwined with each other through trade, investment, and travel. The proof of the stability of the system and the power of these new norms and connections, ironically, is evident in the pushback against Chinese efforts to assert itself in its periphery.

The international environment is more peaceful and stable today than it was one hundred years ago, despite enduring rivalry with China over what Japan terms "remote islands."[19] Although China and Japan bicker over the Senkaku/Daioyu islands, neither China nor Japan has even begun the steps to war – neither country puts sanctions on the other or attempts to restrict the other's massive bilateral trade and investment; fishermen and coast guards contend with each other,

[18] Seo-Hyun Park, *Sovereignty and Status in East Asian International Relations: Imagined Hierarchies* (Cambridge, UK: Cambridge University Press, 2017); Ji-Young Lee, *China's Hegemony: Four Hundred Years of East Asian Domination* (New York: Columbia University Press, 2016).

[19] "Japan Enacts Law to Help Keep Remote Islands Inhabited," *Kyodo*, April 2, 2016, www.japantimes.co.jp/news/2016/04/20/national/politics-diplomacy/japan-enacts-law-help-keep-remote-islands-inhabited/#.WBtyoxIrLGJ.

but navies do not exchange fire. Perhaps most importantly, both sides unquestioningly accept the existence of the other country – neither has any intention of conquering or colonizing the other. So while accidents may happen, and they should be managed with care, that possibility is different from a situation in which countries plan to eliminate each other from existence or subjugate them and their people.

South Korea and Japan have an intense maritime dispute, too, and like the Chinese, Koreans have bitter memories of Japan's past actions. But as with China–Japan relations, a South Korea–Japan war is highly unlikely, and the two appear prepared to contend their claims through means other than war. Frictions persist and tensions ebb and fall, but there is an understanding among Japanese and South Korean politicians and publics of the value and importance of a positive bilateral relationship. Disputes between the two countries are loud and bitter, but there are constraints to how far the ill will can drive the relationship.

In sum, there is almost no evidence that Japan is remilitarizing. Plainly, there is no indication that Japan's national survival is at stake. Absent that existential threat, mustering the national will to create and sustain a military that could project power or threaten its neighbors will not occur. Indeed, Abe may be the "high water mark" of attempts in that direction. If Abe cannot succeed in this last gasp effort to make Japan more vigorous and leaderlike, given larger trends, it is not clear who can. It will probably be a generation before there is another attempt in the direction of greater activism in Japanese foreign policy. Japan's defense policies are evolving to keep pace with a changing regional environment, but the idea that Tokyo will be able to threaten its neighbors is just not credible. There is no will, nor the capability to do so.

Moreover, the international environment has been transformed. While military conflict is not impossible, norms governing the use of force have changed from one hundred years ago. At this moment, a cornerstone of the Abe administration's foreign policy is the rejection of the right of any state to arbitrarily or unilaterally change the status quo. The fundamental premise behind the threat of a remilitarized Japan is rejection of exactly that principle; otherwise, any such policy shift is merely defensive in nature, to prevent unilateral action being taken against Japan.

A second and important conclusion is that Americans and others who hope for an assertive, ambitious Japan risk being disappointed. Japan will be stronger and safe, but it is unlikely to truly be an activist country on the international stage over the long term. It is important that the United States keep its hopes for Japan in context and scale back expectations about Japan's foreign policy to those that are more realistic, to ensure that this strong alliance endures. Japan can be a problem-solving country, an active and inspiring example of how to be a rich and democratic country that passes through social, demographic, and economic transitions. But it might not be the partner that America envisions. As Grant Newsham concludes, "One should not assume this trajectory towards a more assertive Japan will continue."[20]

Australia Between China and the U.S.

Australia has long been viewed as a stalwart American ally, and indeed, U.S.–Australia relations are close and warm. However, this should not be interpreted as meaning Australia views the world the same way as America does. Australia is deeply tied into the regional economy, and Australians increasingly see their future tied up with the future of East Asia. Australia, while valuing its American alliance, has also moved in significant ways to embrace East Asian relations across diplomatic, economic, and security issues. The election of Donald Trump, and the rocky first interactions between Trump and Australian Prime Minister Malcolm Turnbull, were not the cause, but rather only served to highlight these deeper trends.

Although Australia has long been proud of its position as one of America's closest allies in the Asia-Pacific, and although that support of American presence and overall policies remains strong, there are indications that Australia is potentially moving toward a more independent stance regarding the United States, China, and its own grand strategy toward the region. Although Australians may side with the United States on certain issues, the days of automatic and unquestioned Australian support for an American agenda have probably passed. As Nick Bisley points out, "there is a discernible divergence of opinions about China and the United States, respectively between strategic policy specialists and Australian business elites."[21] These different

[20] Grant Newsham, "Note to Washington: Enjoy Abe While You Have Him," *Interpreter*, April 12, 2016, www.lowyinterpreter.org/post/2016/04/12/Note-to-Washington-Enjoy-Abe-while-you-have-him.aspx.

[21] Nick Bisley, "Australia's Strategic Culture and Asia's Changing Regional Order," NBR Special Report No. 60 (December 2016), 17.

perspectives have become more obvious in recent years, especially with the arrival of president Trump in the United States.

For example, former Australian Prime Minister Paul Keating has forcefully argued that Australia – and the United States – need to respect China's rise as legitimate and important. Keating has written that "The U.S. cannot remain No. 1; it will not remain No. 1. The US must recognize that stability in Asia can no longer be imposed by a non-Asian power, least of all by the direct application of US military power."[22] Hugh White, former Australian deputy secretary in the Department of Defense, has argued that neither China nor America "can hope to win a competition for primacy outright, so both would be best served by playing for a compromise."[23] Peter Leahy, former Australian Chief of the Army from 2002 to 2008, recently argued that "By substantially increasing its close relationship with the US, Australia may unduly complicate its relationship with China … As a sovereign nation Australia should maintain the ability to say no to the US and separate itself from its actions."[24]

That there is growing debate about Australia–U.S. relations should come as no surprise. There is consistent and solid evidence that Australians do not view China as a major threat. Opinion polls from 2016, for example, revealed that 47 percent of Australians view Islamic extremism as the most important security threat. The second largest fear was economic, with 29 percent responding that a major economic slowdown in China was the country's biggest threat. Only 4 percent said "disruption of trade from conflict over the South China Seas" (Table 8.2). Australia sees economic relations with China as most important, not political or security relations.

Perhaps even more significant in understanding shifting Australian attitudes, only 20 percent of Australians view the alliance with the United States as helping Australia's relationships in Asia either a little

[22] Paul Kelly, "Australia Must Heed the Shift in the US–China Power Balance: Keating," *The Australian*, December 24, 2016, theaustralian.com. au/opinion/columnists/australia-must-heed-the-shift-in-the-uschina-power-balance-keating/news-story/8fa56d25c1a135cc82a4bfeff0fadebd.

[23] Hugh White, *The China Choice: Why We Should Share Power* (Oxford: Oxford University Press, 2013), 66.

[24] Peter Leahy, "We Must Not Get Too Close to the US," *The Weekend Australian*, April 12, 2012, www.theaustralian.com.au/national-affairs/opinion/we-must-not-get-too-close-to-the-us/news-story/670505ac9707a97f70e6bf02a709833b.

Table 8.2. *Greatest threat to Australia?*

Islamic extremism	47
Major economic slowdown in China	29
Internal political instability in Australia's Asian neighbors	9
Australia involved in a military conflict involving China	7
Disruption of trade from conflict over the South China Sea	4

Source: "Survey on America's Role in the Asia-Pacific," Asian Research Network (University of Sydney, Australia, June 2016).

or a great deal, yet a surprising 40 percent of Australians see the alliance with the United States as "hindering" Australia. When asked whether Australia's alliance with the United States makes external threats more or less likely, 39 percent said "much more likely" or "more likely," and only 11 percent said threats were "less likely" or "much less likely" (Table 8.3). Other polls have largely replicated these findings. For example, the Lowy Institute's annual poll of Australians found that in 2016 Australians viewed the United States and China as equally important, with both at 43 percent.[25] Furthermore, younger Australians see China as more important than the United States. Australians under age forty-five saw China (51 percent) as more important than the United States (35 percent), while an almost identical proportion of those older than forty-five saw the United States as more important (51 percent) than China (36 percent). Paul Carr noted that "For the first time, there is a huge chasm between the Australian values and those of the U.S. administration – his [Trump's] abandonment of free trade in favor of protectionism, his dumping of support for international action on climate change, his insistence on America first instead of alliances and multilateralism."[26]

These attitudes toward their security threats have been reflected in both Australian military spending and in the choice of weapons being purchased. Australian defense spending has remained low and fallen over the years, to below 2 percent of GDP (Figure 8.2). Australia has offered to house 2,500 U.S. marines at the port city of Darwin, although

[25] Alex Oliver, "The Lowy Institute Poll 2016" (Lowy Institute for International Policy, June 7, 2016).
[26] A. Odysseus Patrick, "Australia Debates Future of U.S. Alliance as Trump Era Nears," *The Star*, December 12, 2016, www.thestar.com/news/world/2016/12/12/australia-debates-future-of-us-alliance-ahead-of-trump-era.html.

Table 8.3. *Does Australia's alliance with the United States make the threat more or less likely?*

Much more likely	10
More likely	29
No difference	50
Less likely	8
Much less likely	3

Source: "Survey on America's Role in the Asia-Pacific," Asian Research Network (University of Sydney, Australia, June 2016).

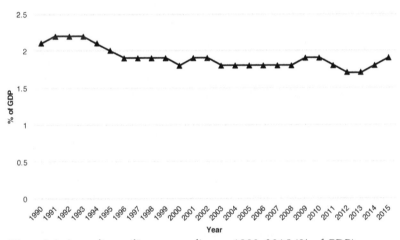

Figure 8.2 Australian military expenditures, 1990–2015 (% of GDP). *Source:* SIPRI 2016.

implementation of that agreement has taken far longer than anticipated. Far from devoting extensive resources to their military, Australians have consistently decided to reduce that spending. The military plays an important role in Australian politics and defense planning, but those involved in military and defense issues comprise only small handful of elites within the larger policy-making and business communities. In fact, Nick Bisley points out that Australia has not had a defense minister with military experience in almost three decades.

While Australians appear fairly clearly not to view China as a threat, and while military expenditures are low, in economic relations China has rapidly become important to Australia. China is Australia's largest economic partner – China took 34 percent of Australia's exports in 2014. Australia also is the second largest recipient of Chinese foreign direct investment, after the United States. China and Australia signed a free-trade agreement in December 2015, and over ninety thousand Chinese study in Australia.[27] In short, China and Australia have a deep and growing economic and social relationship. Australia has also "taken political steps that are at some remove from Washington's preferences, such as joining the Asian Infrastructure Investment Bank and leasing the port of Darwin to the Chinese company Landbridge."[28]

So far has Australia moved from its position of automatic support of the United States that there is speculation that Australia may not side with the United States if it takes a harder line on the one-China policy. While Australia is still a close U.S. ally, it is clear that its interests and even values may be drifting slightly away from those in the United States. There is tremendous goodwill in both Canberra and Washington, DC, and both sides work closely together on a number of issues. But that should not blind us to the differences in the two sides, as well, which are real and greater than before.

Singapore and Indonesia

Indonesia and Singapore in Southeast Asia are illustrative of how the region is managing the unfolding question of how to interact with both China and the United States. These countries have strong and close economic and diplomatic relations with the United States and want to increase that relationship. They also want strong relations with China as well. This is a refrain that has been repeated throughout this book, and Indonesia and Singapore are simply two more important cases that reflect this fact. Neither country sees military force as its primary tool in their dealings with each other and the region. Neither is sending costly signals to China.

Indonesia, for example, has maintained a general preference against having a single dominant, external power in Southeast Asia. This preference is consistent with the core and long-standing principle of a

---

[27] Joe Myers, "5 Things to Know About China and Australia's Economic Ties," *World Economic Forum*, April 11, 2016, www.weforum.org/agenda/2016/04/5-things-to-know-about-china-and-australia-s-economic-ties/.
[28] Nick Bisley, "Australia's Strategic Culture," 15.

"free and active" foreign policy, where Jakarta refrains from joining alliances with major powers and instead strives to carve out its own niche diplomacy and activism in regional and international affairs. Indonesian President Jokowi has recently highlighted Indonesia's strategic opportunity to emerge as a key actor in maintaining the delicate security balance in the region, where Indonesia would serve as a "global maritime fulcrum" through which global trade, commerce, and maritime traffic would pass through the country and link the Pacific and Indian oceans. As Aaron Connelly concludes, "despite resolute rhetoric on maritime rights, Jokowi's administration has been eager to ensure it does not offend Beijing."[29]

Indonesia formally declares that it is not a claimant in the larger South China Sea disputes, a claim that allows it to attempt to play the role of honest broker in the region. This is because the issues in the South China Seas are far more complex than simple Chinese assertiveness, and managing piracy, illegal fishing, and commercial relations are as important and pressing. For example, Indonesia has a far larger problem with illegal Vietnamese fishing than it does with illegal Chinese fishing. Of fifty-seven fishing boats captured near Natuna Island by Indonesia in spring 2016, forty-nine were Vietnamese. Furthermore, as noted previously, the biggest practical maritime issue is piracy and kidnapping, leading Indonesia, Malaysia, and the Philippines to create joint patrols.

Rather than siding exclusively with the United States or China, Indonesia envisions a strategic opportunity for regional littoral states to increase access to all of the major power markets, all the while benefiting from military assistance, reassurances, and training from any combination of these powers. Indonesian Foreign Minister Marty Natalegawa commented in 2013 on the U.S. agreement to base troops on Australian port city of Darwin by saying, "What I would hate to see is if such developments were to provoke a reaction and counterreaction precisely to create that vicious circle of tensions and mistrust."[30] Prominent Indonesian security analysts Sabam Siagian and Endy

---

[29] Aaron L. Connelly, *Indonesia in the South China Sea: Going It Alone* (Sydney: Lowy Institute, December 2, 2016), 2.
[30] Stephen McDonnell and Helen Brown, "China, Indonesia Wary of US Troops in Darwin," *ABC News (Australia)*, April 25, 2013, www.abc.net.au/news/2011-11-17/china-indonesia-wary-of-us-troops-in-darwin/3675866.

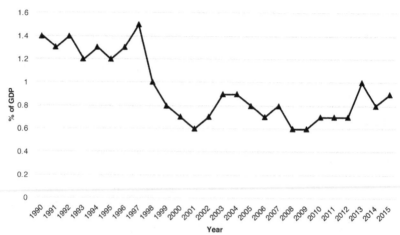

Figure 8.3 Indonesian military expenditures, 1990–2015 (% of GDP).
Source: SIPRI 2016.

M. Bayuni have argued that "Washington will be better off negotiating new power-sharing arrangements with Beijing, instead of seeking to contain the rise of China by rounding up its allies and friends in the region. Asia would welcome a U.S. policy that will, of necessity, be vastly different from the 2011 pivot, and one that is more realistic and less gung-ho."[31]

Indonesian military spending is low and shows few signs of increasing. The Yudhoyono administration (2004–2014) set the target of 1.5 percent of GDP for defense spending, but actual expenditures remained below 1 percent for the duration of his administration (Figure 8.3). President Jokowi actually proposed a 6 percent *reduction* in military expenditures for 2016.[32] That Indonesia has had sustained military expenditures before 2 percent is an indicator of its view of its security environment and priorities. Indonesia has a fairly robust navy, with eleven principal surface combatants in 2016. These have been used primarily to patrol the border and fight piracy.

---

[31] Sabam Siagian and Endy M. Bayuni, "Why Should the US Be Involved in Asia?" *Jakarta Post*, October 9, 2013, www.thejakartapost.com/news/2013/10/09/why-should-us-be-involved-asia.html.

[32] Natasha Hamilton-Hart and Dave McRae, *Indonesia: Balancing the United States and China, Aiming for Independence* (Sydney: United States Studies Center at the University of Sydney, 2015), 7.

Table 8.4. Which country is most hostile toward Indonesia?

Malaysia	51
Australia	23
United States	8
South Korea	5
India	4
China	4

Source: "Survey on America's Role in the Asia-Pacific," Asian Research Network (University of Sydney, Australia, June 2016).

Table 8.5. With which country does the Joko Widodo government have closest ties?

China	39
United States	34
Saudi Arabia	10
Japan	7

Source: "Survey on America's Role in the Asia-Pacific," Asian Research Network (University of Sydney, Australia, June 2016).

Indonesian public opinion is consistent with these other indicators and reveals consistently positive views of China. In an opinion poll from June 2016, 51 percent of Indonesian respondents named Malaysia as the country most hostile to Indonesia, followed by 23 percent naming Australia (Table 8.4). Both China and India were named as hostile by only 4 percent of respondents, less than even those 5 percent of Indonesians who view South Korea as hostile. When asked which country does Indonesia have closest ties with, 39 percent named China, and 34 percent named the United States (Table 8.5). These recent results are consistent over time. In 2005, a Pew Research Center poll found that 60 percent of Indonesians welcomed a strong China, and in 2010, 58 percent of respondents had a favorable view of China.[33] In short, Indonesians view China positively.

These public perceptions reflect a larger focus in Indonesia on economic growth and regional economic ties. Jokowi's administration

---

[33] Polls cited in Evan Laksmana, "The Domestic Politics of Indonesia's Approach to the Tribunal Ruling and the South China Sea," *Contemporary Southeast Asia* 38, No. 3 (2016): 382–388, 384.

is focused on economic growth, and Jokowi's successful presidential campaign saw him emphasize his experience as a mayor who
achieved results for his people. China is Indonesia's largest trading
partner, with over $47 billion in trade in 2014. China has also been
an important source of investment for Indonesia. The Jokowi government awarded a $6 billion high-speed rail contract to a Chinese and
Indonesian consortium in 2015, despite what was widely regarded as
a superior Japanese offer. Although the overall level is low, Chinese
foreign direct investment in Indonesia has increased at a rapid pace.
In 2003, there was $54 million in total Chinese FDI in Indonesia. By
2013, the total stock of Chinese FDI in Indonesia had increased to
$4.6 billion.

As the largest Muslim country in the world, Indonesia has a different perspective on the United States than many other countries in
the region. Indonesians overwhelmingly opposed George Bush's war
on terror, seeing it as unfairly targeting Muslims. Trump's avow-
edly anti-Muslim rhetoric during the presidential campaign made
some Indonesian observers wary about how a Trump presidency
might affect Indonesia. Officially, Indonesian leaders took a wait-
and-see stance. In early 2017, Foreign Minister Retno Marsudi said,
"We will wait until President Trump releases his real policies. So
far we've only seen his campaign promises. We will see if President
Trump will go through with his promised foreign policies or adjust
them here and there. We will determine our stance once he's made
up his mind."[34]

Like Indonesia, Singapore is an important case that does not con-
form to easy categorizations about its views and strategies in the
region. Singapore is often viewed by Americans as staunchly pro-U.S.,
and often viewed by Chinese as staunchly pro-China. However, like
many East Asian countries, Singapore is attempting to have good relations with both major countries. Singaporean leaders have long argued
for good relations with both China and the United States and for an
important regional role for both countries.

While Singapore has warm relations with the United States,
Singaporean officials have consistently warned the United States that

---

[34] "Indonesia to Take Wait-and-See Approach with President Trump's Foreign
Policies," *Jakarta Globe*, January 2, 2017, jakartaglobe.id/news/indonesia-take-
wait-see-approach-president-trumps-foreign-policies/.

they would not welcome a return to containment policies. While the U.S. press and observers often emphasize the fact that Singapore's Changi Naval Base will now house four Littoral combat ships from the United States, those same observers often also overlook the very clear and consistent message Singaporean officials have been telling the United States – that Singapore sees warm relations with China as important, that American influence is as much economic as it is military, and that Singapore has no intention of choosing sides. Regarding U.S. attempts to contain China, Singaporean Foreign Minister Shanmugam said in 2015:

They [China] are rational actors. At the same time, as they grow in power, they demand their rightful place in the world. And if the US and the West does not accommodate legitimate requests then China will look for alternate means ... They have the second largest economy in the world. But their legitimate request with respect to the IMF which your administration has negotiated has been blocked in Congress. And China today is in a position such that you block them there, they are able to set up another international bank, to which a lot of countries subscribe to. So you have to understand, it is a multipolar world. It's not a world you can completely dominate all by yourself ... And if you don't you will find alternate multilateral institutions being set up where you are completely excluded. Your influence will not grow, it will reduce. That is one aspect, it requires a certain – for a want of a better word – an adult approach towards dealing with some of these issues.[35]

Over the past generation, Singapore has also reduced its military expenditures (Figure 8.4).

Significantly, a 2017 opinion piece in the *Straits Times* asked whether it was time for Singapore to "move away from Uncle Sam's embrace."[36] That a government-influenced newspaper would allow open speculation indicates that such sentiments are at least being discussed. As Hugh White points out, "For [America's allies] American

---

[35] Jeremy Au Yong, "With Free Trade, US Faces Stark Decision on Asia – Is It In or Out? – Minister Shanmugam," *Straits Times*, June 16, 2015, www.straitstimes.com/news/world/united-states/story/free-trade-us-faces-stark-decision-asia-it-or-out-minister-shanmugam-#3.

[36] Michael Tan Ngee Tiong, "Time for Singapore to Move Away from Uncle Sam's Embrace?" *Straits Times*, January 7, 2017, www.straitstimes.com/opinion/spore-china-ties-at-a-crossroads.

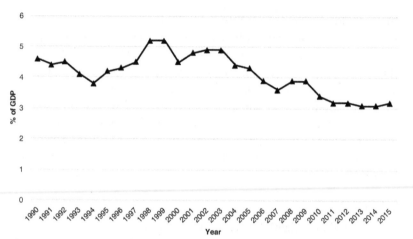

Figure 8.4 Singapore military expenditures, 1990–2015 (% of GDP).
Source: SIPRI 2016.

primacy has no intrinsic value. They have welcomed and supported it for the last forty years only because it has been the foundation of peace and stability in Asia. They will continue to support it as long as that remains true, but not otherwise."[37] This is, in fact, what many of East Asia's most serious and thoughtful leaders have been telling the United States. Singapore's Foreign Minister K. Shanmugam gave a speech in Washington, DC, in February 2012 saying:

Domestic pressures in the US and the demands of elections have resulted in some anti-China rhetoric in domestic debates ... Americans should not underestimate the extent to which such rhetoric can spark a reaction which can create a new and unintended reality for the region. Such rhetoric is a mistake on many levels ... The world and Asia are big enough to accommodate a rising China and a reinvigorated US.

The evidence from a number of Southeast Asian countries clearly leads to the conclusion that many regional countries – especially those not directly involved in maritime disputes – view the region as fairly stable. They view China with equanimity, if not warmth. And they want the United States to emphasize economics and diplomacy as much as military issues.

[37] White, *The China Choice*, 85.

Conclusion

Japan, Australia, Indonesia, and Singapore want good relations with both China and the United States. None is sending costly signals about a commitment to use force to settle their disputes. These countries clearly have different perceptions than what is generally assumed in the United States. None face war or invasion, and all want good relations with both China and the United States. Japan may be the most reliable American ally in the region, but Japan's capacity and desire for regional leadership may be more dependent on one leader – Abe Shinzo – and less enduring than may be expected. Furthermore, Japan's capacity to lead is declining by the day, and it still has unresolved tensions and historical enmities with its closest neighbors of Korea and China.

For their part, Australia, Singapore, and Indonesia are all key regional countries. All have more sanguine views of China than is often expected in the United States. It also appears unlikely that any containment coalition is about to arise that would be based upon these countries. All view diplomacy and institutional mechanisms as key tools for dealing with each other, and there is little indication that any of these countries see military options as the first tool in their foreign policy toolkit.

9 | Powerful Patron: America's Changing Relations with East Asia

Japan is better if it protects itself against this maniac of North Korea ... We are better off frankly if South Korea is going to start protecting itself ... they have to protect themselves or they have to pay us ... We can't be the policeman to the world.

– Donald Trump, April 3, 2016[1]

Previous chapters have shown that East Asian countries are pursuing comprehensive security with each other. They have deepening and widening economic, diplomatic, and institutional relations with each other, in addition to managing their military and security relations. Regional integration is also proceeding, particularly as a central element of continued growth and stability of the region. Detailed case studies of the Philippines, Vietnam, South Korea, and a number of other countries revealed that these countries are also not relying principally on costly signals or military strategies for their national security nearly to the extent as is sometimes believed.

Yet it is sometimes argued that these East Asian countries send few costly signals and have low military expenditures and low threat perceptions because of the U.S. security presence in the region. It is widely believed that the U.S. military presence in the Pacific dampens regional conflicts, reassures allies, and deters regional states from seeking hegemony. Indeed, almost all theory about alliances takes for granted that the smaller power desires an alliance more than the larger power. For example, a common criticism about too robust a U.S. security guarantee is that it allows allies to underspend on their own defense. Barry Posen argues that:

---

[1] Tim Hains, "Trump: 'We Are Like the Policeman to the World ... We're Not Properly Reimbursed'," *RealClearPolitics*, April 4, 2016, www.realclearpolitics.com/video/2016/04/04/trump_we_are_like_the_policeman_to_the_world_were_not_properly_reimbursed.html.

Another problematic response to the United States' grand strategy comes from its friends: free-riding. The Cold War alliances that the country has worked so hard to maintain – namely, NATO and the U.S.–Japanese security agreement – have provided U.S. partners in Europe and Asia with such a high level of insurance that they have been able to steadily shrink their militaries and outsource their defense to Washington.[2]

Logically, however, a strategy of too heavily relying on a distant and easily distracted powerful patron has inherent weaknesses. After all, the powerful patron can always change its mind, leaving the smaller protégé badly exposed and underprepared to face security threats on its own. Indeed, as we have seen in this book, smaller East Asian countries are often careful about relying too heavily on a patron for their security.

Given that the United States still has formidable forward military deployments in East Asia, the hypothesis that East Asian states are mainly or solely relying on external balancing relies heavily on a counterfactual: if the United States weren't forward deployed in East Asia, then East Asian states would feel more insecure and thus would spend more on their militaries, leading to greater arms racing and increasing the tensions in the region. This world may be about to test that hypothesis, because what grand strategy a Trump administration will take toward East Asia is still coming into focus.

During the election campaign, Trump advocated a wide variety of positions in foreign policy, many of them contradictory. The contours of a Trump administration stance are only slowly becoming clear, and a "Trump doctrine" toward Asia could take years to truly emerge. By summer 2017, for example, many key positions in the Trump national security apparatus were unfilled, and some key ambassadorial positions in East Asia still did not even have nominees. What had become clear, however, was that it was unlikely a Trump administration would continue a mainstream focus on diplomacy, economics, and security alliances. Rather, Trump's two most consistent stances emphasized either more nationalism and confrontation in security affairs toward countries such as China and North Korea, or more isolation and protectionism in economic affairs than the United States has pursued

[2] Barry Posen, "Pull Back: The Case for a Less Activist Foreign Policy," *Foreign Affairs* 92 (2013): 116–123.

since World War II. For example, Trump announced even before he was inaugurated that the United States would no longer consider joining the Trans-Pacific Partnership, a massive economic trade and investment pact involving eleven East Asian countries and the U.S. Whether East Asian countries embrace or resist this emerging U.S. approach will thus be critical to both the success of the policy and regional stability.

American Allies and Nonallies

Previous chapters have shown that South Korea, the Philippines, and Vietnam are placing only minimal reliance on the U.S. forward presence in the region. Here we look more broadly and ask whether we can find any systematic difference in behavior between U.S. allies and nonallies. While it is plausible that the United States would defend its treaty allies from a direct threat to their national survival, it is far less clear that the United States would engage in a potentially devastating war with China over strategically marginal disputes in which it has no direct stake.[3] This arises because of moral hazard in alliances: too clear a U.S. commitment to its allies may embolden them to take risky actions because they believe the United States will support them, drawing the United States into a war that it does not want to fight.[4] The United States is thus careful about clarifying or extending its security guarantees to its alliance partners. Put differently, there will always be a gap between what the level of security provision an ally desires and the level of security provision the United States provides. From the perspective of East Asian states, the U.S. alliance system may reassure about national survival, but it is unlikely to ever be a complete military guarantee against all contingencies.

And, smaller states must prepare for that gap. In short, from the perspective of smaller states that rely on the United States, the concern is primarily that the United States will choose not to help in times of need. External balancing will never be a complete guarantee against all contingencies, and allies will always have to be prepared for the possibility that their powerful patron will be preoccupied, distracted, engaged in a different crisis, or simply decide not to intervene. This is

---

[3] White, *The China Choice*.

[4] Benson, *Constructing International Security*; Benson, Bentley, and Ray, "Ally provocateur"; Fang, Johnson, and Leeds, "To Concede or To Resist."

especially likely under a Trump administration. President Trump has consistently been suspicious of being the "world's policeman," having numerous times shown skepticism about involving the United States too quickly in issues around the world. At the same time, Trump has also shown a willingness to be more confrontational than most. How both these tendencies play out during his actual administration will not be clear for some time. As Evan Osnos noted, despite many different and contradictory statements over the years, Trump has been consistent on three main issues:

One of them is his belief that the United States is fundamentally being damaged by immigration. Number two is his belief that trade deals have done more damage to the United States than they have helped. And number three is his belief that the United States does too much for the world. As he said in 2015, "I want to take back everything that the United States has given the world."[5]

There are actually a number of logical and empirical reasons to avoid assigning too much causal weight to the U.S. role in keeping the peace in East Asia. Logically, the U.S. military presence is clearly not a public good that is available to all. Only some countries shelter under a U.S. military umbrella, and only these countries might expect the United States to provide aid, and thus only these countries might have lower defense spending than might be expected. For example, it is unlikely that the U.S. forward military deployment in the Philippines would benefit Malaysia. It is also unlikely that the United States would intervene in a Malaysia–Indonesia border skirmish, for example. And as was shown in Chapter 7, while Vietnamese leaders may enjoy having an occasional U.S. warship dock at Cam Ranh Bay, they are probably not so naïve as to think this is a guarantee of U.S. military support in the unlikely event of a Vietnam–China war. As Hugh White points out: "It is far from clear that America's interests in the Spratly Islands are worth a war with China."[6]

[5] Evan Osnos, quoted on "Could Trump 'Undermine the Legacy of the Obama Presidency' with the Stroke of a Pen?" *Fresh Air*, November 15, 2016, www.npr.org/2016/11/15/502157875/could-trump-undermine-the-legacy-of-the-obama-presidency-with-the-stroke-of-a-pe.

[6] White, *The China Choice*, 97.

Before speculating about what Trump may do in the future, is there empirical evidence that U.S. allies have historically been underspending on defense because a U.S. security umbrella allows them a free ride? It should be possible to distinguish differences in military expenditures between countries that free-ride and those that do not. If this were the case, then we would expect systematic differences in behavior between allies and nonallies. We should easily be able to find that non-U.S. allies are spending more on their defense than are U.S. allies, because nonallies cannot rely on the U.S. to protect them the way that allies can.

Testing this proposition is straightforward, because only some countries shelter under a U.S. military alliance (Table 9.1). Only five East Asian countries have a defense pact with the United States: Japan (1951), the Philippines (1951), South Korea (1953), Australia (1951), and Thailand (1962).[7] However, it is difficult to find evidence that U.S. allies behave systematically differently than nonallies in their security policies. There is virtually no evidence that U.S. allies are underspending and free-riding. Perhaps most tellingly, the empirical evidence reveals that East Asian countries with a U.S. alliance and those lacking a U.S. alliance have similar military expenditures (Figure 9.1).[8] There was a notable difference in defense spending at the end of the Cold War in the late 1980s, with U.S. allies directing a much smaller share of their GDP to defense than those without a U.S. alliance. However, defense expenditures between the two types of countries rapidly converged. Both allies and nonallies now devote an average of less than 2 percent of their GDP to their militaries – indeed, allies and nonallies were identical in averaging 1.7 percent of GDP to defense in 2015. This empirical observation needs to be emphasized: we have virtually no evidence of free-riding by U.S. allies.

This similarity in defense policies between allies and nonallies exists partially because of clear limits of U.S. military commitments to its allies, and, as has been shown, because many East Asian states do not particularly fear for their survival. The Philippines is a good example. It faces no threat to its existence, and also the areas of conflict covered

[7] U.S. Department of State, "US Collective Defense Arrangements," www.state.gov/s/l/treaty/collectivedefense/.

[8] Treaty allies, from U.S. Department of State, "U.S. Collective Defense Arrangements," www.state.gov/s/l/treaty/collectivedefense/.

Table 9.1. *U.S. relationships with key East Asian countries*

Mutual Defense Treaty	
Japan	The Treaty of Mutual Cooperation and Security between Japan and the United States was signed in 1960.
Korea	The United States and the Republic of Korea signed a Mutual Defense Treaty in 1953.
Philippines	The Manila Declaration signed in 2011 reaffirmed the 1951 U.S.–Philippines Mutual Defense Treaty.
Australia	The ANZUS security treaty, concluded in 1951, serves as the foundation of defense and security cooperation between the countries.
Friends	
Taiwan	Despite no formal diplomatic recognition from the United States, the 1979 Taiwan Relations Act provides the legal basis for the unofficial relationship between the United States and Taiwan, and "enshrines the U.S. commitment to assist Taiwan in maintaining its defensive capability. The United States insists on the peaceful resolution of cross-Strait differences, opposes unilateral changes to the status quo by either side."
Thailand	Despite the dissolution of the South East Asia Treaty Organization (SEATO) in 1977, the Manila Pact remains in force and, together with the Thanat–Rusk communiqué of 1962 and the 2012 Joint Vision Statement for the Thai–U.S. Defense Alliance, constitutes the basis of U.S. security commitments to Thailand. In 2003, the United States designated Thailand a Major Non-NATO Ally.
Singapore	Strategy Partner, 4 Littoral Combat Ships (LCS) stationed at Changi.
New Zealand	Left the Australia, New Zealand, and Unites States Security Treaty (ANZUS) in 1986 after declaring itself a nuclear-free weapons zone and refusing passage to U.S. nuclear capable warships.

Sources: U.S. Department of State, "U.S. Bilateral Relations Fact Sheets" (www.state.gov/r/pa/ei/bgn/index.htm).

by the U.S.–Philippines mutual defense treaty are vague: "... an armed attack on either of the Parties is deemed to include an armed attack on the metropolitan territory of either of the Parties, or on the island territories under its jurisdiction in the Pacific Ocean, its armed forces,

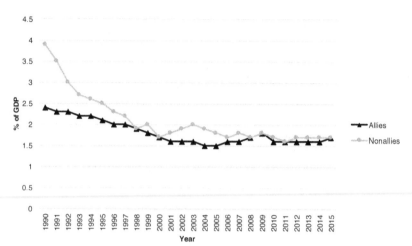

Figure 9.1 U.S. allies' and nonallies' military expenditures, 1990–2015 (% of GDP). U.S. allies: Japan, Korea, Philippines, Thailand, Australia. Nonallies: China, Indonesia, Malaysia, Vietnam, and Taiwan. *Source:* SIPRI 2016.

public vessels or aircraft in the Pacific." As Ricard Saludo wrote in the *Manila Times*:

> Big question: If the island attack is not in the Pacific, is Uncle Sam obliged to fight? … Unless maps are mistaken, Philippine-claimed islands, shoals and waters, including Pag-asa, are in the South China Sea, not the Pacific Ocean. Perhaps that explains why the U.S. has done nothing but talk when China took over Recto Bank and Panatag Shoal, and now threatens Ayungin … if the PLA targets Philippine troops and vessels in the Spratlys, the treaty won't apply. We're on our own.[9]

A good example of the complex security dynamics countries face is Taiwan. Trump's phone call with Taiwanese President Tsai Ing-wen in early December 2016 was hailed by some as a much-needed show of strength from the U.S. president-elect, one that would support democratic Taiwan. It also broke four decades of clear U.S. policy of not communicating directly with the head of state of Taiwan and set off a firestorm of controversy. Significantly, however, and consistent with

---

[9] Ricardo Saludo, "Big Holes in the Philippines–US Defense Treaty," *The Manila Times* (March 20, 2014), http://www.manilatimes.net/big-holes-in-the-philippines-us-defense-treaty/84117/.

theoretical expectations that a small protégé would fear abandonment, many Taiwanese were more worried than emboldened.

The phone call was reportedly long planned and was a careful move by the incoming U.S. president. But in Taiwan, reacting too enthusiastically to an American overture would be rash. Taiwan, not the United States, would be the main target of retaliation by China. Furthermore, Trump at any time could become distracted or change his mind about support for Taiwan, leaving the country totally exposed. Former Taiwanese deputy defense minister Lin Chong-pin said that Taiwan should be wary of Mr. Trump's overtures to Taiwan, which might not be sincere. "When he [Trump] turns, carrots can immediately become sticks."[10] As such, reaction in Taiwan was muted, and Taiwanese President Tsai said that "One phone call does not mean a policy shift. We all see the value of stability in the region."[11] The vice-president of an influential Taiwanese think tank, Lin Ting-hui, said that "We have to let Trump know that Taiwan is very important and it cannot be a bargaining chip," while a member of the ruling Democratic Progressive Party, Lo Chih-Cheng, said that a trade war between the United States and China "would be an indirect impact on Taiwan's economy, and we don't want to be on the bargaining table."[12] While U.S. policy toward Taiwan is unlikely to change under Trump, the relevant point is that Taiwanese leaders will be cautious about embracing too quickly perceived changes in U.S. policy and are not necessarily embracing a more activist U.S. foreign policy.

The question of who will abandon whom goes both ways, as well. U.S. allies do not appear eager for a showdown with China, as previous chapters have shown. That reluctance to join American initiatives by some U.S. allies has not gone unnoticed in the U.S. military. Indeed, if President Trump is actually as confrontational toward Beijing as some fear, it is quite likely that many East Asian countries – even close

---

[10] Andrew Browne, "Wooed by Donald Trump, Taiwan Trembles," *Wall Street Journal*, December 6, 2016, www.wsj.com/articles/ wooed-by-trump-taiwan-trembles-1481014830.

[11] Donna Leger, "Taiwan: Trump Call Was Not China 'Policy Shift'," *USA Today*, December 6, 2016, www.usatoday.com/story/news/2016/12/06/phone-call-trump-taiwan-president/95027782/.

[12] Both quotes are from William Kazer, "Taiwan Fears Becoming a Pawn in Donald Trump's Game," *Wall Street Journal*, January 19, 2017, www.wsj.com/ articles/taiwan-fears-becoming-a-pawn-in-donald-trumps-game-1484821803.

American allies – may attempt to distance themselves from American policies. East Asian countries may want American power and leadership as a potential bulwark against too domineering Chinese power, but they fairly clearly do not want an American containment strategy against China, either. Few countries would risk being caught in the middle of a U.S.–China dispute. As Admiral Harry Harris testified at a hearing on U.S. military strategy in the Asia-Pacific region before the Senate Armed Forces Subcommittee on September 17, 2015:

As far as the allies go, we have 5 treaty allies in the Pacific of varying degrees of capability but whether they would be with us in every fight is a matter for them to decide and the fight at-hand, so while I count the delta in numbers between us and China I try not to count the quantity of assets our allies have because depending on the situation at hand and their own national decisions we might have to fight alone.[13]

Another significant and often overlooked indicator of regional stability has been the reception of East Asian countries to a steady reduction in American military deployments to the region. The United States has reduced its military deployments in East Asia over the past thirty years, without any of the panic that pundits have predicted would follow a significant U.S. drawdown. Furthermore, although China is not yet anywhere near a match for the U.S. military, the gap has narrowed. U.S. military personnel deployments to East Asia are now 90 percent lower than they were in 1970. Those numbers may have been artificially inflated due to the Vietnam War, but even excluding deployment in Vietnam, U.S. military personnel have been reduced by two-thirds since 1970 (Table 9.2). Naval deployments have followed a similar trend of reductions (Table 9.3). Although the U.S. maintained 101 principal surface combatants in the Asia-Pacific in 1975, by 2015 the U.S. deployed 51 principal surface combatants in the region.

The Congressional Budget Office released a report in March 2015 concluding that the overall U.S. fleet appears set to decline from the current 275 ships today to somewhere between 208 and 251 ships.[14]

---

[13] U.S. Congress, Senate, Committee on Armed Services, *Maritime Security Strategy in the Asia-Pacific Region*, 114th Cong., 1st sess., 2015, www.c-span.org/video/?328185-1/hearing-us-maritime-security-strategy-asiapacific&live, 1:21:35 to 1:22:13.

[14] Congressional Budget Office, *Preserving the Navy's Forward Presence with a Smaller Fleet* (Washington, DC: Congressional Budget Office, March

Table 9.2. *U.S. military deployments in East Asia, 1970–2016*

	1970	1980	1990	2000	2005	2016
Vietnam	390,278	0	0	16	13	4
South Korea	52,197	38,780	41,344	36,565	30,983	24,189
Japan	82,264	46,004	46,593	40,159	35,571	38,807
Thailand	39,212	95	213	526	114	296
Philippines	23,440	13,387	13,863	79	55	36
Taiwan	8,813	0	0	0	0	9
Australia	559	644	713	175	196	187
Indonesia	34	55	32	51	23	24
Malaysia	13	15	14	18	16	13
Singapore	10	23	50	411	169	175
% compared to 1970		16.6	17.2	13.1	11.2	10.7
% compared to 1970 (excluding Vietnam deployments)		47.9	49.8	37.8	32.5	30.9
Total	596,820	99,003	102,822	78,000	67,140	63,740

Source: U.S. Department of Defense, PERSONNEL & PROCUREMENT STATISTICS (siadapp.dmdc.osd.mil/personnel/MILITARY/miltop.htm).

Table 9.3. *U.S. naval deployments in East Asia, 1970–2015*

	1975	2000	2015
Aircraft carriers	8	6	5
Principal surface combatants	101	68	51
Submarines	44	60	41

Source: IISS, *The Military Balance*, various years.

President Trump has called for an increase to a 350 ship navy, a massive expansion in the army and marine corps, and greater spending across the board. A main Trump adviser, Peter Navarro, calls this "Peace Through Strength," arguing that "the U.S. Navy is perhaps the greatest source of regional stability in Asia ... the mere initiation of the Trump naval program will reassure our allies."[15] Yet this appears to be wishful thinking, as it is totally oblivious to the question of whether the United States would actually follow through on its commitments and how long it would take.

Despite the best of intentions, any major expansion of American military forces will face difficulties. It is fairly clear that U.S. military priorities are actually in the Middle East, and that is unlikely to change under a Trump administration. President Obama tried to focus on East Asia and yet was consistently pulled back into issues in the Middle East. For example, a Council on Foreign Relations study in 2015 found that even during the Obama "rebalance to Asia," from 2010 to 2015, "overall security aid to Southeast Asia fell by 19 percent since 2010 ... assistance to US treaty allies Thailand and the Philippines fell by 79.9 percent and 8.8 percent, respectively."[16] Furthermore, the

2015), 1, www.cbo.gov/sites/default/files/114th-congress-2015–2016/reports/49989-ForwardPresence-2.pdf.

[15] Alexander Gray and Peter Navarro, "Donald Trump's Peace Through Strength Vision for the Asia-Pacific," *Foreign Policy*, November 7, 2016, foreignpolicy.com/2016/11/07/donald-trumps-peace-through-strength-vision-for-the-asia-pacific/. For an assessment, see Ronald O'Rourke, *Navy Force Structure: A Bigger Fleet? Background and Issues for Congress* (CRS Report No. R44635) (Washington, DC: Congressional Research Service, 2003), fas.org/sgp/crs/weapons/R44635.pdf.

[16] Council on Foreign Relations, "Rebalance to Asia Led to Drop in Security Assistance for Southeast Asia," *World Post*, May 4, 2016, www.cfr.org/asia-and-pacific/rebalance-asia/p37516?cid=nlc-public-the_world_this_week--link8-20160429&sp_mid=51268757&sp_rid=am9obi5nZXJzaG1hbkBueXUuZWR1S1S0#!/.

study found that U.S. security assistance to Europe "dwarfs" aid to Southeast Asia: total European security assistance was three times as large as aid to Southeast Asia in 2015.

In sum, even if the Trump administration is dramatically more confrontational than its predecessors, and even if it attempts to devote virtually unlimited resources to the U.S. military, it is not clear whether the focus on East Asia or massive increases in military spending can be sustained over the long run. In terms of alliance theory, a major move toward confrontation and containment in U.S. grand strategy for East Asia would likely raise uncertainty in the region, uncertainty that would not necessarily be welcomed by East Asian countries, even U.S. allies. Although Trump could sustain attention to his initiatives for a while, whether a major change in U.S. grand strategy would survive a four- or eight-year Trump administration would be key questions East Asian countries will ask themselves. The greatest risk for East Asian countries would be that they embrace a new Trump doctrine only to see Trump change his mind. In other words, East Asian states are likely to react cautiously to Trump's overall approach to Asia.

The Social and Economic Dimensions of U.S. Grand Strategy

America's relationship with East Asia is wider and deeper than simply its military presence. This book has argued that East Asian countries view their grand strategies and national security in comprehensive terms, and see economics, diplomacy, and regional integration as central to their national security and survival. The region itself is home more to business than to war. Yet often overlooked or neglected in discussion about U.S. grand strategy in Asia are the economic and diplomatic dimensions. This is regrettable, because the story of East Asia is as much economic as it is political. The last half-century has seen phenomenal and near-miraculous economic transformation across the region – from Japan, South Korea, and Taiwan to China and much of Southeast Asia. The United States was central to that economic dynamism, and the growth in East Asia also spurred economic growth in America as well. Looking only at security relations in East Asia will often obfuscate the width and depth of American interactions with Asia.

East Asia's increasing closeness to China has been accompanied by evidence of declining American economic attention to East Asia. From the troubles with the Trans-Pacific Partnership to the waffling over the Asian Infrastructure Investment Bank (AIIB), the United States in 2017 had begun to pull back from regional economic leadership to a degree that was unthinkable even a few years ago. While much of this may have been mere rhetoric, and while much of Trump's ire has been directly solely at China, his policies will have regionwide implications. How Trump's economic policies actually manifest themselves could potentially weaken U.S. influence. After all, as Richard Katz pointed out, "U.S. leadership rests on others' perception of it as a benign hegemon. By undermining such perceptions, one-way street notions of free trade pose a far greater threat to national security than any free-trade agreement that China could create."[17]

And indisputably, Asia has become a key American trading and investment region: China is America's largest trading partner, comprising 16 percent of total trade in 2015 (Table 9.4). Japan, Korea, Taiwan, and India are all top ten trading partners of the United States. As for investment, Japan is the second-largest investor in the United States, with a cumulative $393 billion invested over time. As a block, ASEAN's largest trading partner was China (14 percent of total trade), while the United States was fourth (8.2 percent).[18]

However, despite the clear economic importance of Asia to the United States, Americans still overwhelmingly think Europe is more important than Asia. For example, a Pew Research Poll of 2016 found that Americans continue to believe that European ties are far more important than Asian ties for the United States.[19] Fifty-two percent of Americans believed that European ties were most important, compared to 32 percent who believed Asia was most important. Two decades ago, in 1997, 49 percent of Americans thought Europe was most important, and 31 percent thought Asia was more important. Put differently, Americans have consistently seen Europe as more important than Asia by almost 20 percentage points, and that shows no signs of changing in 2016.

[17] Richard Katz, "Free Trade and the TPP," *Foreign Affairs*, October 7, 2015, www.foreignaffairs.com/articles/united-states/2015-10-07/free-trade-and-tpp.

[18] Nargiza Salidjanova and Iacob Koch-Weser, "China's Economic Ties with ASEAN: A Country-by-Country Analysis," Staff Research Report, U.S.–China Economic and Security Review Commission, March 17, 2015, 4.

[19] Pew Research Center, "Public Uncertain, Divided over America's Place in the World," May 5, 2016, www.people-press.org/2016/05/05/public-uncertain-divided-over-americas-place-in-the-world/.

Table 9.4. U.S. trade partners, 2015 (U.S.$ in billions,% of total trade)

Rank	Country	Total trade (US$ billion)	% of total U.S. trade
1	China	598.1	16.0
2	Canada	575.5	15.4
3	Mexico	531.1	14.2
4	Japan	193.6	5.2
5	Germany	174.1	4.6
6	South Korea	115.3	3.1
7	United Kingdom	114.2	3.0
8	France	77.7	2.1
9	Taiwan	66.6	1.8
10	India	66.3	1.8

Source: U.S. Census Bureau, "Top Trading Partners – Year to Date Total Trade 2015," (www.census.gov/foreign-trade/statistics/highlights/top/top1512yr.html).

This focus on Europe is reflected not just in opinion polls, but also in where the few Americans who actually study overseas go to study. Over half (53 percent) of all college students studying abroad went to Europe in 2014, according to U.S. data.[20] Seven out of the top ten destinations for college students studying abroad were Western. The most popular destination is the United Kingdom: 12.6 percent of all Americans studying abroad studied in the United Kingdom alone.[21] Only 4.5 percent of all Americans studying abroad went to China, and only 6.5 percent of all American students abroad went anywhere in Asia.

For its part, although Asia's economic strategy had focused mainly on the United States during the mid-twentieth century, that began to change in the 1990s. The widening of Asia's diplomatic, economic, and institutional order to include the United States but also to move beyond the United States began in earnest in the wake of the Asian financial crisis of 1997. Following that crisis, two mutually exclusive viewpoints emerged about the role of American-dominated

[20] "Trends in U.S. Study Abroad," Association of International Educators (NAFSA), www.nafsa.org/Policy_and_Advocacy/Policy_Resources/Policy_Trends_and_Data/Trends_in_U_S__Study_Abroad/?.
[21] "Open Doors Data: U.S. Study Abroad," Institute of International Education, January 5, 2016, www.iie.org/Research-and-Publications/Open-Doors/Data/US-Study-Abroad#.WA-jYOErLGI.

international institutions – such as the IMF, the World Bank, and the Asian Development Bank (ADB). One, largely centered in the United States, sees these institutions as more transparent, careful, and reliable. The other view, largely centered in East Asia, sees these institutions as promoting American power and pushing a particular ideological perspective.

Although largely overlooked in the United States, East Asian debates about the role of the IMF and America's influence on the choices and type of international economic institutions have continued to today. As Evan Feigenbaum recently pointed out, "the crisis of 1997–98 ... left a particularly searing legacy on many Asian countries. The US was perceived to be disconnected and aloof."[22] Criticisms of the IMF's political and economic role became more obvious – when the Thai bhat collapsed in 1997, "many blamed the IMF for forcing the country to open up its financial markets before there was a proper regulatory infrastructure in place."[23] Austerity measures imposed by the IMF after the crisis as part of the conditions for receiving IMF bailouts included slashing government budgets, which meant slashing important social services so that the IMF could be repaid first. Unemployment spiked, leading to widespread public protests.

Donald Emmerson observes that:

While it would be unfair to blame the AFC [Asian financial crisis] on the US Treasury, the United States had favored open capital markets ... Washington was reproached for hostility, or indifference, or both – for torching the region's economies and then letting them burn.[24]

The United States also opposed a Japanese initiative to create an Asian Monetary Fund in the late 1990s, which was perceived across Asia as being more about retaining American control and power than any substantive reason for opposition.[25] The roots of searching for

---

[22] Evan Feigenbaum, "The U.S. Must Adapt to Asia's New Order," *East Asia Forum*, March 22, 2015, www.eastasiaforum.org/2015/03/22/the-us-must-adapt-to-asias-new-order/.

[23] Rebecca Liao, "Out of the Bretton Woods: How the AIIB Is Different," *Foreign Affairs*, July 27, 2015, www.foreignaffairs.com/articles/asia/2015-07-27/out-bretton-woods.

[24] Donald Emmerson, "What Do the Blind-Sided See? Reapproaching Realism in Southeast Asia," *Pacific Review* 18, no. 1 (March 2005): 1–21.

[25] Phillip Lipscy, "Japan's Asian Monetary Fund Proposal," *Stanford Journal of East Asian Studies* 3, no. 1 (2003): 93–104.

alternative or complementary institutional means and relations by which to deal with their economic and security situations are thus not new, and not directly or even mainly a function of China's rise. Rather, East Asian states have always engaged in what Evelyn Goh calls "complicity and resistance" to the United States.[26] Indeed, East Asian institution building rapidly increased after the 1997 crisis, and T. J. Pempel observed only a decade later in 2008 that "Asia is more complex, more institutionalized, and more 'Asian' than it was when the crisis struck."[27] As Vinod Aggarwal and Min-kyo Koo point out, "the lament that Asia lacks regional trade institutions has now been replaced by the criticism of the excessive number of institutional for in the region."[28]

Not only have East Asian countries become more skeptical of U.S.-led institutions, the past thirty years have also seen China more clearly included in discussions of regional economic policy. As Saadia Pekkannen notes, "Chinese actions increasingly demonstrate it has the money bags and the brains as well ... One by one, or so it seems, the United States' closest allies in Europe and Asia are joining emergent institutions of a new world order that China is putting into motion."[29] Although the remarkable economic growth in Japan, South Korea, and Taiwan was due in part to exports to the United States during the middle of the twentieth century, the arrival of China in the late-twentieth century as an economic powerhouse rapidly changed Asian countries' focus. The speed with which these countries shifted their economic focus to China was astounding. Focusing on these larger diplomatic and economic initiatives in the region places regional security issues within this larger context. In many areas, such as trade and investment, Asian countries are rapidly increasing their ties with China, rather than limiting them. China, for example, is ASEAN countries' largest trade partner, where two-way trade stands at $367 billion

---

[26] Goh, *The Struggle for Order.*

[27] T. J. Pempel, "Restructuring Regional Ties," in Andrew MacIntyre, T. J. Pempel, and John Ravenhill, eds, *Crisis as Catalyst: Asia's Dynamic Political Economy* (Ithaca, NY: Cornell University Press, 2008), 165.

[28] Vinod Aggarwal and Min Gyo Koo, "Designing Trade Institutions for Asia," in Saadia Pekkanen, ed., *Asian Designs: Governance in the Contemporary World Order* (Ithaca, NY: Cornell University Press, 2016), 35.

[29] Saadia Pekkanen, "Introduction," in Saadia Pekkanen, ed., *Asian Designs: Governance in the Contemporary World Order* (Ithaca, NY: Cornell University Press, 2016), 3.

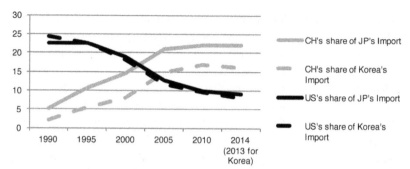

Figure 9.2 Chinese and American shares of East Asian imports, 1990–2014.
Sources: World Integrated Trade Solution (WITS), World Bank, 2016; Trade Statistics of Japan, Ministry of Finance, 2016.

in 2014, or 14.5 percent of Southeast Asia's total trade volume.[30] Between 2012 and 2014, Chinese investment flows to ASEAN grew by nearly 6 percent and is the only country besides Australia and South Korea to increase foreign direct investment (FDI) to Southeast Asia for each of the last three years (Figure 9.2).[31]

The rapid East Asian economic embrace of China plays into theoretical debates about costly signals and information. If China's neighbors fear China, why do China and its neighbors not substitute less costly modes of conflict, such as the imposition of sanctions or other attempts to limit Chinese economic growth? If countries fear China, why do they not attempt to limit Chinese influence over their own economies? As noted in Chapter 2, attempts to limit an adversary's economic growth, and even economic sanctions, are a key method of sending costly signals about disputes that a country cares deeply about. As Andrew Coe writes, "Certainly, when faced with extremely high costs of war, the U.S. and the Soviet Union made ample use of all these alternative modes of conflict to prosecute their disputes."[32] Yet

[30] "ASEAN External Trade Statistics," *ASEAN*, as of December 21, 2015, www .asean.org/?static_post=external-trade-statistics-3.
[31] Investment from the European Union (EU) region also increased over that time period, but the EU is a region, not simply one country. ASEAN Foreign Direct Investment Statistics Database as of May 26, 2015 (data are compiled from submission of ASEAN Central Banks and National Statistical Offices through the ASEAN Working Group on International Investment Statistics [WGIIS]), asean.org/?static_post=foreign-direct-investment-statistics.
[32] Andrew Coe, "An Economic Theory of Peace" (unpublished manuscript, University of Southern California, 2017), 12.

East Asian countries are not pursuing economic isolation of China to limit its power and retard its economic growth. Rather, the opposite has occurred – it was China's decision in 1978 to engage the region, and East Asian countries rapidly engaged China economically, as well.

As has been seen by the response of countries to the founding of the Chinese-originated Asian Infrastructure Investment Bank (AIIB) in 2014, many countries are even ignoring direct pressure from the United States and actively joining the China-sponsored bank. Key American allies such as Australia, South Korea, the Philippines, and Thailand were all founding members of the AIIB. India, Vietnam, Indonesia, and Malaysia were also founding members.[33] This is because countries forge security policy woven in with economic and diplomatic policies. The region has continued to evolve and morph over the past three decades in ways that make the region more focused on itself, and less focused simply on the United States. Australia's decision to join the AIIB came from the recognition that there is an estimated infrastructure financing gap of nearly $8 trillion in the region over the decade, and that participating in the bank's projects would provide a significant opportunity for Australia to boost its exports of raw commodities and minerals, agriculture, and services to the region.

In the wake of the founding of the AIIB, the *New York Times* editorialized that "The Obama administration, to its embarrassment, has been spurned by Western allies flocking to a China-led Asian development bank, defying White House pleas to stand back."[34] Treasury Secretary Jacob Lew admitted that "It's not an accident that emerging economies are looking at other places because they are frustrated that, frankly, the United States has stalled a very mild and reasonable set of reforms in the IMF." An unnamed American source in the administration said that "We are wary about a trend toward constant accommodation of China, which is not the best way to engage a rising power," quoted in the *Financial Times*.[35] As Gideon Rachman observed, "By

---

[33] Malaysia, the Philippines, and Thailand have signed AIIB's founding charter but have yet to join on the bank's establishment date.

[34] The Editorial Board, "U.S. Allies, Lured by China's Bank," *New York Times*, March 20, 2015, www.nytimes.com/2015/03/20/opinion/us-allies-lured-by-chinas-bank.html.

[35] Geoff Dyer and George Parker, "U.S. Attacks UK's 'Constant Accommodation' with China," *Financial Times*, March 12, 2015, www.ft.com/content/31c4880a-c8d2-11e4-bc64-00144feab7de.

setting up and then losing a power struggle with China, Washington has sent an unintended signal about the drift of power and influence in the 21st century."[36] Significantly, this trend occurred even before the Trump administration.

America's putative concerns about the AIIB concerned its organization, that it would not function as professionally or transparently as the IMF or World Bank. As Saori Katada notes, one reason Japan was one of the few Asian countries not to join the AIIB at its founding came from Japan's commitment to the existing order: "Japan worries about the AIIB diluting the influence of post-WWII Bretton Woods institutions such as the IMF and the World Bank, as well as the ADB ... Japan's own political influence in these institutions is also at stake."[37] Yet Japan was the only major East Asian country not to join the AIIB at its founding, and even Japan later expressed interest in joining both the bank and China's larger economic initiatives.[38]

As the United States grapples with a rapidly changing regional institutional and economic environment in which many countries see their economic future tied to that of China, it intensifies the dilemma of how countries will manage their relationships with the United States, China, and each other. Beyond military and security-related issues, a much more integrated, interactive region is emerging, a region in which countries want U.S. engagement but is also increasingly searching for alternative, complementary, institutional, and diplomatic arrangements. American foot dragging looks less like rule building and more like churlish unwillingness to face a changing East Asian reality.[39]

The Changing Nature of American Hegemony in Asia

Even if a "Trump doctrine" for East Asia begins to emerge, it has become increasingly clear that U.S. leadership and policy toward

[36] Gideon Rachman, "China's Money Magnet Pulls in U.S. Allies," *Financial Times*, March 16, 2015, www.ft.com/content/cd466ddc-cbc7-11e4-aeb5-00144feab7de.

[37] Katada, "At the Crossroads," 6.

[38] Naoya Yoshino, "Abe's Belt and Road Pivot Signals Push to Improve Bilateral Ties," *Nikkei Asian Review* June 6, 2017, http://asia.nikkei.com/Spotlight/The-Future-of-Asia-2017/Abe-s-Belt-and-Road-pivot-signals-push-to-improve-bilateral-ties.

[39] Joshua Kurlantzick, *State Capitalism: How the Return of Statism is Transforming the World* (Oxford: Oxford University Press, 2016).

East Asia is in the midst of a major change. No matter what overall U.S. grand strategy emerges under and even after President Trump, the post–World War II approach and institutions appear to be in question in ways they never were before. Trump's administration and the actions that Trump takes may accelerate a trend in East Asia that has already been under way. The region has widened its economic and institutional focus beyond the United States. The United States used to be the sole social and economic focus, but now it is only first among equals. Investment, trade, and financial flows between Northeast Asian countries and China continue to increase rapidly, despite political rivalry that dominates the headlines. More than 1 million Taiwanese now conduct business in mainland China – almost 5 percent of the entire Taiwanese population.[40] Thus, while there is fear about potential Chinese economic domination, regional firms and individuals have clearly voted with their feet, and there is no hint of any move in Taiwan to limit or retard economic interactions between the two countries.

For its part, the United States' decision to withdraw from the Trans-Pacific Partnership (TPP) – one of the most important economic pacts of the past few decades – has already had a major effect in East Asia. While he was president, Barack Obama advocated strongly on behalf of the TPP, saying that "The Asia-Pacific region will continue its economic integration, with or without the United States. We can lead that process, or we can sit on the sidelines and watch prosperity pass us by."[41] In June 2016, Singapore's Foreign Affairs Minister Vivian Balakrishnan said that American support of the TPP was a "litmus test" of American resolve and commitment to the region. Balakrishnan said, "There are many leaders in Asia who have gone out on a limb to support the TPP. If, having marched everybody up the hill, you march down now, it will have been better if you never even started on this journey. So getting it passed is

[40] Keith B. Richburg, "Despite a Government Standoff, People of China and Taiwan Increasingly Mingle," *Washington Post*, July 20, 2010, www .washingtonpost.com/wp-dyn/content/article/2010/07/19/AR2010071905247 .html.

[41] Barack Obama, "President Obama: The TPP Would Let America, Not China, Lead the Way on Global Trade," *Washington Post*, May 2, 2016, https://www .washingtonpost.com/opinions/president-obama-the-tpp-would-let-america-not-china-lead-the-way-on-global-trade/2016/05/02/680540e4-0fd0-11e6-93ae-50921721165d_story.html?utm_term=.1c4c62f84103.

absolutely crucial."[42] The message from Singapore on this point has been particularly consistent and clear. Kishore Mahbubani, the dean of the Lee Kuan Yew School of Public Policy in Singapore, said bluntly in June 2016 that "If America kills the T.P.P., then China becomes the main center of economic gravity."[43] Singaporean Foreign Minister K. Shanmugam pointed this out during a visit to Washington in 2015:

If you don't do this (TPP) deal, what are your levers of power? How integrated are you into the Asian economies? ... So the choice is a very stark one: Do you want to be part of the region or do you want to be out of the region? And if you are out of the region ... not playing a useful role, your only lever to shape the architecture, to influence events is the Seventh Fleet and that is not the lever you want to use. Trade is strategy and you're either in or you're out.[44]

Yet the decision by Donald Trump to abandon the TPP heralds a major shift in U.S. leadership in the region. U.S. leadership can no longer be taken for granted. Barma, Ratner, and Weber have been particularly clear in arguing that, in fact, the world is moving beyond Western institutions. They write that "what is happening instead is a concerted effort by the emerging powers to construct parallel multilateral architectures that route around the liberal order and will likely reshape international politics and economics in fundamental ways."[45] Countries such as China (and India) are not challenging or simply assimilating to existing institutions. Rather, they are creating complementary and even parallel institutions.

The search for economic and multilateral alternatives to existing institutions is not simply an isolated case of the AIIB. In the past few

[42] Simon Marks, "Singapore Concerned US May Be at 'Inflection Point': Vivian Balakrishnan," *Channel News Asia*, June 10, 2016, www.channelnewsasia .com/news/singapore/singapore-concerned-us/2860474.html.

[43] Keith Bradsher, "In Trade Stances Toward China, Clinton and Trump Both Signal a Chill," *New York Times*, June 29, 2016, www.nytimes.com/2016/06/ 30/business/international/hillary-clinton-donald-trump-trade-china.html.

[44] Jeremy Au Yong, "With Free Trade, US Faces Stark Decision on Asia – Is It In or Out? – Minister Shanmugam," *Straits Times*, June 16, 2015, www.straitstimes.com/world/united-states/ with-free-trade-us-faces-stark-decision-on-asia-is-it-in-or-out-minister.

[45] Naazneen Barma, Ely Ratner, and Steven Weber, "Welcome to the World Without the West," *National Interest*, November 12, 2014, nationalinterest. org/feature/welcome-the-world-without-the-west-11651.

years, an ASEAN initiative, the Regional Comprehensive Economic Partnership (RCEP), encompassing all members of ASEAN and the countries they have free-trade agreements with, has made steady progress. RCEP would represent 27 percent of global trade. APEC member countries agreed in 2014 to explore a free-trade area of the Asia Pacific (FTAAP) that would include China. Both India and Pakistan have joined the Shanghai Cooperation Organization. China has been one of the founding members the ASEAN Regional Forum (ARF), the ASEAN Plus Three (APT), the East Asian Summit (EAS), and the ASEAN Defense Ministers' Meeting Plus Eight (ADMM-Plus). China is pursuing a Silk Road initiative. Cheng-Chee Kuik notes that "Because of the growing economic importance of China to virtually all U.S. allies and partners, it is not unthinkable that an increasingly closer intra-Asian collaboration might over time erode the very foundations of U.S.–Asia ties."[46] There is tremendous skepticism in Western circles about the actual effectiveness of these numerous organizations. But, as Evan Feigenbaum points out, "Washington's first problem is that it cannot simply reject every pan-Asian idea out of hand ... Indeed, the proliferation of Asia-only pacts and institutions over the last two decades has won support in more than a few Asian capitals, even in countries that are ambivalent about China's rise and among U.S. allies and partners."[47]

American hegemony is changing in other ways, as well. Perhaps most visibly, the election of Donald Trump as U.S. president led to massive declines in trust in the United States around the entire globe. In East Asia alone, respondents' "confidence in the U.S. president to do the right thing" under Trump dropped dramatically compared to the end of the Obama administration. Seventy-eight percent of Japanese had confidence in Obama, and only 24 percent for Trump. In Korea, 88 percent trusted Obama, 17 percent trust Trump. Australia saw a decline from 84 percent to 29 percent, and Indonesia from 64 percent trust in Obama to 23 percent trust in Trump. This decline may be temporary,

---

[46] Cheng-Chwee Kuik, "An Emerging 3rd Pillar in Asian Architecture? AIIB and Other China-Led Initiatives," *Asia-Pacific Bulletin* no. 305, March 26, 2015, www.eastwestcenter.org/system/tdf/private/apb305.pdf?file=1&type=node &id=35025.

[47] Evan Feigenbaum, "The New Asian Order: And How the United States Fits In," *Foreign Affairs*, February 2, 2015, www.foreignaffairs.com/articles/east-asia/2015-02-02/new-asian-order.

of course, and Donald Trump is only one president. It is quite likely that a different president, or different circumstances, could change opinion again and America could easily regain its position as a leading normative and moral force in the region. However, whether that occurs remains to be seen, and at least in 2017, there is a growing chorus of discussion wondering whether the American era is on the wane.[48]

Conclusion

The American relationship with Asia is wider and deeper than simply a military commitment to containment. While security scholars naturally tend to focus on the military aspects of American grand strategy, the reality is that economic and social relations are perhaps more consequential on a daily basis than are military ones. There is actually little evidence that the American forward military deployment is as unalloyed a positive, as some have argued. A major economic initiative such as the trans-Pacific Partnership has foundered after years of effort. President Trump most likely will pursue either a more confrontational, or more isolationist, line in selected issue areas, although it is not clear at this point whether or how his overall policy will emerge.

There is also plentiful evidence that East Asian states conduct their foreign economic policies with one eye on the United States and one eye on the rest of the world. As U.S. grand strategy toward the region changes and evolves, East Asian countries have moved forward along parallel tracks: working with the United States on some issues, creating other institutions and relationships on their own. The United States will remain important to East Asia, and East Asia will be important to the United States. The issue is not whether East Asian-designed institutions will eventually win out over Western ones; or whether the "West" can retain its hegemonic role. Neither is likely to happen. In fact, there is little evidence of any competition at all. Rather, the conclusion is that the region will have parallel, overlapping, complementary, and occasionally competing institutions in East Asia.

---

[48] Pew Research Center, "U.S. Image Suffers as Publics Around World Question Trump's Leadership," June 26, 2017, http://www.pewglobal.org/2017/06/26/u-s-image-suffers-as-publics-around-world-question-trumps-leadership/.

Significantly, this slow evolution of the broader American presence in East Asia is consonant with the absence of costly signals from regional countries towards China. The evidence consistently shows that East Asian countries appear to be relying less on an American forward military presence than is often believed within the Washington beltway. There is less demand or desire for American leadership than is often asserted in D.C. East Asian countries are not sending dangerous costly signals to each other, and they are not simply free-riding on a U.S. presence. There is little evidence of free-riding by American allies in the region; and indeed a fair amount of evidence exists that even American allies are cautious about too eagerly or quickly supporting American confrontation of China. The implications for American grand strategy, and for continued American leadership in the region, are profound, and are the subject of the concluding chapter.

10 | *A Minimalist American Grand Strategy Toward Asia*

I fully understand the One-China policy. But I don't know why we have to be bound by a One-China policy unless we make a deal with China having to do with other things, including trade.[1]

– Donald Trump, December 11, 2016

The research in this book leads to some fairly clear conclusions: there are no arms races in East Asia. Few states are sending costly signals of the type identified in bargaining theory that show clear resolve and a willingness to risk the cost of a war. The region is more peaceful, stable, and prosperous now than at any time in the past century. Rather than engaging in military competition, East Asian countries are pursuing *comprehensive security* with each other, with China, and with the United States: a wide range of diplomatic, institutional, and economic strategies – as well as military strategies – are being pursued in their dealings with each other.

Half a century ago, Japan, then Korea and Taiwan, and then other East Asian countries began economic growth so unprecedented that it was called miraculous. The high-growth era of the 1960s and 1970s transformed much of East Asia, and that era ended with the crushing Asian financial crisis of 1997–1998. What is often overlooked, however, is that these countries recovered from that crisis quite quickly, and growth since then has continued to outpace the rest of the world, even if it no longer was the glittering double-digit growth of before. These countries have experienced over two generations of increasing regional integration and spectacular economic growth. Leaders and publics have crafted peaceful, outward-looking foreign policies that attempt to navigate diplomatic, economic, and security issues as a

---

[1] Caren Bohan and David Brunnstrom, "Trump Says U.S. Not Necessarily Bound by 'One China' Policy," *Reuters*, December 12, 2016, www.reuters.com/article/us-usa-trump-china-idUSKBN1400TY.

whole. China's return as the regional center of gravity is deeply inter-woven with this larger regional rise, and is just one element of the increasing economic, diplomatic, and social integration of East Asia. All countries in the region have to live with each other. No country appears eager for a containment policy of China. All countries want good relations with both China and the United States.

Within this situation, then, an American grand strategy that empha-sizes a confrontational approach to China is unlikely to attract many Asian participants. Rather, it is more likely that East Asian countries will avoid being caught between the United States and China, and indeed will back slowly away. While it is too early to clearly discern what a Trump strategy to East Asia might be, there are early indica-tions that he will favor more confrontation, more protectionism, and less active diplomacy. But a United States that abandons economic leadership and multilateral institutions in favor of nationalist protec-tionism will also not find many enthusiastic supporters in East Asia. A United States that denigrates diplomacy and nuance in favor of blus-ter and confrontation will likely find few Asian countries eager to join. In short, containment and confrontation of Chia is unlikely to find many supporters in East Asia.

As a Trump approach to the region emerges, some scholars have worried that too confrontational a U.S. approach might embolden our allies and lead to moral hazard: allies taking more risks because they think the United States will back them. But the research in this book points to a different conclusion: that the more confrontational the United States becomes toward China, the more that regional countries will back slowly away from the United States. After all, leaders in East Asia clearly want good relations with both China and the United States; and few countries wish to choose one side or the other. To get caught in the middle of a spat would be the worst outcome for most regional countries, hence they will most likely not become more risk taking with respect to China, but rather carefully avoid getting involved. This is likely to be especially true because it is not at all clear that a Trump administration would sustain its atten-tion to the region. For regional leaders, to embrace a confrontation of China and then be left hanging by a distracted U.S. president is perhaps the worst possible outcome. In short, there is very good evi-dence that an East Asian containment coalition against China will not emerge.

Although superficially Japan is a staunch U.S. ally, the reality is a bit more complex. Japan is clearly the most skeptical country with regard to China, and Japan is defending its maritime claims in dispute with China, the Koreas, and Russia. Japan may even alter its constitution and remove Article IX, the famous "peace" constitution. Yet Japanese military expenditures remain very low, and even Japan shows very little signs that it plans to contain or join a balancing coalition against China. An NHK poll from June 2016 found that only 26 percent of voters support constitutional revision, while over 70 percent of Okinawans want to remove all or significant proportion of U.S. bases.[2] As Jeff Kingston notes, "can Japan become the U.K. of the Far East that many hawkish security wonks in Washington desire? Nope. Abe has led them on."[3] Japan shows few signs of being a regional leader, and even fewer signs of dramatically halting or even turning around its increasingly inward focus.

For its part, South Korea is more skeptical of Japan than it is of China, and it views China more warmly than it does Japan. Neither Japan nor South Korea show any signs of changing their fundamental postures toward regional security, and as a result, relations in Northeast Asia are likely to be considerably complex for the foreseeable future. South Korea's pursuit of its own national interests is increasingly being coopted into the larger U.S.–China strategic rivalry, thereby generating a misinterpretation about the country's behavior and the likelihood of it taking sides. Perhaps the most important lesson is that the ROK will probably never have the strategic priorities that Americans may expect or desire. South Korea has just as often chosen to make decisions that avoid cleaving too closely to the United States, and this pattern is unlikely to change in the future. South Korea has an enduring and close relationship with the United States, but it also desires good relations with its regional neighbors, particularly China.

---

[2] NHK poll quoted in Jeff Kingston, "How Rights and Liberties Might Be Downsized Under the LDP," *Japan Times*, July 9, 2016, www.japantimes.co.jp/opinion/2016/07/09/commentary/rights-liberties-may-downsized-ldp/; "Over 40 Percent of Okinawans Want Bases Withdrawn and 53 Percent Want Marines Withdrawn," *RyukyuShimpo*, June 3, 2016, english.ryukyushimpo.jp/2016/06/10/25179/.

[3] Jeff Kingston, "Empire of the Setting Sun," *Foreign Policy*, August 15, 2016, foreignpolicy.com/2016/08/15/japan-shinzo-abe-war-constitution-article-9-revision-public-sentiment/.

In Southeast Asia, some countries have maritime disputes with China, and those have not yet been resolved. But even those countries do not plan to contain or balance China, and indeed have been busily increasing their economic and diplomatic relations with China. The key long-term task for these countries is to learn how to live with each other, China, and the United States. As the region becomes more integrated economically and diplomatically, they have begun the long process of crafting stable relations with each other. These countries welcome more interaction with the United States, but they are not chasing America; rather, America is chasing East Asian countries.

Furthermore, this book has shown that there is ample evidence that countries not involved in disputes view China far more warmly than many Americans might expect. In short, there is no evidence that a balancing coalition is forming to counter China's rise. There is no incipient containment on the horizon. Rather, most countries are moving closer to China, rather than farther away. If a balancing coalition against China's rising power is both incipient and inevitable, then it is quite possible that the United States can retain primacy in East Asia with general support from most countries in the region other than China. On the other hand, if few countries consider containment an option, then a U.S. attempt to lead or create such a coalition may backfire. As Aaron Friedberg noted:

Although concern over China is growing, there is no appetite for a full-blown rivalry ... Even if American strategists concluded that it was necessary, the democratic countries that are its principal strategic partners in Asia are simply not ready to abandon engagement and sign on to a policy of containment.[4]

East Asian leaders and peoples are clearly telling the United States that while they share some U.S. concerns about China, they also have other serious concerns – such as continued economic growth; border control over migration, piracy, and trafficking; regional institution building and integration; and unresolved territorial and historical disputes. These other issues are of central importance to leaders and publics in the region.

[4] Aaron L. Friedberg, "The Debate over US China Strategy," *Survival* 57, no. 3 (2015): 107.

If this is the case, then what are the implications for American grand strategy to the region?

Liberal Hegemony: A Mainstream American View

There is a long-running and consistent view about American grand strategy toward the world in general, and East Asia in particular. This view emphasizes defending American primacy and taking a muscular, military-first approach to deterring Chinese assertiveness at every step. This view might be called "liberal hegemony," and although liberal interventionists and neoconservative hawks may disagree about the particulars, this view might even be a mainstream Washington beltway consensus from both left and right. A strategy of liberal hegemony begins with the view that "the United States should dominate the world militarily, economically, and politically ... and needs to preserve its massive lead in the global balance of power, consolidate its economic preeminence, enlarge the community of market democracies, and maintain its outsized influence in the international institutions it helped create."[5] The United States has started two bloody and expensive wars in the Middle East, tried to instigate regime change in a number of other countries, defends human rights, and tries to install democratic regimes around the world. Much of this is laudable in goal, but questionable in whether it is realistically likely to achieve things without making them worse.

When applied to East Asia, this view is focused almost exclusively on China. Regional issues are viewed through a lens as to how they affect U.S.–China relations. It sees American unwillingness to contain and confront China as a sign of weakness. In this view, the only way to continue American primacy is to vigorously intervene anywhere China might appear to be making headway against a presumably total American hegemony in the region. Dan Blumenthal has argued that "rather than increase its deterrence of China – a natural move given the uncertainty attendant to the rise of any great power – the United States has let its Pacific forces erode and will do so further."[6] As Tuan

---

[5] Posen, "Pull Back," 116.
[6] Dan Blumenthal, "The Top 10 Unicorns of China Policy," *Foreign Policy*, October 3, 2011, foreignpolicy.com/2011/10/03/the-top-10-unicorns-of-china-policy/.

Pham wrote in July 2016, "Beijing is revealing its new maritime strategy. America must be ready to stop it … the stakes are American preeminence."[7] Michael Pillsbury calls this a "hundred-year marathon," in which he identifies "China's secret strategy to supplant the United States as the world's dominant power, and to do so by 2049."[8]

But rarely is the need or rationale for American preeminence ever articulated. Hegemony is taken for granted. Rather, the need for American primacy is usually taken as self-evident, as an end in itself, so obviously important that it need not be justified. The "Lessons of Munich" school sees every challenge to the United States everywhere as interconnected, and thus the United States must respond anywhere it is challenged. This interventionist view believes that American credibility is fragile, thus requiring an extraordinary overkill response to every challenge. For example, despite calling for a reduced U.S. presence globally, even supposed realists such as John Mearsheimer and Stephen Walt unquestioningly accept the need for American primacy. In 2016, they asked, "If China continues its impressive rise, it is likely to seek hegemony in Asia. The United States should undertake a major effort to prevent it from succeeding … Ideally, Washington would rely on local powers to contain China, but that strategy might not work … The United States will have to coordinate their efforts and may have to throw its considerable weight behind them."[9]

Yet Mearsheimer and Walt do not explain why the United States must contain China; what the benefit of primacy is to the United States; and, most pragmatically, whether there is any realistic way to contain China if regional states do not wish it. The research presented in this book has made abundantly clear that a containment coalition is highly unlikely to occur in East Asia and that "local powers" are almost certainly not going to contain China. In this case, if the United States follows the Mearsheimer and Walt strategy, it would find itself

---

[7] Tuan N. Pham, "America Has a Chance to Beat Back China's South China Sea Strategy," *National Interest*, July 5, 2016, nationalinterest.org/feature/america-has-chance-beat-back-chinas-south-china-sea-strategy-16851.

[8] Michael Pillsbury, *The Hundred-Year Marathon: China's Secret Strategy to Replace America as the Global Superpower* (New York: St. Martin's Griffin, 2015), i.

[9] John Mearsheimer and Stephen Walt, "The Case for Offshore Balancing: A Superior U.S. Grand Strategy," *Foreign Affairs*, June 13, 2016, www.foreignaffairs.com/articles/united-states/2016-06-13/case-offshore-balancing.

unilaterally devoting massive resources to containing China, with no obvious goal or measure of success.

This preoccupation with primacy tends to lead to military-first policies, with continual calls for increased U.S. defense spending. Although coming from different ends of the political spectrum, both tend to agree on the need for a muscular, military-first, interventionist American grand strategy. For example, despite the United States being by far the largest spender on defense in the world, Kagan and Rubin argued in 2016 that "an urgent first step ... is to significantly increase U.S. national security and defense spending."[10] In East Asia, this view leads to a military first, containment view of American grand strategy to the region.[11] Harry Kazianis argues that the "Scarborough 'Shoaldown'" is "an opportunity to push back against China," although how and to what end is not clear.[12] This focus on primacy for its own sake means meeting almost every and any challenge to total U.S. hegemony anywhere, usually beginning with military force.

Perhaps most important is that advocates of this liberal hegemonic perspective care more about the "hegemonic" side than the "liberal" side. Neocons and the GOP don't actually believe in the liberal order. What they really believe in is U.S. dominance. This is an important difference. U.S. primacy is an end in itself. A G-2 regional concert with China is, ipso facto, a nonstarter. This type of U.S. exceptionalist ideology makes it hard to accept any negotiated solutions with China. After seventy years of hegemony and relentless cheerleading about the end of history and all that, some Americans are cognitively struggling to accept anything less than Chinese capitulation. There is a large constituency for this kind of thinking in parts of the U.S. foreign policy-making establishment. If many in the U.S. mainstream foreign policy

---

[10] Robert Kagan and James Rubin, *Extending American Power: Strategies to Expand U.S. Engagement in a Competitive World Order* (Washington, DC: Center for a New American Security, May 21, 2016), p. 3.

[11] For similar approaches to American strategy, see Blackwill and Tellis, *Revising U.S. Grand Strategy Toward China* (New York: Council on Foreign Relations), Council Special Report No. 72 (March 2015); Richard K. Betts, "The Lost Logic of Deterrence," *Foreign Affairs* (March/April 2013); and Kazianis, "Get Ready, America."

[12] Harry Kazianis, "Scarborough 'Shoaldown': An Opportunity to Push Back Against China," *The National Interest*, April 25, 2016, nationalinterest. org/blog/the-buzz/scarborough-%E2%80%98shoaldown%E2%80%99-opportunity-push-back-against-china-15919.

community view the Iran deal as the worst deal ever, how would they respond to any serious concession to China?

The dangers in this type of American exceptionalist and interventionist thinking accords closely with Jack Snyder's *Myths of Empire*, where he points out that empires often overextend themselves because domestic politics pushes leaders to be overly ambitious.[13] There is an argument to be made that credibility is wildly overrated as a cause for U.S. actions.[14] Furthermore, as Steven Stashwick points out, there is an "exaggerated myth" about military showdowns between China and the United States, where relatively benign military interactions are reportedly breathlessly as "threatening" and "ominous," by even supposedly reputable sources such as the *New York Times*.[15] Alastair Iain Johnston has pointed out that much of the hype about China's new assertiveness comes from the change in reporting about China in the United States, not necessarily any new behavior on the part of China.[16] Lyle Goldstein points out the exaggeration of Chinese aggression:

There is the curious notion that China's recent actions in the South China Sea portend a spasm of aggression spanning East Asia, spilling into the Indian Ocean and then through the Middle East, Africa and beyond. Almost

[13] Jack Snyder, *Myths of Empire: Domestic Politics and International Ambition* (Ithaca, NY: Cornell University Press, 1993).

[14] Jonathan Mercer, "Bad Reputation: The Folly of Going to War for 'Credibility'," *Foreign Affairs*, August 28, 2013, www.foreignaffairs.com/articles/syria/2013-08-28/bad-reputation.

[15] Steve Stashwick, "What 2 Russian Jets Can Teach Us About a US-China Clash in the South China Sea," *The Diplomat*, April 15, 2016, thediplomat.com/2016/04/what-2-russian-jets-can-teach-us-about-a-us-china-clash-in-the-south-china-sea/.

[16] Johnston, "How New and Assertive Is China's New Assertiveness?" Johnston later pointed out that although both the *New York Times* and the *Christian Science Monitor* claimed in 2014 that Chinese antiforeign propaganda had "spiked," neither newspaper provided any evidence to back up their claims. In fact, careful measurement of Chinese propaganda from 1988 to 2014 revealed that there had been no dramatic increase in this antiforeign messaging. Johnston notes that "by far the greatest frequency of articles referring to foreign hostile forces was in the Deng Xiaoping period in the immediate aftermath of the Tiananmen crackdown in 1989." Alastair Iain Johnston, "Anti-foreigner Propaganda Is Not Spiking in China," *Monkey Cage (Washington Post)*, December 2, 2014, www.washingtonpost.com/news/monkey-cage/wp/2014/12/02/anti-foreigner-propaganda-is-not-spiking-in-china/.

as fanciful is the idea that Beijing is about to erect figurative toll barriers around the South China Sea, only admitting the ships of nations that agree to perform the infamous 磕头 [kowtow]. Presumably, naval vessels requesting admittance would require either multiple prostrations or at least some very fat 红包 [red envelopes].[17]

From this perspective, taking a military-first response to China's increasing influence in the region may even be counterproductive. Would the United States truly be willing to risk war with China over maritime disputes in which it has no direct claim or stake? Would the United States risk a war when even regional claimants are not willing to fight and are making no costly signals about their resolve?

The United States has made abundantly clear that it would protect its treaty allies – the Philippines, South Korea, and Japan – if another country threatened their national survival. But even the interventionist hawks do not claim that China threatens the national survival of the Philippines or other claimants. But if China is not threatening Philippine existence, then what are the stakes for the United States? If the Philippines itself clearly says it will not fight over the Spratly Islands, will the United States fight for them over a stake in which it has no direct claim? Chas Freeman puts it, "who would go to war with China with us on behalf of Filipino claims to worthless sandbars, rocks, and reefs? Surely it would be better to promote a diplomatic resolution of competing claims than to help ramp up a military confrontation."[18]

It would be the ironic if, after decades of clearly telling East Asian states that the maritime disputes in the South China Sea are not worth fighting over, that the United States itself decided to fight over them simply because somebody else wants them. After all, the United States has consistently maintained that it takes no stance on sovereignty in regional maritime disputes. The United States runs great risks if, simply because the United States opposes China, it ignores generations of U.S. policy and at the same time ignores international law and arbitrarily and unilaterally decides sovereignty. In fact, many American

[17] Lyle J. Goldstein, "The South China Sea Showdown: 5 Dangerous Myths," *National Interest*, September 29, 2015, nationalinterest.org/feature/the-south-china-sea-showdown-5-dangerous-myths-13970.

[18] Chas W. Freeman, Jr., "The End of the American Empire," *War on the Rocks*, April 11, 2016, warontherocks.com/2016/04/the-end-of-the-american-empire/.

policy analysts have voiced skepticism about whether it would be worth it for the United States to fight over the Senkaku Island or in the South China Seas, referring to them as "strategically marginal territory."[19]

As Robert Kelly points out, interventionist prescriptions

almost always [involve] more hawkish chest-thumping, rejection of any deals or negotiations, accusations of appeasement and retreat, higher military spending, and so on … neocon high-handed moralism and American exceptionalism in this business-like region will fail spectacularly. Neoconservatism will make an enemy of China, permanently end the possibility of any nuclear deal with North Korea (unlikely to be sure, but that is for Seoul to work out, not us), and frighten American allies/friends, like South Korea or Vietnam, that we are war-mongers. No one out here wants a repeat of Iraq in North Korea or Southeast Asia. No one wants grandstanding, culturally-ignorant American exceptionalists lecturing the region about the "freedom agenda."[20]

Much of the scholarship on a more forward-leaning U.S. policy toward Asia emphasizes the dangers of moral hazard: the idea that American allies could be emboldened to take increased risks because they believe the United States will back them. However, the research in this book leads to the opposite conclusion: that East Asian countries are not eager for a more confrontational United States and that they are unlikely to join a containment coalition. Rather, East Asian countries are likely to view a more muscular American foreign policy with alarm, as threatening an increasingly stable East Asian order.

It is perhaps not unfair to characterize current U.S. grand strategy toward East Asia as backward looking: emphasizing 1940s-era economic institutions, 1950s-era military defense treaties with three countries, and a Cold War–era containment military-first posture. In short, current U.S. policy tends to be reactive, and defensive; trying

---

[19] See, for example, Emma Ashford, "Realism Restrained: The Washington Playbook Strikes Back," *War on the Rocks*, May 2016, warontherocks.com/ 2016/05/realism-restrained-the-washington-playbook-strikes-back/; and Posen, "Pull Back," 122.

[20] Robert Kelly, "A Note to Congressional Republicans: Why the Neocon Formula Won't Work in Asia," *The Interpreter*, April 20, 2015, www .lowyinterpreter.org/post/2015/04/20/A-note-to-Congressional-Republicans .aspx.

to hold on to what it has. This policy is aimed at sustaining for as long as possible a U.S. role of primacy as it existed during some imagined golden era of the recent past: when U.S.-backed institutions and U.S. alliances were the central elements of East Asian peace and prosperity. But clinging too much to the past might mean overlooking the ways that the region is changing now.

The key pillars of this American grand strategy are over half a century old, and while it worked very well in the past, it is also clear that they have not solved the remaining issues that face the United States and East Asian countries in the twenty-first century. Most clearly, the most important issue is how to incorporate China's rise into a regional order that is stable across economic, diplomatic, and military dimensions. Another set of issues is the continued maritime disputes between many countries in the region – these disputes do not threaten the survival of any country, but they are a source of continued friction.

Nowhere is America's backward-looking and yet incomplete and contradictory grand strategy more clear than in its use of the catchphrase "international rules and norms." Many of the Westphalian rules and norms have worked very well, and are accepted unquestioningly by all states in the region, including China. It often goes overlooked how deeply institutions such as passports, nationality, sovereignty, and diplomatic recognition have been internalized around the globe, and by China itself.[21]

However, if two hundred years of Westphalian rules and norms have not solved remaining issues, they may never solve them. This leads to what might be considered a somewhat provocative implication: the solution to the remaining issues may not lie in current rules and norms. In fact, the remaining territorial issues in East Asia are actually created by the Westphalian need to precisely demarcate a series of zero-sum boundaries in which overlapping or mutual sovereignty is impossible. What may be needed are new, or at least innovative, means of resolving the remaining differences. After all, as Ryan Griffiths argues:

China's territorial claims are not based on claims over other sovereign states; or on key sections of their landmass. There are important disputes, to be sure, such as with India, but these do not lay claim to vital sections of

---

[21] Allen Carlson, *Unifying China, Integrating with the World: Securing Chinese Sovereignty in the Reform Era* (Stanford, CA: Stanford University Press, 2005).

the Indian state ... Does ambiguity imply that the norm can be stretched to cover all claims and that the powerful can casually determine whose integrity is threatened? The answer is no. The existing territorial grid has already been determined through diplomacy, war, and the other practices, both fair and unfair, that shape international relations. Of course, conflicting claims over territory do exist on the margins of that grid – Taiwan being one of the most prominent – and it is precisely in cases such as these, where territorial integrity can be invoked by both sides, that conflict becomes more likely. But these cases are limited in number, rooted in history, and not simply conjured whole cloth. The existing territorial grid would shape China's ability to call on the territorial norm.[22]

If the solution were easy or obvious, regional states would have figured it out by now. Rather, a stable solution to maritime disputes will require new cooperation and diplomacy between China, the United States, and all regional countries. Even the existing UNCLOS and other international bodies do not address underlying claims of sovereignty. As Barma and his coauthors point out, "the fundamental problem in the South China Sea is not China seeking to overturn some existing order or that China is refusing to integrate. It is that the prevailing order is so thin as to be meaningless."[23] Chin-hao Huang's important scholarship points out that China is more likely to adhere to international norms when the norm is clear, when other countries are all following the norm, and when the consequences of not following are clear.[24] In the South China Seas, none of those scope conditions is met.

The norms, principles, and rules are changing, as are the actors and their interests. The question is not whether East Asia will develop and evolve rules and norms and institutions – it already has and it is continuing to do so – but rather how. As Evelyn Goh writes, "East Asian states have reconstructed the US hegemonic order to incorporate a layered hierarchy with more complex social processes of maintenance ..."[25] American leadership can be most influential in showing

---

[22] Ryan Griffiths, "States, Nations, and Territorial Stability: Why Chinese Hegemony Would Be Better for International Order," *Security Studies* (forthcoming).

[23] Naazneen Barma, Ely Ratner, and Steven Weber, "The Mythical Liberal Order," *National Interest* (March/April 2013): 64

[24] Chin-hao Huang, *"Power, Restraint, and China's Rise"* (ms.) (Singapore: Yale-NUS College, August 2016).

[25] Goh, *The Struggle for Order*, p. 7.

a way forward. But to date that has not yet happened as much as needed. Creating and maintaining a stable status quo in the region will not be a result of an imposed military balance of power. The solution will not arise from current rules and norms, because these rules and norms are incomplete. Rather, enduring stability will require new ideas and forward-thinking leadership.

It is thus likely that Trump will accelerate, but not begin, the slow changes in American grand strategy. Some have written about the end of the American-led international order, and that may happen.[26] But Trump will not begin that process, only accelerate it, if it does happen.

A Minimalist American Policy for East Asia

The research presented in this book provides an important perspective on this debate about American grand strategy to East Asia. Looking at what regional countries are doing, as well as what they are saying, leads to the conclusion that states in the region do not wish to choose between the United States and China and are not planning to fight over the remaining issues in the region. East Asian states show no signs of planning containment-style balancing in which they clearly choose one side or the other. These countries are not sending costly signals about their resolve. They are not spending on their militaries. There is no evidence of an arms race in East Asia. Rather, East Asian states are also utilizing all tools at their disposal – institutional, diplomatic, and economic – to interact with and deal with both the United States and China.[27]

A strong military is one component of that larger American strategy, but there is also a need for American economic and diplomatic attention to the region. The evidence provided in this book leads fairly clearly to the conclusion that a diplomacy-focused, economic, and multifaceted American grand strategy toward East Asia is more likely to contribute to peace, stability, and prosperity for both America and East Asia.

---

[26] Amitav Acharya, *The End of the American Order* (Cambridge, UK: Polity Press, 2014).

[27] On this point, see Evelyn Goh, "Meeting the China Challenge: The U.S. in Southeast Asian Regional Strategies," *Policy Studies*, No. 16 (Washington, DC: East-West Center, 2005).

In fact, on the other side of the debate about American grand strategy to East Asia are those who emphasize a multifaceted approach, and who view economic and diplomatic measures as important as militarily measures. In contrast to those favoring liberal hegemony, this perspective sees any enduring stabilization or settlement of the outstanding issues in East Asian regional security as clearly requiring a larger diplomatic and economic solution. As Kurt Campbell, former assistant secretary of state for Asia under Barack Obama's administration, wrote in 2016, U.S. strategy toward China and Asia is a "careful, calibrated mixture of cooperation, competition, and interdependence developed over decades ... [and] goes beyond simply the requirements of the US–China relationship to embrace a deeper American engagement in the region as a whole, from Japan to Korea to Southeast Asia, Australia, and India. [This approach] seeks to harness the optimism and sense of possibility that has always animated life in Asia."[28] The Senate Foreign Relations Committee concluded in 2015 that the United States "should make clear that [American] policy is about broadening U.S. engagement, not containing China; the rebalance seeks to expand economic growth, ensure regional security, and improve human welfare for the benefit of all, not the detriment of one."[29] Less flamboyantly, Andrew Erickson has emphasized:

The need to avoid an insular approach, combined with the increasing inability for Washington to exercise undifferentiated global preeminence, makes it necessary to craft a coherent Asia-Pacific Strategy ... Failure to craft an explicit comprehensive Asia-Pacific Strategy will complicate efforts to "see the big picture" across the entire diplomacy, information, military, and economic (DIME) spectrum and beyond.[30]

---

[28] Kurt Campbell, "'The Pivot': A Reply to Hugh White," *Interpreter*, July 5, 2016, www.lowyinterpreter.org/post/2016/07/05/The-Pivot-A-reply-to-Hugh-White.aspx.

[29] U.S. Congress, Senate, Committee on Foreign Relations, *Rebalancing the Rebalance: Resourcing U.S. Diplomatic Strategy in the Asia-Pacific Region*, 113th Cong., 2nd sess. 2014, 3.

[30] Andrew Erickson, testimony before the House Armed Services Committee Subcommittee on Seapower & Projection Forces, Hearing on "China's Naval Modernization: Implications and Recommendations," Hearing on "U.S. Asia-Pacific Strategic Considerations Related to PLA Naval Forces," Rayburn House Office Building, Washington, DC, December 11, 2013, docs.house.gov/meetings/AS/AS28/20131211/101579/HHRG-113-AS28-Wstate-EricksonA-20131211.pdf.

A particular version of this approach calls for reduced intervention. Barry Posen calls this a strategy of "restraint," one that "gives up on global reforms and instead sticks to protecting narrow national security interests."[31] Chas Freeman has argued that, "Whatever the cure for our foul mood and foreigners' doubts about us may be, it is not spending more money on our armed forces, piling up more debt with military Keynesianism, or pretending that the world yearns for us to make all its decisions for it or to be its policeman."[32]

A focus on diplomacy first – and a concomitant reduced emphasis on military-first policies – is consistent with the larger American public's views. A 2015 poll by the University of Chicago found that only 27 percent of Americans think the United States should be more involved in dealing with various troubles facing the world; 38 percent would rather the United States reduce its involvement.[33]

The United States has already begun to abandon important elements of its international leadership and the postwar order. The failure of the Trans-Pacific Partnership was not only the failure of years of economic diplomacy, it was a reflection of a much wider problem for the United States. Perhaps the most important element of a minimalist foreign policy for the United States is to have a forward-looking economic agenda that engages the world. The TPP was a key element of an American economic agenda for the region, and to fail to embrace the region economically will be to severely harm American interests and influence in East Asia. If the United States begins to pursue economic nationalist protectionism or an antiglobalization economic agenda that reduces rather than increases our embrace of East Asia, the United States will be firmly placing itself outside of the mainstream in the region and isolating itself and losing the key and main source of its influence and leverage in the region. To not pass TPP, and thus to only have the tenuous reed of a military that may or may not be used to counter a purported Chinese threat, would leave the United States sidelined in the most important and dynamic region of the world.

---

[31] Posen, "Pull Back," 118.

[32] Chas W. Freeman, Jr., "The End of the American Empire" (speech, Barrington, Rhode Island, April 2, 2016), chasfreeman.net/the-end-of-the-american-empire/.

[33] "Global Issues: Americans' Foreign Policy Priorities" (Chicago: Associated Press – NORC Center for Public Affairs Research, July 2015), www.apnorc .org/projects/Pages/HTML%20Reports/global-issues-americans-foreign-policy-priorities.aspx.

The pessimistic interventionists may be right, and – just wait – the region may be heading toward a classic bipolar confrontation where containment, blocs, and military deterrence are at the forefront. It may be that soon most East Asian countries make a clear choice and openly ask for U.S. primacy and begin outright balancing against China. China and the United States may also divide up the region into two blocs. But neither has yet happened. Indeed, the evidence provided in this book leads to the conclusion that although the region does contain potential flashpoints, countries are seeking ways to manage relations with each other, the United States, and China that emphasize institutional, diplomatic, and economic solutions rather than purely military solutions.

American observers and policy makers might be wise to consider how best to implement a strategy that retains U.S. influence in East Asia by addressing key issues and avoiding making regional countries take sides.[34] The region still seems to see a pathway that avoids either the capitulation or containment of China as achievable. How decisions are made from here forward are important – nothing is inevitable. The key to continuing the almost half-century of peace, stability, and prosperity in East Asia will be diplomatic, not military.

The United States wants China to play a constructive role regionally and globally, one that follows international law and respects international institutions. The United States needs to ensure that China plays by rules set out by the international community, not outside it. While renewed U.S. attention to the region is welcome, it is important that the American grand strategy not be framed or perceived as an either/or proposition, with regional states being forced to choose between the United States and China. The United States should devote as much attention to economic and diplomatic issues as it does to military issues, and present a clear economic agenda for the region, while avoiding viewing American interests in Asia in purely strategic terms. As Joseph W. Prueher and his coauthors write, "The solution is not for the United States to double down militarily, spending vast amounts of money in a futile attempt to remain militarily predominant across all

[34] Bates Gill, Evelyn Goh, and Chin-Hao Huang, *The Dynamics of US–China–Southeast Asia Relations*, (Sydney: United States Studies Center at the University of Sydney, June 2016).

of maritime East Asia … Washington needs to adapt its security posture in the region to one that the U.S. economy can sustain."[35]

This might be called a "smart power" position – the U.S. should stay involved in Asia, but in an intelligent way that respects the region's particularities. No one could argue with that, but in practice it may be nearly impossible. A U.S. presence, especially a heavy political-military one like it has now, means America will all but inevitably get sucked into the region's issues and problems. That is basically unavoidable. Very predictably then (as has been the case with U.S. involvement in the Middle East), the United States will act in ways it thinks are helpful ("We're Americans!") but which locals will not see that way and which will set off all sorts of unwanted second-order effects. Asia is big, old, and complicated. Americans don't understand it well and still focus more on other regions of the world than Asia. The languages and religions are hard. The conflicts are a cross-cutting tangle. That strongly suggests that U.S. action will have huge second-order effects that cannot be predicted. That is why U.S. "reactive" behavior may be best. Complaints against this approach equates "doing something" with progress. In a highly complex environment with low information and many jockeying parties, that is not at all obvious.

Furthermore, America's forward presence will tempt East Asian countries to use its immense power for their own ends, as various factions in post-Saddam Iraq tried, or as South Korea and Japan and other East Asian countries do against each other. Participants in regional conflicts are likely to see the United States as a powerful tool to pursue their own preferences in those conflicts if they can recruit the United States to their side. Not only is America unqualified, morally and intellectually, to sort out regional conflicts, but the United States is a huge pot of resources tempting any entrepreneurial leader to recruit to pursue his or her own goals in those conflicts and possibly make them worse. There will be no durable solution until the Southeast Asian countries and China take ownership and forge some kind of working compromise. A solution cannot be imposed, and it will not be military. It will have to involve recognition and legitimacy

[35] Joseph W. Prueher, J. Stapleton Roy, Paul Heer, David M. Lampton, Michael D. Swaine, and Ezra Vogel, "How America Can Lead in Asia," *National Interest*, December 12, 2016, nationalinterest.org/feature/how-america-can-lead-asia-18720.

of the solution on all sides. Once again, a heavy or confrontational U.S. presence can easily distort this by encouraging maximalists in all camps, creating weird incentives and temptations, and fueling hardliner paranoia in the Chinese leadership.

The implications for the United States are direct and clear: get out of the way. There are way too many conflicts, they are a cross-cutting tangle, Americans don't understand them, the United States has no clear moral authority in the eyes of the region to act as an umpire for those conflicts, and the regional actors themselves don't really know how to solve them. Yet America blunders in anyway. Furthermore, a forward-leaning U.S. presence just as easily serves to freeze a region's conflicts in place (e.g., the Middle East) as alleviate them (Europe). It is not at all clear that the United States is actually improving stability and resolving Asia's conflicts through its presence, or that the United States even can improve them. Indeed, if the number of articles that use European history to explain contemporary Asia is any indication, most Western observers have no interest in putting in the hard work to truly understand Asian languages, history, and culture, much less understand contemporary issues, perceptions, and intentions. Why bother with all that work if knowing some factoids from Greek history is enough?[36]

Hence, the actual end-point implication from the research presented in this book is for the United States to just get out of the way. This would appear to be a really obvious lesson about the Mideast, but one that neocon hawks and liberal interventionists are ideologically and professionally committed to refusing to learn. So in practice, restraint and minimalism is the approach to pursue. Given the heroic assumptions needed for smart power, the next choice the research in this book

---

[36] Graham Allison's *Destined for War* argues that twelve out of sixteen previous power transitions ended in war. But these sixteen power transitions were cherry picked entirely from the past four hundred years of European history. Allison thus argues that there were only seventeen power transitions in the entire scope of world history: one that occurred in fourth century BCE between two villages in what is now present-day Greece, and sixteen that began with the France/Hapsburg transition in the late-sixteenth century. Evidently nothing that happened in Asia over the past 2,500 years, or anywhere else around the world, for that matter, that is important enough to study. This is what passes for careful historical research. Allison, *Destined for War: China, America, and the Thucydides Trap* (Boston: Houghton Mifflin Harcourt, 2017).

suggests is to just not get involved so much in order to not make big blunders, like accidentally sparking a South China Seas war. This most clearly does not mean an abrogation of U.S. security treaties, nor does it mean a unilateral military withdrawal of the forward-deployed U.S. military assets around the region. This is most clearly not an isolationist argument.

To repeat: a minimalist strategy does not mean America should leave. There is no possible way for the United States to leave the region economically, militarily, and diplomatically anyway – American relations with the region are too wide, multifaceted, and enduring. A minimalist policy also includes a vigorous economic component, as well. However, in security matters it does mean that the United States should probably be quiet and reactive. Asians will have to figure out as Asian problems, just as the EU was intended to solve European problems, and no amount of U.S. intervention in the Middle East solved their problems and, in fact, made them worse.

Here is the difference between this approach and the standard D.C. neocon hawk/liberal internationalist approach. I am vastly more pessimistic that the United States can significantly shape outcomes in a proactive way. A lot of that is wishful-thinking hubris, the product of the natural arrogance that comes from unipolarity, plus the ideology of American exceptionalism. The United States can prevent some outcomes – like an North Korea invasion of South Korea – but it almost certainly cannot proactively, positively generate specific outcomes, like a democratic China or Chinese commitment to norms the South China Seas. From this perspective, the 2017 U.S. discussion of a permanent naval presence in the South China Seas considers precisely the wrong strategy to take: rather than allowing regional states to work out the issue for themselves, the United States is mulling an even greater, and more militarized, intervention into a complex issue that almost certainly will make matters worse, not better.

And the tragedy of an exceptionalist, interventionist U.S. mindset is that it has created this impression among some Americans – that America can do anything; that unipolarity equals omnipotence; and that if the United States isn't seeing the outcomes it wants, the reason is a lack of will or appeasers at home, rather than the more obvious explanation that locals will do want they want, don't take their cues from America, and will probably try to use U.S. power for their own ends. As Geoffrey Wheatcroft notes about American foreign policy: "Is there larger conclusion to be drawn? If the unilateral intervention of the previous [Bush] administration was a total failure, and if the alternative policies followed under Obama have met with very limited success, might it not be time fundamentally to reassess the American role as a would-be but not very successful global superpower?"[37] Or, as Leslie Gelb put it, the United States will have the "power to lead, but no longer to command."[38]

This book began by pointing out that East Asia is measurably richer, more stable, and more integrated today than twenty-five years ago. East Asian defense spending is measurably lower as well, and shows no signs of increasing. East Asian countries are moving closer to China, not farther away. An America that embraces these trends will benefit itself and also the region. An America that works against these trends will find itself increasingly isolated, or even worse. All countries in the region, and the United States, have to live with each other. The future has not yet been written, and the actions and decisions that American, Chinese, and East Asian leaders take today will be critical for determining the future of East Asian security and prosperity.

[37] Geoffrey Wheatcroft, "Is a Rational American Foreign Policy Even Possible?" *National Interest*, August 1, 2016, nationalinterest.org/blog/the-skeptics/rational-american-foreign-policy-even-possible-17204.

[38] Leslie Gelb, "The Future of U.S. Primacy: Power to Lead, but No Longer to Command," *The National Interest*, July 27, 2016, nationalinterest.org/blog/the-skeptics/the-future-us-primacy-power-lead-no-longer-command-17149.

Index